The Bracero Program

THE BRACERO PROGRAM

Interest Groups and Foreign Policy

by RICHARD B. CRAIG

UNIVERSITY OF TEXAS PRESS AUSTIN & LONDON

International Standard Book Number 0–292–70145–4
Library of Congress Catalog Card Number 74–165914
© 1971 by Richard B. Craig
All Rights Reserved
Type set by G&S Typesetters, Austin
Printed by Capital Printing Company, Austin
Bound by Universal Bookbindery, Inc., San Antonio

TO THE OLE MAN

Would that he had lived to see his son become a starter

CONTENTS

TABLES

PREFACE

However one views its lineage, the Mexican labor program—or bracero[1] program, in the vernacular—survived one world war, a major "police action," several political administrations, and countless political skirmishes in both domestic and international arenas. Under its auspices more than 4.5 million Mexican nationals were legally contracted for work on United States farms over a twenty-two–year period. During these years the bracero program never ceased to be a controversial issue. At one system level or another it was perpetually involved in a vortex of political conflict. It is this conflict and its group combatants which provide the focal point of this study.

Within the broader contexts of interest groups and the political process, four phenomena are considered: (1) the international agreements that served as bases for bracero contracting, (2) United States Public Law 78, which provided the legal framework within which the conflict among competing domestic interest groups took place, (3) conflicting domestic and international inter-

[1] Literally translated, the term "bracero" means one who works with his arms. The nearest English equivalent is "field hand." As used in this study, the term "bracero" signifies a legally contracted Mexican farmworker, while the term "wetback" indicates an illegal entrant.

ests in a changing political environment, and (4) the impact of the international environment on the domestic political process.

After a brief theoretical perspective, the first chapter examines the bracero program within a binational environmental context. A discussion of the group processes surrounding bracero importation during the period 1942–1951 provides the substance of chapter 2. Group processes and the institutionalization of imported Mexican labor are analyzed in chapter 3. Chapter 4 examines the bracero program during the era of stabilization: 1952–1959. The fifth chapter analyzes the demise of the statutory foundation of imported Mexican labor. Finally, a summary and conclusions are found in chapter 6.

INTRODUCTION

Theoretically, the Mexican migrant-labor program may be viewed from an international, a national, or a subnational perspective. Realistically, however, it presents a classic example of the inseparability of domestic and foreign policy, thereby necessitating both a micro and a macro approach. As a consequence, the theoretical framework around which this study is structured is an amalgam of two approaches to the study of the political process: interest-group theory and systems analysis.

In regard to the latter approach, the entire bracero question illustrates a system that is at once an integrated whole and simultaneously a composite of interrelated parts. As our investigation of the program unfolds, its fundamentally systemic nature is increasingly evident. The following observation by a noted student of international systems theory could have been made with the bracero program in mind: "As the observer shifts his gaze from the system to one of the constituent parts, he discovers that the part itself is internally a system. This progression of revealing the inner makeup of a complex system reminds one of the taking apart of a Chinese puzzle box. Inside each box is another that appears as soon as the preceding one is removed."[1]

[1] Charles A. McClelland, *Theory and the International System*, pp. 20–21.

In our analysis of the Mexican labor program several levels of interaction are investigated. From an international, or macro, perspective, the Mexican labor agreement involves three interlocking relationships: government with government, group with government, and group with group. On the intermediate, or national, level, primary attention is focused upon three sets of interactions: group with government, group with group, and government agency with government agency. Two relationships merit particular scrutiny at the micro, or subnational, level: group with government and group with group. Like a system, each of these relationships is reciprocal, each is interrelated with the other, and each is affected by a change in the other. At one stage in our investigation of the bracero program attention is directed to particular relationships at the national level. At another stage the primary level of analysis is international, thereby transferring the center of attention to different political actors and their interaction. The macro perspective afforded by systems theory facilitates a smooth shifting of systemic levels and simultaneously permits employing the more restricted interest-group approach in a detailed analysis of the group struggle at national and subnational levels.

Interest Groups and United States Political Culture

The group phenomenon has long been a point of interest in the United States. Through the years there seems to have emerged, normatively and empirically, what might be termed a "group legend" of the American polity. Not all scholars have accepted the thesis entirely, but it is clear that, on a comparative basis, Americans are prone to group membership.[2] It is one thing, however, to

---

[2] This collective tendency among Americans has been noted by foreigner and native alike. For examples of the former who were impressed with the propensity of Americans to join voluntary associations, note the following: Alexis de Tocqueville, *Democracy in America*, esp. p. 181; Lord Bryce, *The American Commonwealth*, pp. 281–282; and Gunnar Myrdal, *An American Dilemma: The Negro Problem and Modern Democracy*, esp. chap. 33.

On this question, American observers have differed. For writers who view the United States as essentially one large interest group, see Thomas A. Bailey, *The Man in the Street: The Impact of American Public Opinion on Foreign*

concede the existence of such a group syndrome; it is quite another to look upon it with favor.

In his analysis of the nature of interest groups, Alfred de Grazia reminds us that the term "interest" has a "shady past" in United States political culture.[3] From contemporary United States history there has appeared what might be called the "demon legend" of interest groups. Void of its emotional tapestry, the legend contends that interest groups and democracy, or pressure groups and the national interest, are essentially incompatible.

Although some observers of the American political scene continue their preoccupation with the evils of organized groups, the great majority has faced up to the problem in a more realistic manner. Among these realists there are two discernible schools. The first school of thought includes those scholars who accept as inevitable the group nature of contemporary democratic society, with all its accompanying debits and credits. Although they acknowledge the oligarchic tendencies in voluntary associations as well as the dangers these groups pose to individualism and the national interest, these observers do not foresee therein the demise of a democratic way of life. Instead, they place their faith in group self-discipline, overlapping membership, and the evolution of countervailing groups, while simultaneously urging increased vigilance to avert the worst evils of the group-dominated society.[4]

Policy, p. 292; and Donald C. Blaisdell, *American Democracy under Pressure*, p. 66. Contrariwise, note Mancur Olson, Jr., *The Logic of Collective Action: Public Goods and the Theory of Groups*, p. 20. Other American scholars concur with the joiner thesis, but with reservation: E. E. Schattschneider, *The Semi-Sovereign People: A Realist's View of Democracy in America*, pp. 30–36; and V. O. Key, Jr., *Public Opinion and American Democracy*, pp. 502–503.

On a comparative basis, recent empirical scholarship substantiates the thesis that the United States is a nation of joiners: David McClelland, *The Achieving Society*, pp. 199–201; Gabriel Almond and Sydney Verba, *The Civic Culture: Political Attitudes and Democracy in Five Nations*, pp. 246–251.

[3] Alfred de Grazia, "Nature and Prospects of Political Interest Groups," *Annals of the American Academy of Political and Social Science* 319 (September 1958):32–40.

[4] Such a perspective is well illustrated by Bertram Gross, who states: "The process of group conflict itself—harsh and cruel though it may be—provides a

A second group of contemporary scholars appears to have discovered a rainbow behind the gray cloud of pressure groups. Far from perceiving organized interest groups as the scourge of democracy, they look upon the group phenomenon as virtually prerequisite to the survival of democratic principles in mass society. They contend that only through participation in voluntary associations may the individual escape the evils of atomization and share meaningfully in the political process. This school of thought goes so far as to discount the contemporary possibility of meaningful democracy in a groupless society. Not only are interest groups not anathematic to the democratic polity, but they also represent its very lifeblood.[5]

On balance, there are elements of truth in both schools of thought. The power of interest groups may, if unchecked, pose a danger to individualism, the national interest, and the survival of democracy itself. On the other hand, one would be hard pressed to visualize a viable contemporary democratic polity without a substantial network of voluntary associations. On the subject of democ-

---

check-and-balance system of protection far more powerful and meaningful than the constitutional arrangements envisaged by the Founding Fathers against the harshness and cruelties of unguarded guardians" (*The Legislative Struggle: A Study of Social Combat*, p. 36). For additional illustrations of this school of thought, note the following: David B. Truman, *The Governmental Process: Political Interest and Public Opinion*, Chap. 5; Gabriel Almond, *The American People and Foreign Policy*, pp. 235–236; Raymond Bauer et al., *American Business and Public Policy: The Politics of Foreign Trade*, p. 226; and John Kenneth Galbraith, *American Capitalism: The Concept of Countervailing Power*.

[5] This point of view appears to have been well substantiated by recent empirical studies. Almond and Verba are emphatic in this respect. In line with their theme that the democratic citizen is one who speaks the "language of demands," they see in political interest-group membership a process whereby "fusion occurs at the heart of the democratic process—the process by which the ordinary citizen exercises some control over his government" (*The Civic Culture*, p. 154). In a similar vein, see Harmon Zeigler, *Interest Groups in American Society*, pp. 37–40; Seymour M. Lipset, *Political Man: The Social Basis of Politics*, p. 201; Robert E. Lane, *Political Life: Why People Get Involved in Politics*, pp. 187–188; William Kornhauser, *The Politics of Mass Society*, pp. 74–84; and Herbert McClosky et al., "Issue Conflict and Consensus among Party Leaders and Followers," *American Political Science Review* 54(June 1960):406–427.

racy's need for intermediary organizations, V. O. Key writes, "If the system of organized groups did not exist, it would have to be contrived."[6]

Interest Groups and Mexican Political Culture

In this study of interest-group conflict, primary attention is focused upon the American political process. However, a critical international and comparative aspect is also involved, due to Mexico's role in the bracero program. Such a dimension need not conceptually alter our group perspective. As in any democratic polity, interest groups play an indispensable role in the Mexican political process. However, the group–political process relationship in Mexico is somewhat unique and meaningful only if viewed within the context of a dominant one-party political culture.

Viewed comparatively, crucial, though by no means clear-cut, differences exist between the interest-group milieu of the United States and that of Mexico. Granted that an understanding of the nature of pressure groups is requisite to a meaningful understanding of the political process in both states,[7] the following differences must be noted: First, much of Mexico's group conflict is *intra*party in nature; the same struggle generally takes place on an *intragovernmental* level in the United States. While pressure groups do function outside Mexico's dominant Revolutionary party (PRI)—for example, business associations, the Catholic church, and the military as an organized entity—and within opposition parties,

---

[6] V. O. Key, Jr., *Politics, Parties, and Pressure Groups*, p. 149.

[7] Such an assumption is indeed not universal among students of Mexican politics. Essentially, the controversy concerns the role and nature of the Partido Revolucionario Institucional (PRI) and is well illustrated in the works of three American scholars. Frank Brandenburg views the PRI as little more than a subsidiary of the Mexican executive. Mexican government is seen as a benevolent despotism, while interest groups are relegated to a position of relative impotence (*The Making of Modern Mexico*, pp. 3–7). Contrariwise, Robert Scott pictures the PRI as a dominant, yet democratic, political party, which, through its function as aggregator of demands emanating from politically potent interest groups, functions as the vortex of the Mexican political process (*Mexican Government in Transition*, Chap. 6). Assuming a compromise stance between the two polar positions is L. Vincent Padgett, *The Mexican Political System*.

most meaningful group conflict occurs on an intraparty basis. Second, Mexican politics tends to combine relationship and function between the PRI and politically potent interest groups; in the United States, on the other hand, political parties and interest groups generally perform different functions. A third difference, which stems from the Mexican tradition of *personalismo*, is that Mexico's interest-group universe is not characterized, as is the United States', by the phenomenon of overlapping membership.[8] Accordingly, one should not expect to encounter in Mexico the tone of moderation among competing interest groups that typifies the United States political process.

Fourth, and perhaps most important, is the omnipotent position of the president in the Mexican political process.[9] It is one thing to deem the president of the United States "powerful" because he heads the majority party in Congress and receives the electoral acclaim of the populace at large. The connotation of the same term is vastly different when one refers to the leader of the only meaningful political party. Deemed to personify the Revolution of 1910 and acting as the focal point of his nation's political process, the Mexican president, in league with the dominant Revolutionary party, occupies an all-but-unchallenged position in the face of interest-group demands. Like the United States president, Mexico's chief executive must respond to pressures from organized interests, but in so doing he enjoys far more power and leeway than his American counterpart. As final interpreter of the national interest, Mexico's president played a decisive role during twenty-two years of bracero contracting.

In conclusion, it may be said that interest groups play an important role in the Mexican political process. Conversely, one need not accept verbatim Robert Scott's contention that Mexico possesses an "informal but very real semicorporative form of government" in order to grant the paucity of a group approach to the Mexican

---

[8] For a salient examination of Mexico's group milieu, see Scott, *Mexican Government*, pp. 22–23. I have relied heavily on his analysis for comparative purposes.

[9] Padgett, *The Mexican Political System*, Chap. 6.

political process.[10] In fact, one observer has prophesied for Mexico what amounts to a form of interest-group "demon legend" in reverse. Raymond Vernon contends that Mexico's political process is so preoccupied with accommodating all important interests that dynamic, innovating leadership has not been forthcoming.[11] Be that as it may, group theory appears equally applicable to the political systems of Mexico and the United States and is especially pertinent to an investigation of the binational ramifications of the bracero program.

Summary

The effort at theoretical combination employed in this study appears logical and is perhaps requisite given the topic at hand; it is, in any case, hardly a novelty among students of the political process. David Easton has observed that "concepts are neither true nor false; they are only more or less useful."[12] With this in mind, the framework contained herein is derived for the sole purpose of providing a conceptual perspective through which the politics of the bracero program might be more accurately described and analyzed. If the use of group theory in conjunction with systems analysis accomplishes this, it will have fulfilled its conceptual purpose.

[10] Scott, *Mexican Government*, p. 32.

[11] Raymond Vernon, *The Dilemma of Mexico's Development: The Role of the Private and Public Sectors*, esp. pp. 188–193.

[12] David Easton, *A Framework for Political Analysis*, p. 33.

The Bracero Program

CHAPTER 1

The Environmental Context

Like other political phenomena, the group struggle surrounding the importation of Mexican farm labor must be viewed within its environmental context if it is to be properly understood. This chapter places the bracero program in its proper milieu: the historical conditions under which it grew are discussed as well as the intricate and multifaceted nature of the program.

THE BRACERO PROGRAM: A CAPSULE ANALYSIS

Legislation for large-scale importation of Mexican agricultural labor into the United States expired on December 31, 1964. At the time of this study, some Mexicans were still employed on southwestern farms, but for all practical purposes United States agriculture has been sans Mexicans since January 1, 1965.[1] Mexicans

[1] In 1965, there were 20,084 braceros in United States agriculture; in 1966—

had worked in United States fields long before 1951, yet it was not until that year that formal authority was granted nationally and internationally for the massive and highly routinized utilization of braceros in United States agriculture. Although extended coverage of the international and group processes surrounding the inauguration and content of the bracero program is presented in chapter 3, it is necessary to consider its basic structure at this point.

From 1942 until July, 1951, braceros were admitted into the United States as temporary farmworkers under various governmental authorities. In 1951, Congress approved Public Law 78, which added Title V to the Agriculture Act of 1949 and which served as the statutory basis for bracero contracting until it expired in December, 1964. Under its provisions, the United States was specifically authorized to negotiate an agreement with Mexico for admitting Mexican nationals as farmworkers. Public Law 78 restricted the use of braceros to areas where the secretary of labor certified that (1) a bona fide shortage of domestic farmworkers existed; (2) the employer seeking braceros had attempted, but without success, to hire native labor at wages and hours comparable to those offered Mexicans; and (3) the use of braceros did not adversely affect the wages and working conditions of domestics.[2]

In accordance with the provisions of the Mexican labor agreement of 1951, the Mexican government established several regional recruiting centers throughout Mexico at which potential braceros gathered in hopes of securing work in the United States. At these centers they were examined by Mexican and United States officials and then transported to one of several United States reception cen-

---

8,647; in 1967—6,125 ("Long-Term Trends in Foreign-Worker Employment: Table 3, Foreign Workers Admitted for Temporary Employment in U.S. Agriculture," *Farm Labor Developments*, February, 1968, p. 10; hereafter cited as "Foreign Workers Admitted for Temporary Employment").

[2] U.S., Department of Labor, *Information Concerning Entry of Mexican Agricultural Workers into the United States. Public Law 78, 82d Congress, as Amended; Migrant Labor Agreement of 1951, as Amended and Pertinent Interpretations; Standard Work Contract, as Amended and Pertinent Interpretations; Joint Operating Instructions*, pp. iii–iv.

ters, where employers or their representatives signed a standardized work contract with individual braceros.

The contract, legally supported by the United States government, afforded the bracero the following guarantees: (1) payment of at least the prevailing area wage received by natives for performing a given task, (2) employment for three-fourths of the contract period, (3) adequate and sanitary free housing, (4) decent meals at reasonable prices, (5) occupational insurance at employer's expense, and (6) free transportation back to Mexico once the contract period was completed.[3]

A careful reading of this brief summation reveals the rather ambiguous nature of the bracero program. Like numerous other agreements, it contained a great deal of vagueness. In 1951, the United States and Mexico came forth with little more than a skeletal guideline. The flesh and blood of the bracero program took shape in subsequent years from a course that spanned the entire political process spectrum. Defining and clarifying such phrases as "prevailing wage," "adverse effect," "reasonable effort," and "adequate and sanitary," involved two political systems, several administrations, legislatures, executives, bureaucrats, judges, and a wide array of pressure groups. Even at its expiration there was anything but consensus on the program's terminology. Thus, not only was there disagreement concerning the need for the program; there was, in addition, discord about its contents once it came into existence. Yet under the terms of P.L. 78 and its accompanying international agreement, more than four million Mexican farm laborers were legally employed in the United States during a fourteen-year span.[4] It is not surprising, therefore, that the bracero program was so controversial.

UNITED STATES IMMIGRATION POLICY

The Mexican farm labor program must first be analyzed in the context of United States immigration policy. The United States, as

---

[3] Ibid., pp. 1–34.
[4] The exact number was 4,216,754 ("Foreign Workers Admitted for Temporary Employment").

an expanding industrial nation, has long been a country of immigrants. We have been, through several historical immigration
cycles, a country in need of the talents of those outside our national
frontiers. The flow of immigrants into the country has varied in
intensity through the years. Barriers have been erected in the guise
of socioeconomic class, numbers, race, and political affiliation. Yet,
legal restrictions have never halted the flow entirely.

Just as the United States has long been a nation of immigrants,
so too has she long witnessed a more temporary migrant phenomenon: the contracting of foreign workers for brief periods of employment to compensate for domestic labor shortages. In the main,
the great percentage of these imported workers has been of the
agricultural variety. During the mid–twentieth century, the overwhelming majority of agricultural importees was Mexican.[5]

Although the use of Mexican workers in the fields of the Southwest is hardly a recent development,[6] it was not until World War
I that a large influx of Mexican labor became evident.[7] The war
years reflected also the fundamental interest group conflict that has
surrounded the question of imported labor from the very beginning. Early in the century the Immigration and Nationality Act

[5] Of the 5,073,475 foreign workers legally admitted for temporary employment in United States agriculture during the 1942–1967 period, 4,681,255
(or more than 92%) were Mexicans. Ibid.

[6] Estimates vary on how long Mexicans have been employed in United
States agriculture. For example, a recent report by the Department of Agriculture contends that the practice goes back more than a century (Robert C.
McElroy and Earl E. Gavett, *Termination of the Bracero Program: Some Effects on Farm Labor and Migrant Housing Needs*, p. 3). Another author re-
duces this estimate by 50 percent (Pauline R. Kibbe, *Latin Americans in Texas*,
p. 169). One time president of Mexico, Adolfo de la Huerta, contends that the
exodus began in earnest during the Porfirio Díaz presidency (*El Universal*,
June 24, 1951).

[7] It is reported that approximately 73,000 Mexicans were admitted for temporary employment from 1917 to 1921 (U.S., Congress, House, Committee on
the Judiciary, *Study of Population and Immigration Problems, Administrative
Preservations [III], Admission of Aliens into the United States for Temporary
Employment, and "Commuter Workers": Hearing before Subcommittee*, 88th
Cong., 1st Sess., June 24, 1963, p. 27; hereafter cited as House Judiciary Committee Hearings, 1963).

of 1917 became law. The act revealed, even at this early date, the power of agricultural interests vis-à-vis organized labor. The statute, though highly restrictive, contained a loophole in the area of labor importation. Under the terms of the ninth proviso to Section 3 of the act, the commissioner general of immigration was authorized to admit for temporary employment various classes of workers, among them agricultural laborers.[8]

Section 3 of the 1917 act remained the basis for legally admitting temporary agricultural labor until a series of statutes was enacted in the early 1940's, designed specifically to meet emergency labor needs during the World War II era.[9]

Since there exists no reliable evidence on the flow of temporary Mexican labor from the turn of the century until the passage of these wartime measures, we must rely on data drawn from traditional immigration records. Although statistics on annual permanent immigration from Mexico during this period do not reveal the extent of contract labor importation, let alone account for a substantial yet illegal international ebb and flow, they do, nonetheless, divulge a number of radical seasonal fluctuations stemming, in the main, from the restrictive immigration act of 1924 and the effects of a severe economic depression in the early 1930's.[10] A lack of concrete data notwithstanding, the flow of farm labor to and from Mexico continued in a sporadic pattern during the interwar years.[11]

The World War II statutes, prompted by an acute manpower shortage and enacted in accordance with a United States–Mexican agreement, waived virtually all barriers to the importation of nonpermanent foreign labor and facilitated an uninterrupted demand-based flow for the war's duration. Simultaneously, this series of statutes appropriated funds from the federal government for the specific purpose of contracting and importing foreign workers.

[8] Ibid., pp. 24–25.

[9] Ibid., p. 25.

[10] U.S., Bureau of the Census, *Historical Statistics of the United States, Colonial Times to 1957*, p. 58.

[11] Report of the President's Commission on Migratory Labor, *Migratory Labor in American Agriculture*, pp. 37–38.

With the expiration of the last of the wartime statutes, the ninth proviso of Section 3 of the 1917 immigration act was again the sole basis for admitting contract workers on a temporary basis.

However, in the early 1950's, again under a wartime manpower emergency, Congress passed the Agricultural Act of 1949 and then enacted the Immigration and Nationality Act of 1952. These two laws were subsequently the bases for the legal importation of Mexican labor. In July, 1951, Congress amended the 1949 agricultural act, adding Title V in order to govern the admission of Mexican braceros. This amendment became known as Public Law 78. Second, Congress passed an entirely new immigration act the following year: the Immigration and Nationality Act of 1952, which repealed the Immigration Act of 1917 and subsequently came to be known as either the McCarran-Walter Act or Public Law 414. Any Mexican legally admitted to the United States as a temporary farmworker for the period 1951–1964 gained entry under the provisions of either Public Law 78 or Public Law 414.

LABOR UNIONISM IN AGRICULTURE

A second historical context that must be considered if the pressure-group struggle over imported Mexican farm labor is to be properly understood is organized labor's long struggle to unionize agricultural workers.

The efforts of organized labor in agriculture have closely paralleled those of the federal government. It is no oversimplification to view the entire history of governmental action in the area of farm labor as a series of attempts to bring hired farm labor within the range of federal statutes governing nonagricultural workmen. Success in this endeavor has been, at best, modest and sporadic. Before the demise of the bracero program, proponents of a greater federal government role in the area of farm-labor legislation failed repeatedly to enact a minimum wage for agriculture and succeeded only in bringing farmworkers under the coverage of the social security (OASI) program. Farmer groups, in league with other conservative sectors, were successful in excluding farm labor from provisions of other important federal labor programs, such as the

National Labor Relations Act, the Fair Labor Standards Act, and several unemployment compensation laws.[12] Just as the proponents of a greater role by government in the area of farm labor have proved none too successful, so, too, have the supporters of unionization in agriculture fought a sporadically victorious, but largely futile, uphill battle.

Labor unionism in United States agriculture is hardly a recent phenomenon. The first known attempt to unionize farmworkers is said to have been undertaken by the Industrial Workers of the World (IWW) at the turn of the century. Following some early successes in organizing field workers in the 1920–1940 period, a clearly discernible trend away from organizing field labor and toward organizing the processors of field crops became more apparent.[13] During World War II, the drive by organized labor in agriculture lapsed into virtual nonexistence. With the war's termination, the movement again gained some momentum in the Southwest, only to be thwarted in the early 1950's by another wartime labor shortage in agriculture and the resultant federal sanction of legislation anathematic to the very existence of a unionized agriculture sector—the bracero program.

Coupled with an ever-mounting tide of illegal migrants from Mexico (the so-called wetbacks),[14] the legalized importation of Mexican farm labor appeared for a time to be more than the unionization effort could stand. In the long run, however, P.L. 78 may have proved to be a blessing in disguise. As the bracero program was extended into the post–Korean War period, the unionization operation in agriculture united with other movements concerned about the plight of domestic migrant labor. Together, they were to form a common front against a clearly discernible enemy: the bracero program. From the struggle against a common antagonist

[12] Spencer A. Rich, *United States Agricultural Policy in the Postwar Years, 1945–1963*, p. 77.

[13] Alice C. Kinkead, *Labor Unionism in Agriculture: A Brief History and Summary of Pro and Con Arguments*, pp. 1–8.

[14] While the Mexican uses the term "bracero" to describe all farmworkers, he too distinguishes between legal and illegal entrants, terming the latter *espaldas mojadas*.

emerged a revitalized union movement in southwestern agriculture, a movement that, at this writing, continues a struggle begun half a century earlier.

AGRICULTURAL MECHANIZATION

The third historical fact is the relentless march of mechanization in United States agriculture. In a word, the machine has all but replaced the man on the mid-twentieth-century United States farm. As the use of machinery has increased, so has the number of farms, farmers, and farmworkers decreased.

The postwar period has been an era of accelerated mechanization on the farm. Machines have replaced farmworkers of all types, including permanent employees, temporary local workers, seasonal domestic migrants, and imported foreign laborers. In the period 1949 through 1965, while its total population increased some 45 million, the United States farm population dropped from 24,194,000 (or 16.3 percent of the total population) to 12,363,000 (or 6.4 percent of the total population). During the same period (1949–1965), the average number of persons employed on United States farms fell from 9,964,000 in 1949 to 5,610,000 in 1965. The number of farm wage workers dropped from 4,140,000 in 1949 to 3,128,000 in 1965. Unfortunately, the number of migrant farmworkers did not decline during the same years, rising slightly from 422,000 in 1949 to 466,000 in 1965.[15] Thus, more domestic migrants were competing for a sharply reduced number of jobs.

Equally revealing, the total number of farmworkers dropped 41 percent during the 1950–1960 decade. This amounted to the largest percentage reduction during any ten-year period in United States history.[16] During the 1949–1961 period, the number of man-hours used in agricultural production declined an enormous 41 percent.[17] Even more important was the phenomenal reduction in total man-hours devoted to cotton during the 1950–1964 period. If one keeps in mind that most braceros worked in some phase of cotton produc-

15 U.S., Department of Agriculture, *Agricultural Statistics, 1966*, pp. 446–449.
16 *New York Times*, October 3, 1962.
17 Ibid., November 9, 1962.

tion during the early and mid-1950's, the following statistics assume particular relevance: The total man-hours devoted to cotton in an average year during the 1950–1954 period were approximately 1.5 billion. This figure was reduced to 961 million in the average year from 1955 to 1959. By 1964, the figure had slumped to 590 million man-hours in United States cotton.[18] In 1950, approximately 8 percent of United States cotton was machine harvested.[19] By 1964, the final year of bracero contracting, the figure had risen to 78 percent. In Arizona and California, two of the principal bracero-using states, 97 percent of the 1964 cotton crop was machine harvested.[20]

These figures reveal irrefutably that fewer people on fewer farms, hiring fewer laborers and utilizing a maximum amount of machinery and technology, are producing more than ever before. For the seasonal farm laborer, be he domestic migrant or Mexican importee, one paramount conclusion emerges: the machine has taken his place. For the hired native agricultural laborer the ultimate and perhaps invincible opponent may prove to be the machine and not the imported bracero.

UNITED STATES–MEXICAN RELATIONS

A fourth historical context within which the bracero program must be considered is that of United States–Mexican relations. The impact of imported Mexican labor on our relations with Mexico gave the entire question its diplomatic overtones. If the bracero program had definite repercussions on our relations with Mexico, it also, by logical extension, affected United States Latin American policy and United States diplomacy in general. It is the overall diplomatic ramifications of the question, and its impact on United States relations with Mexico in particular, that render the bracero

[18] Robert G. Ainsworth, "Causes and Effects of Declining Cotton Employment," *Farm Labor Developments*, September–October, 1967, p. 32.

[19] James Nix, "Effects of Cotton Harvest Mechanization on Hired Seasonal Labor," *Employment Security Review* 30 (January 1963):12.

[20] Table 21, Upland Cotton: Percentage Harvested by Hand and Mechanically, by States and the United States, 1960 to Date, in *The Cotton Situation*, May, 1965, p. 21.

program a fit topic for study by students of American diplomacy.

Before the bracero program terminated in 1964, the flow of Mexican farm labor to the United States was of fundamental importance to relations between Mexico and the United States. In fact, the question was at least as prominent as any single issue between the two nations during the postwar era.[21] The entire process of labor importation from Mexico revolved around the 1951 agreement between the United States and Mexico. Past experience with direct employer contracting led Mexico to insist that the process be placed on an official international basis. For both governments concerned, the international dimensions of the bracero program were as crucial as its intranational ramifications.

The Bracero Program: A Multifaceted Phenomenon

From the preceding outline of the bracero program's environmental context, one might inadvertently assume an overly simplistic view of the question. Nothing could be further from the actual truth. The program's milieu did encompass national immigration policy, unionization efforts, agricultural mechanization, and Mexican–United States relations. Omission of any of these factors would render hollow any analysis of the question. However, a great deal more was involved.

In many respects, the entire question of imported Mexican farm labor was akin to an iceberg. On the exterior the aforementioned components were clearly visible. Lying beneath the surface, however, was a virtual labyrinth of interrelated and multidimensional processes. One could spend a lifetime and never thoroughly trace each primary component of the bracero question, let alone analyze the multitude of secondarily related ingredients. Still, an effort in

[21] Writing in 1964, Frank Brandenburg placed the bracero question on a par with four other crucial issues between the two nations: (1) tariffs on lead and zinc, (2) water rights and boundary questions, (3) American "pirating" in what Mexico considers to be her national fishing waters, and (4) racial discrimination (*The Making of Modern Mexico*, pp. 233–234). Writing in 1965, Paul Kennedy classified the bracero program along with the question of water salinity as "two of the most serious obstacles at the moment to binational harmony . . ." (*New York Times*, February 21, 1965).

this direction is requisite to the study at hand. Although several avenues are available through which to analyze the multifaceted nature of the question, I have chosen to postpone for the moment specific consideration of the bracero program's diplomatic ramifications and have selected instead a more restricted country-by-country approach.

Mexico and the Bracero Program

If one views the bracero program through Mexican eyes, it is possible to reduce its many dimensions to an oversimplified set of opposites: (1) those conditions favoring the exodus of workers, or what I shall call the "positive factors"; and (2) those forces opposing the exodus, or the "negative factors." Of the former category, it may be said that four interrelated Mexican conditions aided the migration (whether legal or illegal) of farmworkers to the United States: (1) topographic conditions, (2) demographic factors, (3) sociopsychological variables, and (4) economic-political factors.

The Positive Factors. Mid-century Mexico presents a classic example of one of the dilemmas facing many contemporary developing nations: an overwhelming peasant population without the topographic base required to sustain it.[22] Mexico is ill equipped topographically to support its burgeoning rural population. Rainfall in Mexico's vast northern reaches is wholly insufficient in normal years, and this problem was exacerbated by a prolonged drought during the 1950's. Much of the country is mountainous, with only one-third of the land being level. To compound this problem, an overwhelming percentage of Mexico's arable land either lies in the tropical, agriculturally unproductive southern peninsula or is found on high-altitude plateaus where the climate is unfavorable to most crops.[23] In short, Mexico's total arable acreage

---

[22] A concise review of Mexican topography is contained in Howard F. Cline, *Mexico: Revolution to Evolution, 1940–1960*, Chap. 4; and Nathan L. Whetten, *Rural Mexico*, pp. 108–123.

[23] In 1950, approximately 70 percent of Mexico's total land area was in farms, while only 10 percent of her total land area was classified as "tillable." Of this 10 percent (some 49 million acres), approximately 46 percent (some 22 mil-

is overwhelmingly disproportionate to the size of her largely rural population. Nature has proven topographically unkind to the majority of Mexico's citizenry and, thus, has given cause for migration.

On the other hand, Mother Nature seems to have smiled rather cynically in the area of demography. Again in the mold of the model underdeveloped nation, Mexico suffers from overpopulation. It appears that religion and the cult of *machismo* ("virility" or "masculinity") have combined during recent decades to produce a population explosion.[24] Mexicans face a dearth of arable land in a predominantly rural country and have responded in a nontextbook manner by producing more children to populate an already overcrowded agricultural sector.[25] Thus, like the proverbial snowball, a second positive ingredient is added to the phenomenon of Mexican migration.

The sociopsychological climate within which the typical rural Mexican is reared constitutes a third positive factor in the outward flow of manpower. Social and psychological attributes of the Mexican peasant worked in combination to provide an approximate personality prototype for the role of bracero. To toil endless hours in stifling heat and under generally adverse conditions demanded more than mere physical attributes. Granted, a unique and indeed remarkable physical specimen was required to successfully perform the arduous endless hours of stoop labor demanded of the field hand in southwestern agriculture. Such physical attributes alone, however, were not enough.

---

lion acres) lay fallow (Kathryn H. Wylie, *Mexico as a Market and Competitor for U.S. Agricultural Products*, p. 10).

[24] During the first half of this century, Mexico's population increased at a rate of approximately 3.5 percent annually. Even more crucial for the purposes of this study was the phenomenal population boom from 1940 to 1950. During these ten years Mexico's population rose from approximately 19.5 million to 25.5 million—an increase of more than 30 percent (Dirección General de Estadística, *Compendido Estadístico, 1951*, pp. 7–9 and 72; hereafter cited as *Compendido Estadístico*).

[25] In 1950, for example, approximately 58 percent of all Mexicans were employed in agriculture (John A. Crow, *Mexico Today*, p. 312).

The various tasks performed by such a laborer required, in addition, a somewhat unique personality type: one accustomed to living, and indeed thriving, in a virtual state of physical and mental peonage. The Mexican peasant, by virtue of his rather unique sociopsychological background, was ideally suited for the task. The transition from *ejidatario* or *minifundista* to bracero was generally accomplished with utmost ease by the Mexican. Indeed, the average bracero or wetback probably found little except language (and not always that) to distinguish between the *patrón* and the straw-boss. It would appear, in sum, that the sociopsychological milieu in which the average Mexican peasant was reared prepared him ideally for his role as the servile, hard-working, seldom complaining, perpetually polite bracero.[26]

The economic-political variable must also be considered when analyzing the domestic factors favoring a northbound flow of Mexican labor. In approaching the task of nation-building, Mexico, like her fellow developing nations, has placed the industrial cart before the agricultural ox. For various reasons, not the least of which is the ubiquitous phenomenon of hypersensitive nationalism, Mexican development has, in the face of counsel to the contrary,[27] been somewhat unbalanced in favor of the industrial sector. That Mexico has made remarkable strides in the industrial area of her economy is undeniable. It is likewise beyond debate that she has done so at the expense of the agricultural sector.[28] With the possible ex-

[26] Descriptions of the sociopsychological milieu within which the typical rural Mexican is reared are numerous. Particularly revealing are Oscar Lewis, *Life in a Mexican Village: Tepoztlan Restudied*; and Richard H. Hancock, *The Role of the Bracero in the Economic and Cultural Dynamics of Mexico: A Case Study of Chihuahua.*

[27] Stanford A. Mosk, *Industrial Revolution in Mexico*, pp. 304–311.

[28] This is not to contend that the entire agricultural sector has been neglected. It is meant only to emphasize that, in comparison to the urban resident, the lot of the average Mexican peasant has not improved in recent years. In fact, many rural Mexicans are worse off today than in past decades. Thus, while substantial funds have been allotted to the mechanized, market-oriented segments of Mexican agriculture (cotton, in particular), little has been done to improve the subsistence-level segment—that segment of Mexican agriculture which supports the great majority of Mexico's rural poor (Hancock, *The Role*

ception of the Cárdenas years (1934–1940), the Mexican peasant
has been relegated to a secondary position vis-à-vis his urban
counterpart.

Contemporary Mexican politicians have thus found it expedient
to allot, on a comparative basis, the choice slices of Mexico's developmental pie to the industrial arm, while allocating only the left-
overs to the peasant-dominated segment of agriculture. The results,
accordingly, have been anything but surprising.[29] Mexico has witnessed a substantial rural-urban migration in recent years. Simultaneously, the ever-present multiplier effect has seen to it that rural Mexico remains overpopulated. Those peasants not migrating
to the cities chose one of two remaining alternatives: continued
bare subsistence off the land, or migration north to the United
States. It was the latter alternative that proved so magnetic to the
average *campesino* during the immediate postwar decades.

Comparatively speaking, the Mexican peasant earns substantially less than his urban counterpart.[30] The latter, in turn, garners
far less than the modal United States citizen, be he agriculturally
or nonagriculturally employed.[31] No elaborate mathematical com-

---

of the Bracero, pp. 29–35; and *Hispanic American Report* 10(September 1957):
402.

[29] Commenting sarcastically on the political neglect of the *campesino*, José
Vasconcelos observes that, while the *ejido* system may have proven politically
effective as a means of organizing farmers behind the PRI, "it has been disastrous economically as thousands of braceros who left not only their land but
their country have shown" (*New York Times*, March 10, 1954). For further
comment on the failure of Mexico's economic prosperity to trickle down to the
rural masses, one may note Oscar Lewis, "Mexico since Cárdenas," in *Social
Change in Latin America Today: Its Implications for United States Policy*,
Richard N. Adams, et al., pp. 291–294.

[30] In 1955, for example, agriculture employed approximately 55 percent of
Mexico's labor force, yet received only 20 percent of the national income. The
average income of the Mexican farmworker was $215 in 1955, while his urban
counterpart earned $1,026. For the total economically active Mexican popula-
tion, the average per capita income for 1955 was $586 (*Hispanic American Re-
port* 10(September 1957):402.

[31] In 1956, the American migratory farmworker, who represented the bottom
rung on the U.S. economic ladder, earned a yearly average of $1,178 (U.S.,
Dept. Agriculture, *Agricultural Statistics, 1966*, p. 449).

putation is needed to reach the conclusion that the average Mexican stands an excellent chance of earning the equivalent of a small fortune if only he can come to the United States. Even if he earned a paltry sum by American standards, the bracero could, through hard work and diligent saving, return home with a substantial nest egg by Mexican standards.[32]

There existed, in addition to the obvious individual attraction of the United States dollar, another economic-political element that must be taken into account: the importance of bracero remittances to the Mexican economy in general and to Mexico's balance of payments with the United States in particular.[33] It has been estimated that during the 1950's official and unofficial remittances of Mexican farmworkers ranged between $22 million and $120 million annually.[34] While nationalistically minded Mexican economists tended to underrate the actual amount of these earnings, one of the most thorough studies of the program's impact on the Mexican economy found that bracero remittances constituted that nation's

[32] Numerous authors have commented upon the enormous discrepancy in earning power that lured the Mexican laborer northward. Representative of their opinions is this observation by Frank Brandenburg: "The Mexican migratory laborer receives more per hour on U.S. farms than he normally earns per day in Mexican agriculture" (*The Making of Modern Mexico*, p. 334).

[33] That bracero remittances were indeed crucial to Mexico's balance of payments was evidenced by a U.S. government study completed three years after the program's termination. The report showed a substantial increase in balance of payments in favor of the United States during the post-bracero years (U.S., Congress, Senate, Committee on Appropriations, *Department of Agriculture and Related Agencies Appropriations. Hearing before Subcommittee on H.R. 10509*, 90th Cong., 1st sess., Fiscal Year 1968, pp. 55–57).

[34] Official Mexican sources list remittances at slightly more than $200 million for the period 1954–1959 (Secretaría de Industria y Comercio, Dirección General de Estadística, *Revista de Estadística* 19:422, 21:112, 22:108, 23:168). Hancock, on the other hand, estimates that the amount of money actually sent or taken home by braceros during 1956–1957 was no less than $120 million annually (*The Role of the Bracero*, p. 37). A U.S. government publication contends that braceros earned approximately $200 million in 1957, of which roughly half reached Mexico (U.S., Department of Labor, *Farm Labor Fact Book*, p. 176). There is, unfortunately, no official compilation of data, in either English or Spanish, that calculates actual bracero earnings.

third largest source of foreign exchange in 1956 and 1957.[35] What is more important, the study continues, is that, unlike other sources of foreign exchange, these remittances went directly to Mexico's most deprived economic group: the peasants themselves and their families.[36]

Since there were 436,290 braceros in 1957, some 2,250,000 people may be assumed to have received all or part of their support from bracero wages during that year. In 1956, 1957, and 1958, years in which braceros numbered over 400,000, it can be said that 4 percent of Mexico's entire economically active population—7 percent of those active in agriculture—found employment in the United States, while over 10 percent of the total rural population was directly dependent to varying degrees on bracero income.[37]

A final economic-political factor that, from the Mexican perspective, appeared to facilitate the exodus of farm labor is what might be termed the "safety valve" dimension of the bracero program. The siphoning off of a substantial number of unemployed and underemployed members of a politically explosive segment of the population acted as a safety valve for the Mexican polity.[38] One of Mexico's truly restless sectors in the postwar era has been the agricultural. The peasant looks upon himself as the forgotten link in Mexico's developmental chain and, led often by radical elements, has made his resentment felt in what was generally a none-too-subtle manner. Seizures of haciendas, mass squatter movements, riots, and occasional premeditated murders characterized Mexico's sporadically violent rural populace in the last quarter-century.[39] During the apogee years of this rural unrest, one of the principal palliatives was the exodus of braceros and wetbacks. It is no exag-

[35] Hancock, *The Role of the Bracero*, pp. 1–2.

[36] Ibid., p. 2.

[37] Ibid., p. 41.

[38] Several students of Mexican political culture have noted this effect, including Robert E. Scott, *Mexican Government in Transition*, p. 37; Hancock, *The Role of the Bracero*, p. 129; and Lewis, "Mexico since Cárdenas," pp. 292–293.

[39] *New York Times*, April 13, 1958; *Hispanic American Report* 7 (February 1954):1.

geration to surmise that many a potential rural agitator became, instead, a contented bracero.

One might mention other plus factors that, from the Mexican standpoint, abetted the migratory flow, such as geographic proximity to the United States border, the agricultural skills and techniques acquired by braceros and put to use on their return,[40] and the culturally broadening experience that being a bracero invariably entailed.[41] On balance, however, the variables of topography, demography, economics, and politics constituted the principal catalytic agent to the exodus of Mexican farmworkers. Yet not all aspects of the bracero program were appealing from the Mexican point of view. For many Mexicans the program's ledger displayed more debits than credits.

The Negative Factors. The flow of Mexican labor to the United States engendered native opposition on religious, economic, and political grounds. The Catholic church of Mexico opposed the migration of braceros for several reasons. The program was said, first of all, to contribute directly to the disruption of family life. While the father was in the United States, his family was said to have suffered various hardships that led, in many cases, to family desertion by the mother.[42] A second ground for church opposition was the immoral life supposedly led by the migrant during his stay

[40] Wide disagreement exists on this point. For examples of those who feel that the bracero did acquire and put to use new agricultural skills, see William O. Freithaler, *Mexico's Foreign Trade and Economic Development*, pp. 77–78; Frank D. Barlow, Jr., and Grady B. Crowe, *Mexican Cotton: Production, Problems, Potentials*, pp. 1–3; and Hancock, *The Role of the Bracero*, p. 122. Lewis, however, assumes the opposing viewpoint ("Mexico since Cárdenas," p. 293).

[41] Whetten, *Rural Mexico*, p. 270; Lewis, "Mexico since Cárdenas," pp. 292–293; Lewis, *Life in a Mexican Village*; and Hancock, *The Role of the Bracero*, pp. 122–124.

[42] Louisa R. Shotwell has described such a condition in a polemic she entitles "Flower Bed: The Adventure of Armando." In this case, Armando, at the urging of naive parents and a lecherous brother, becomes a bracero. He returns laden with money, only to find his wife and children under the naughty brother's roof (*The Harvesters: The Story of the Migrant People*, pp. 49–58). For a more balanced analysis, see Hancock, *The Role of the Bracero*, pp. 38–39.

in this country. Contact with such allegedly ubiquitous phenomena as prostitution, alcohol, and gambling was said to be unavoidable for the national.[43] The third, and perhaps the most fundamental, basis for church antagonism was the migrant's contact with Protestantism. There can be no doubt that the bracero was indeed subjected to non-Catholic religious temptation during his tour. The church did not tarry long, however, in the face of said danger. Beginning in 1953, at the behest of the Vatican, Mexican priests accompanied the migrants for the purpose of providing secular and spiritual aid.[44]

Far more substantial grounds for opposition to the exodus of Mexican labor (whether legal or illegal) were economic in nature. In general, the economic case against migration held that the cream of Mexico's labor crop was being siphoned off by the lure of the United States dollars when they were sorely needed at home. Not only did these men leave during a time of need; many of them never returned, thus registering a net loss for Mexico of thousands of skilled laborers annually.[45]

In addition to the Mexican government, which, by virtue of its position, was generally a *pro forma* opponent of this labor exodus,[46] the three primary sectors of the Mexican economy posed perennial blocks of opposition. Industrialists criticized the outflow of laborers, saying that it deprived Mexican industry of needed skilled and unskilled labor.[47] Mexican unions in general, and particularly the powerful National Farmers Confederation, opposed the program for two reasons: (1) each bracero, had he remained in Mexico as a

[43] Ted LeBerthon, "At The Prevailing Rate," *Commonweal*, November 1, 1957, pp. 122–125.

[44] *New York Times*, May 7, 1953.

[45] As an example of this oft-repeated and dubious contention, one may note *Hispanic American Report* 10(April 1957):118; editorials in *El Universal*, July 19, 1951, and July 25, 1951.

[46] There was one important exception to the Mexican government's *pro forma* opposition to the program—the desertion by farmers of their own private plots in order to become braceros. It is undeniable that such a development was cause for official alarm (*New York Times*, July 21, 1951, July 24, 1952, and February 12, 1956; editorial in *El Universal*, June 18, 1951).

[47] *New York Times*, December 29, 1956.

farmworker, represented a potential unionist; and (2) nothing in the United States–Mexican agreement required the bracero to join a union once he crossed the border.[48] Agricultural entrepreneurs were perennial critics of the migrant exodus. Their opposition was also twofold. They contended, first, that the men were needed to harvest and cultivate Mexican crops.[49] Secondly, and with far greater validity, Mexican cotton growers in particular complained that the use of Mexican labor by United States farmers resulted in a surplus of United States cotton, which was, on occasion, dumped on the world market, thereby undermining the Mexican cotton industry.[50]

Perhaps the most valid economic argument emanating from Mexico against the bracero program was that the flow of laborers fostered an even greater economic dependence on the United States.[51] The very geographic proximity of an industrial giant to her north renders Mexico especially sensitive to United States economic conditions. A large exodus of farm labor only heightened Mexico's general economic dependence, while periodically working particular hardships on bracero-supplying regions.[52] As one scholar observes: "While it can be argued that Mexico is likely to be dependent in any case, the bracero program is very sensitive to United States employment conditions, which can vary sharply from year to year, causing extreme hardship in the areas which provide large numbers of braceros."[53]

[48] *Hispanic American Report* 6(January 1954):10; 7(June 1954):9; and *New York Times*, February 12, 1956.

[49] Given Mexico's chronic rural unemployment, this contention is virtually unsubstantiated. There were, however, instances in which the labor shortage in a given village became chronic due to the bracero exodus (Lewis, "Mexico since Cárdenas," pp. 292–293; and *El Universal*, June 20, 1951). For a thorough rebuttal to this contention by the landowners, see Lesley Bird Simpson, *Many Mexicos*, p. 301; and Mosk, *Industrial Revolution in Mexico*, pp. 304–311.

[50] *Hispanic American Report* 9(August 1956):326; and T. Richard Spradlin, "The Mexican Farm Labor Importation Program—Review and Reform (Part II)," *The George Washington Law Review* 30 (December 1961):321.

[51] *Hispanic American Report* 10(October 1957):453–454.

[52] Hancock, *The Role of the Bracero*, p. 127.

[53] Ibid.

Opposition to the bracero program from Mexico's religious and economic sectors was substantial, even though not always substantiated. It paled, however, alongside the political reaction. The most virulent and sustained Mexican critique had two political bases. In the first instance, domestic politicians often stood in opposition to the extranational employment of Mexican nationals on selfish, yet highly rational, grounds: the restless and potentially explosive nature of the returnee. The lyrics of a popular World War I tune could easily have been applied to the returning braceros: "How ya gonna keep 'em down on the bare-subsistence-level Mexican farm after they've seen L. A.?" The bracero might well return home with needed agricultural skills, but he might also bring with him politically and economically dangerous aspirations.[54] Thus, from a selfish political viewpoint, particular elements within the Mexican populace opposed the migrant flow.

The other political ground for opposing the exodus was far more fundamental and, on a relative basis, constituted the most damning Mexican critique leveled against the bracero program. For the nationalistically sensitive Mexicans, the migration of their nationals to the United States for the avowed purpose of performing admittedly demeaning tasks was nothing short of a conscience gall. To Mexico's political Left, the entire process constituted a classic example of colonial exploitation by capitalistic gringos. For countless political moderates it was clearly an affront to Mexican dignity.[55]

The bracero program proved nationalistically humiliating to the Mexican for numerous reasons, including the fact that (1) his

[54] *New York Times*, July 21, 1951; Whetten, *Rural Mexico*, p. 271; and editorial in *El Universal*, July 19, 1951.

[55] For the reaction of leftist parties, see David G. Pfeiffer, "The Mexican Farm Labor Supply Program—Its Friends and Foes," pp. 98–103. It was perhaps due to the Mexican's wounded sense of pride that the Mexican Political moderate was acutely sensitive to the over-all treatment of his countrymen in the United States. According to one authority, this hypersensitivity was very similar to a previous American concern over the property rights of its citizens in Mexico (Howard F. Cline, *The United States and Mexico*, p. 392).

countrymen were, on occasion, subjected to racial and religious discrimination during their stay in the United States;[56] (2) they performed the most menial of agricultural tasks under salary and working conditions so adverse, by United States standards, as to exclude all but the most desperate domestics; and, above all (3) Mexicans from all walks of life, not just landed peasants, literally inundated recruiting depots, paid sizable bribes, risked imprisonment and even death by illegal border crossing, and literally fought one another tooth and nail for the "privilege" of becoming a temporary migrant to the United States.[57] For these and other reasons, the flow of migrants northward humiliated the Mexican national conscience and resulted in a substantial amount of expressed opposition to the bracero program.

Yet, despite her apparent disgust and humiliation at being the source for such a human stream, Mexico did not terminate the legalized exodus. The United States accomplished this task. With the possible exception of the Catholic church, much of the opposition to bracero contracting on the part of Mexican interest groups and political parties was *pro forma* and to be expected under the circumstances. On balance, Mexico acquiesced to the bracero program because its advantages far outweighed its disadvantages. It was the United States who eventually rejected a program that Mexico by necessity accepted.

[56] Charges and countercharges of racial discrimination were a concomitant to the flow of Mexican labor. For a typical, blatant example, see *New York Times*, June 27, 1959. For a general survey of how Mexicans were accepted in the United States, see Nelson G. Copp, " 'Wetbacks' and Braceros: Mexican Migrant Laborers and American Immigration Policy, 1930–1960," chap. III. The most cogent rebuttal to the ever-present discrimination charge is presented by Richard Hancock. Although he admits that braceros were occasionally the brunt of discrimination, he holds that the vast majority of them was not aware of it: "These men are usually of humble background and often view actions inspired by racial prejudice as the normal behavior of a superior toward an inferior," (*The Role of the Bracero*, p. 127).

[57] Examples of this phenomenon are numerous. For specific instances, note Simpson, *Many Mexicos*, p. 311; *Hispanic American Report* 7 (February 1954): 8; *New York Times*, May 12, 1953, January 24, 1954, January 28, 1954; and *El Universal*, August 19, 1951, and September 7, 1951.

The United States and the Bracero Program

Again, as was the case with Mexico, it is possible to view the bracero system in its United States milieu from an oversimplified perspective of protagonist and antagonist. The case for the program is presented first, and second, the case against.

The Affirmative Case. The forces of agribusiness supported the legalized importation of Mexican agricultural laborers with a seldom equaled political acumen and adroitness. From the very outset of the struggle the American Farm Bureau Federation was at the forefront of these legions. Among other organizations that, from time to time and with varying degrees of ardor and effectiveness, countenanced the bracero program were the National Grange, the Vegetable Growers Association of America, the National Council of Farmer Cooperatives, the National Farm Labor Users Committee, the Amalgamated Sugar Company, the National Beet Growers Federation, the National Cotton Council, state growers' associations in general, and the Council of California Growers in particular. With a collective voice or individually, these forces of agribusiness supported the bracero program on many grounds.

The first argument put forth in behalf of the bracero program was that, in spite of efforts by growers to secure them, domestic farm laborers were simply not available in sufficient numbers when they were needed. Thus, in order to cultivate and harvest their crops, owners were forced to look elsewhere for labor, in this case to Mexico. Farm owners and operators were quick to point out that the type of work they offered was highly seasonal and temporary in nature, that it was difficult stoop labor and often performed under adverse conditions, and that in general it was the kind of work considered repugnant to domestics.[58] Furthermore, failure to secure an adequate labor supply when needed (which often was on very short notice) would mean crop spoilage and financial disaster for the farmer and, if extended to its logical conclusion, would re-

[58] Report of the Senate Committee on Labor and Welfare, *California Farm Labor Problems, Part I*, pp. 110–112; hereafter cited as *California Labor Problems.*

sult in the migration of growers to countries in which a healthier labor climate prevailed.

A second argument in defense of imported Mexican labor was a direct corollary of the initial proposition. It was contended that even among the domestics available for work there was a noticeable lack of skills, dependability, and character. Many of those seeking jobs simply possessed neither the requisite physical stamina nor the skills.[59] The job of the field hand in southwestern agriculture was indeed arduous, to say the least. It took a unique physical specimen to perform twelve hours of back-breaking stoop labor under generally adverse weather conditions. In addition to amazing physical stamina, the field worker had to know his trade. Requisite skills could not be acquired overnight.[60] Like the factory worker, the farmworker required a certain amount of on-the-job training. But, unlike the industrialist, the grower could not afford to offer an apprenticeship. By the time such education was completed, the crops would have spoiled. The bracero, on the other hand, was said to possess both the requisite physical ability and the needed skills. With him the work was done quickly and efficiently.

The Mexican national, in contrast to the native, was also looked upon by farm owners as highly dependable and of excellent character. Growers contended that the domestic field hand could simply not be depended upon.[61] He would promise to appear for work at an appointed time and place and not show up. Once on the job, he could not be trusted to perform his task adequately; he would rest more than he would work. Furnished with adequate housing, domestic workers often destroyed or defaced the premises.[62] In short,

[59] Ibid., p. 113.

[60] For a cogent defense of this contention, see Hancock, *The Role of the Bracero*, p. 128.

[61] An excellent analysis of the attitude of management toward the average domestic migrant laborer is presented by Padfield and Martin. They observe that "fundamental in the grower's view is the general worthlessness of domestic help." Many growers look upon domestics as "vocational rejects" or "bums and winos" (Harland Padfield and William E. Martin, *Farmers, Workers, and Machines: Technological and Social Change in Farm Industries of Arizona*, pp. 256–258).

[62] This contention is well illustrated in a 1960 speech by Senator Harrison A.

fundamental in the owner's mind was the general worthlessness of domestic workers. Not so the bracero. He was dependability personified, always prompt, and never one to shirk his task once the overseer turned his back. The Mexican kept his surroundings spotless and displayed, in general, an admirable character.

A third argument emanating from agribusiness circles held that the use of imported braceros did not adversely affect the wages, working conditions, and employment opportunities of native farmworkers.[63] Domestics were said to be specifically guaranteed protection against any adverse effects of imported labor by provisions of Public Law 78 and its concomitant international agreement. Surely, the owners reasoned, if a sufficient number of skilled, dependable domestic workers could not be found and if the use of braceros could not in any circumstance adversely affect the lot of those natives who were willing and able to work, the utilization of importees was justified.

Fourth, supporters of the bracero program argued that the Mexican national himself benefited immensely from his sojourn in the United States.[64] Financially, the bracero and his family were said to have reaped a bountiful harvest. Socially, his dollar earnings enabled the returnee to accomplish a virtually unknown feat among Mexican peasants—social advancement. It was argued that the cultural horizons of the Mexican national were enlarged enormously during the tenure as a bracero. For many of Mexico's rural inhabitants, a trip to a nearby *municipio* is considered culturally

---

Williams. The opinion of the stereotyped owner toward the typical domestic was paraphrased by the senator as follows: "Well, I've done a lot of things to improve the welfare of migrants on my farm. I've built them new housing, put in toilet facilities, new showers, cooking facilities, nice new bedding, plenty of garbage cans. And what happens? They mark up the walls, kick holes in the window screens, stop up the toilets, pull knobs off the showers and stoves, tear the blankets, and tip over the garbage cans." (Harrison A. Williams, Jr., "For a National Task—A National Program," *Proceedings: Western Interstate Conference on Migratory Labor*, p. 8).

[63] This particular argument by growers is well illustrated in a 1963 letter to the editor of the *New York Times* from O. W. Fillerup, executive vice-president of the Council of California Growers (*New York Times*, November 15, 1963).

[64] *California Labor Problems*, pp. 113–114.

enhancing as well as stature building.[65] By comparison, a six-month stay in the United States was deemed the equivalent of an interplanetary journey, so wordly and prestigious was the returnee deemed by his fellow villagers. Those who championed the Mexican labor program utilized statistics illustrating that a vast majority of braceros were repeaters.[66] How, it was argued, could such a program fail to benefit the bracero if such a large percentage chose to return again and again?

Another defense of the bracero agreement was couched in diplomatic terms. The program was said to be good for United States–Mexican relations. It was argued that Mexico found the program desirable because of its admitted economic impact and because it served as a political safety valve for the restless, overpopulated, unemployed agricultural sector.[67] Mexico was said to also favor the legalized exodus of her nationals because it drastically reduced the flow of illegal wetback traffic, a flow that in the early 1950's became a virtual diplomatic cause célèbre among the xenophobic Mexicans.[68] It was contended, on the other hand, that the United States favored the bracero agreement from a diplomatic standpoint, because Mexico supported it and because it greatly reduced the wetback flood tide.[69] Thus, the backers of imported farm labor added a diplomatic dimension to their list of pro-bracero arguments.

A sixth and final reason for supporting the importation of contracted Mexican laborers was a general economic one. Backers of the bracero pact contended that it was beneficial to the United States in general and to its farmers and consumers in particular. It was said to be good for the United States because a healthy, prosperous agricultural sector was good for the whole country.[70] Some

[65] Note the 1963 letter to the editor of the *New York Times* from Professor Michael Belshaw of Hunter College (*New York Times*, June 14, 1963).

[66] Ibid.

[67] See notes 37 and 38 of this chapter.

[68] Cline, *The United States and Mexico*, p. 393; *Excelsior*, February 26, 1950; editorial in *El Universal*, July 25, 1951; and *El Universal*, August 7, 1951.

[69] *New York Times*, June 8, 1958.

[70] For the position of agribusiness on the interrelationship between agricultural labor, the farmer, and the general well-being of the United States, see

of our greatest farm states were bracero-using states. California, our foremost agricultural state, was the primary utilizer of Mexican nationals during the latter years of the bracero agreement. Braceros, so the argument went, were crucial to California agriculture, which, in turn, was crucial to the whole of United States agriculture. In bracero-using states, those farmers not employing Mexicans were said to benefit from the program, because, if those growers employing braceros turned, instead, to domestics, the small non-bracero-using farmer would have been left with virtually no field laborers.[71] Another particular beneficiary of braceroism was said to be the United States housewife, or whoever purchased bracero-produced items in the supermarket. Since the Mexican was such a hard-working, efficient individual, the grower produced his crop at a lower cost. The savings were, in turn, passed on to the consumer.[72]

The Negative Case. Opponents of imported Mexican farm labor vigorously opposed the pro-bracero arguments. Anti-braceroists refuted, at least to their own way of thinking, every argument put forth by the pro-braceroists and then countered with some original charges of their own. As was the case with the proponents, the foes of braceroism were numerous. Unlike the proponents, however, who were disproportionately agriculturally based, the anti-braceroists were more diversified in composition. Among the organizations opposing bracero importation, the foremost opponents were the representatives of organized labor, that is, the AFL–CIO and its affiliates: the Textile Workers Union of America, the National Agricultural Workers Union, the Agricultural Workers Organizing Committee, the Amalgamated Meat Cutters and Butcher Workmen, and the American section of the Joint United States–Mexico Trade Union Committee.

In addition to organized labor, the opponents of braceroism in-

---

John Zuckerman, "The Migrant Worker in Relation to the Labor Problems of the Farmer," *Proceedings: Western Interstate Conference on Migratory Labor*, pp. 35–40.

[71] *California Labor Problems*, p. 114.

[72] Kinkead, *Labor Unionism in Agriculture*, p. 16.

cluded numerous social reform–human rights organizations, such as the National Council of Churches, the National Catholic Welfare Conference, the National Advisory Committee on Farm Labor, the National Sharecroppers Fund, the National Consumers League, the American GI Forum, the National Association for the Advancement of Colored People, the American Friends Committee, and numerous state-level subsidiaries of the above. As a collective or as individual units the anti-braceroists refuted all six arguments of those supporting the program.

On the contention by growers that, despite their efforts to employ them, domestic farmworkers were not available in sufficient numbers, thus necessitating the use of braceros, critics replied that nothing resembling a verified scarcity of domestic workers existed. Opponents of the bracero program contended, first, that growers made no true effort to secure domestics; or, if any effort was put forth, it involved wage offers so low as to discourage all but the most desperate natives. Growers, the rebuttal continued, had long been labor obsessed. For them a labor scarcity really meant a scarcity of noncompetitive labor. How could growers speak of a dearth of workers when there were so many unemployed individuals who would gladly accept agricultural work if only decent wages and working conditions were offered? For opponents of imported labor there was no shortage of workers, only a shortage of wages.[73]

In reply to the claim that domestics were deficient in skills and character, opponents of the bracero system accused growers of preaching racism when they spoke of the Mexican's inherent physical ability and stamina in contrast to the domestic. Any man, they contended, capable of construction labor could pick cotton or hoe beans.[74] In any event, the great majority of those rejected by

[73] This particular rebuttal was perennial among opponents of the bracero program and is analyzed especially well in a case study of Arizona agriculture (Padfield and Martin, *Farmers, Workers, and Machines*, pp. 256–257). Note also *California Labor Problems*, pp. 117–121.

[74] Lloyd H. Fisher, *The Harvest Labor Market in California*, p. 9; Padfield and Martin, *Farmers, Workers, and Machines*, p. 259.

growers were themselves Mexican-Americans. Had a few years so changed their physical ability? In reply to the claim that natives were unskilled, anti-braceroists retorted that no true skill was necessary to perform field labor. The only requisite was said to be a strong back, and this domestics possessed in abundance.[75] On the bad character reference given domestics, anti-braceroists termed the entire categorization a sham and a good example of mass character assassination. Growers were said to prefer the Mexican's character over the native's because the former was an imported serf, while the latter was every bit a free man and acted accordingly.[76]

Of all the arguments presented in defense of the bracero system, none provoked a more heated rebuttal than the claim that imported labor did not adversely affect the wages, working conditions, and employment opportunities of native farmworkers. Wages in particular were said to have been most adversely affected by the presence of braceros. How else could the growers explain a decrease in wages offered domestics once braceros arrived? Why were domestics being offered less per hour in 1955 for the same work they performed in 1950? The answer was only too obvious: braceros were driving wages down for domestics.[77] They were utilized by the growers as a sword to be held over the heads of United States citizens. Time and again they were told: "Either accept what we offer, or we will use Mexicans."

Likewise, working conditions were said to have been adversely affected by the importation of alien labor. In this instance, critics of the bracero program leveled their criticism against the fringe benefits specifically guaranteed foreigners but denied natives.[78] Not only were the Mexicans guaranteed room, board, and a decent wage, they were also granted various fringe benefits that the native farmworker had not been able to achieve in a century of struggle.

[75] Fisher, *Harvest Labor Market*, pp. 7–8.

[76] F. L. Fernback, "Organized Labor Views Labor Mobility Needs," in *Labor Mobility and Population in Agriculture*, p. 178.

[77] *California Labor Problems*, pp. 115–117.

[78] Ibid., pp. 121–124.

Included among these benefits were medical care, social security, free transportation and subsistence en route, tools and equipment, minimum working standards, and a guaranteed amount of work time.

The bracero program was said also to have adversely affected the employment opportunities of domestics. It was contended that bracero usage became so ubiquitous in California that domestic migrants, who had for years considered certain regions of California prime areas of employment, came to bypass the state in the mid-1950's. Local residents were supposedly piqued initially and subsequently frustrated to despair by the refusal of management to hire them in deference to Mexican nationals. Growers were said to have gone out of their way to discourage local residents either by allotting them the poorest and least profitable areas in which to work, whereby any average man seeking to support a family soon left the field or orchard in despair, or by replying quite bluntly to the prospective domestic: "Sorry, we're only hiring braceros this spring."[79]

A fourth point in the growers' case for the bracero program was its allegedly beneficial impact on the individual Mexican and his family. Since the bracero did earn good wages by Mexican standards, opponents of the system focused attention on the exploitation of the national and on the adverse familial impact of the program. They cited numerous examples of exploitation of individual braceros, such as underpayment for work done, exorbitant prices charged by the company store, racial discrimination, and summary dismissals.[80] Critics of the braceroism held that Mexican family life was disrupted and done irreparable harm by a program that separated a man from his wife and family for extended periods. What good was the money a bracero earned if upon his return he and his family no longer lived under the same roof?[81] In any event, reasoned the critics, the contention that the bracero program bene-

[79] Ibid., pp. 117–121.
[80] Ibid., pp. 124–125; and *New York Times*, June 1, 1958, August 30, 1959.
[81] For the Mexican version of this argument, see Jesus Topete, *Aventuras de un bracero*; and Shotwell, *The Harvesters*, pp. 49–58.

fited individual Mexicans was hardly grounds for United States support. If this were to serve as a rationalization, then surely a system less harmful to the domestic farmworker could be devised.

The claim of proponents that the bracero program fostered improved Mexican–United States relations, was countered by foes of the system with the antithesis. Bracerorism was deemed detrimental to United States–Mexican relations because it exacerbated the perennial anti-American syndrome among the Mexicans.[82] Mexicans knew of the mistreatment and exploitation of their countrymen in the United States. Their pride was severely injured when they were forced to bear daily witness to the fact that thousands of their countrymen were desperate to the point of becoming braceros.[83] The sensitive Mexican knew well enough that he was not materially prosperous in comparison with his giant northern neighbor. Why rub salt in an open wound with such a travesty as braceroism? In any event, the line of reasoning that supported the bracero program on diplomatic grounds was stretching the point to an extreme. If the system were, in fact, a boon to United States–Mexican relations because of its economic-political impact on Mexico, why not replace it with something more rational, such as foreign aid?[84] In that way, the critics observed, Mexico would benefit from the dollar influx while the United States would prosper under the impact of thousands of newly employed farmworkers.

Anti-braceroists replied to the final argument in behalf of imported Mexican labor (that it benefited the United States economically) by again presenting the antithesis. Although they admitted that an end to the system might mean a very slight increase in consumer prices on selected items, foes of the bracero program argued that such an increment would prove infinitesimal compared to the benefits accruing to United States citizens, especially to agricultural workers, as a result of termination. How could the United States prosper as a whole when thousands of farmworkers were deprived of a decent living standard by a system akin to im-

82 Spradlin, "The Mexican Farm Labor Program," pp. 320–321.
83 Cline, *The United States and Mexico*, p. 392.
84 Editorial in the *New York Times*, June 3, 1963.

ported colonialism? As in other cases, the whole was only as good as the sum of its parts.[85] On the local level, bracero-dominated communities were said to be suffering irreparable damage, because Mexican nationals, unlike domestics, sent their earnings back to Mexico. "Would it not be better," asked the anti-braceroists, "if the money earned cultivating and harvesting American crops was spent here at home?"[86]

Summary

The bracero program was indeed a controversial phenomenon. The preceding binational analysis of pro and con arguments may prove highly deceptive unless the reader remembers previous warnings about the program's intricate and multifaceted nature. For purposes of analysis the environmental context of imported Mexican labor may be better understood through oversimplified heuristic models. However, we should never be led by these models to a cut-and-dried set of assumptions concerning the question as a whole.

Not only was the Mexican farm labor question highly involved and multidimensional in both its national and international aspects, but it also encompassed within its broader context a series of anomalies, some humorous, some puzzling, others disturbing. From one perspective there was Mexico, her government and people, placed by the bracero program in a most embarrassing position. It galled the Mexican and his government to admit the desperation of their rural residents. Yet such an admission was made as a matter of necessity.

In addition to the overall dilemma that the bracero program posed for Mexico, it spawned other anomalies for the nation and its citizens. The international agreement that Mexico secured for her nationals displayed provisions that, in effect, guaranteed the Mexican worker more in wages, working conditions, and fringe benefits

[85] Louis Krainock, "Organized Labor Views the Farm Worker Problem," *Proceedings: Western Interstate Conference on Migratory Labor*, pp. 31–33.

[86] *California Labor Problems*, p. 125; and Krainock, "Organized Labor Views the Farm Worker Problem," pp. 31–33.

while in the United States than he had ever received in his native land. During their United States sojourn, individual Mexicans found themselves the object of far greater governmental concern and anxiety than had been the case in their own country. His tour as a bracero or wetback resulted as well in a rare social phenomenon: the peasant, with little or no formal education, often returned to his village a far more wordly man than many of his middle-class countrymen, including some anti-American intellectuals, who had never ventured outside their national boundaries.[87]

Perhaps most ironic, however, from the Mexican standpoint was the development of a movement that might best be described as "back door" braceroism. During the period when desperate Mexican nationals were crossing into the United States, even more desperate Guatemalan braceros were crossing Mexico's southern border to secure jobs entailing working conditions and wages so poor as to prove unattractive to members of Mexico's most depressed economic sector.[88] One is tempted to wonder what effect such an exodus had upon the Guatemalan national conscience.

The bracero program also produced a number of anomalies from the standpoint of the host country. None, however, compared with the fact that the United States government was willing to grant foreign nationals something it refused its own farmworkers: a comprehensive, government-sponsored work program.

Perhaps the ultimate and summary irony of the bracero question was depicted by *New York Times* journalist Gladwin Hill in a caustic parody on *Alice in Wonderland*.[89]

"What are these people doing?" asked Alice, surveying a vast, fertile southwestern valley.

"They're cultivating surplus cotton and lettuce," replied the Red Queen.

"Who are they?" asked Alice, tactfully ignoring the matter of why anyone should produce surplus crops.

"They are Mexicans imported because of the labor shortage," explained the Red Queen.

[87] Hancock, *The Role of the Bracero*, p. 124.
[88] *Hispanic American Report* 9 (January 1957):570–571.
[89] *New York Times*, April 5, 1959.

"Labor shortage?" asked Alice, "I thought we had 5,000,000 unemployed and a million or so migrant farm laborers who need work."

"Obviously," retorted the Red Queen testily, "YOU don't understand the American agricultural system."

That section of United States agriculture involved in the bracero program was indeed a difficult phenomenon to understand. But so was the entire bracero question. All parties involved in the controversy presented cogent, well-reasoned arguments. Yet, they also presented highly emotional polemics. A good case could be made for the program on national and international levels. An equally convincing case could be made against it. Perhaps it is best to recall that the entire question of imported Mexican agricultural labor was one of conflict. Conflict situations rarely afford a clear black-and-white picture. Viewed nationally or internationally, the program was always a struggle. Caught in the center of the encounter was the Department of State. From its very inception the domestic struggle over imported Mexican labor involved heavy diplomatic overtones.

CHAPTER **2**

Group Processes and the Wellsprings of Imported Mexican Agricultural Labor: The Bracero Program, 1942–1951

THE IMPORTATION OF Mexican agricultural labor did not become an institutionalized facet of United States–Mexican relations until 1952. Large-scale use of braceros on United States farms had, however, become an established fact during the 1940's. This chapter analyzes from the perspective of interest groups and the political process two significant stages in the life of the bracero program: the World War II wellspring and the postwar system of direct grower recruitment.

THE WARTIME MEXICAN LABOR PROGRAM, 1942–1947

As a result of severe wartime labor shortages, the United States concluded with Mexico on August 4, 1942, an intergovernmental agreement for the use of Mexican agricultural labor on United

States farms. Though amended several times, the 1942 agreement remained essentially unchanged and served as the basis for bracero importation from 1942 through 1947.

The 1942 agreement marked a significant milestone in United States–Mexican relations.[1] Braceros had entered the United States on a contractual basis during World War I and had been employed intermittently by southwestern farmers during the interwar years. Prior to 1942, however, they had never crossed their northern frontier under the auspices of an international accord. The wartime pact and the events leading up to it not only constitute an important event in our relations with Mexico; they also provide fertile soil for the student of interest-group politics. Despite its international overtones, the bracero program was from its very inception the offspring of an interest-group parentage.

Group Processes and the 1942 Agreement

With the outbreak of war in Europe and the growing involvement of the United States in that war, labor became a more valuable commodity, particularly on United States farms. Long before Pearl Harbor, southwestern growers began to feel the labor shortage. They, in turn, began to relay their discomfort to representatives in state capitals and in Washington. The long-mistreated migrants from Oklahoma and Arkansas were overnight welcomed with open arms, but their majority soon bypassed the fields for more lucrative careers in a burgeoning defense industry. Faced, thus, with what they interpreted as an alarming scarcity of domestic labor, growers turned to a long neglected but never forgotten potential—the Mexican.

Early in 1940, their summons for Mexicans became, in the words of one scholar, "more urgent."[2] Passage of the Selective

---

[1] Although the World War II program was not without its critics, most students of United States–Mexican relations would agree with the assessment of Ernesto Galarza, who termed it "an achievement of great importance in the field of interamerican relations" (Preface to *Los braceros mexicanos en los estados unidos durante el periodo belico*, by Robert C. Jones).

[2] Otey M. Scruggs, "Evolution of the Mexican Farm Labor Agreement of

Service Act in September, 1940, and the National Defense Act in March, 1941, injected even greater urgency into their pleadings. Appeals for foreign help were heard from Texas, Arizona, and California. In September, 1941, California growers directly petitioned the Immigration and Naturalization Service for permission to import thirty thousand braceros.[3] The government, however, proved steadfast in its refusal to sanction such undertakings: "All such applications . . . were denied, since it was found that there was sufficient domestic labor to meet the demand."[4]

Japan's attack on Pearl Harbor altered the thinking of governmental officials on many questions, including imported agricultural labor. Early in 1942, while some officials continued to insist that the supply of domestic farmworkers was adequate,[5] others were already probing the Mexican attitude on the possibility of contract labor. As a result of these informal inquiries, which revealed a steadfast Mexican attitude against contracting on any other than a formal, intergovernmental basis, a special committee was formed that would eventually formulate the United States position on bracero contracting.[6]

With war mobilization and the consequent demands on manpower, it soon became apparent that the United States government would formally approach its Mexican counterpart on the question of imported labor. During 1942, it became increasingly clear that a labor shortage had indeed developed. Grower pleadings for workers to plant, cultivate, and harvest the crops of 1940 and 1941 may have seemed to many a mere repetition of the age-old obsession of

---

1942," *Agricultural History* 34(July 1960):140. I have relied heavily on Scruggs's excellent study of the events immediately preceding the 1942 agreement.

[3] Wayne D. Rasmussen, *A History of the Emergency Farm Labor Supply Program 1943–47*, p. 200. Rasmussen's monograph still stands as the most thorough analysis of farm labor in the United States during World War II.

[4] Gertrude D. Krichefsky, "Importation of Alien Laborers," *I and N Reporter* 5(July 1956):4.

[5] Note the statement of Fay Hunter, head of the farm placement station of the Federal Employment Service, in *New York Times*, January 6, 1942.

[6] Rasmussen, *Farm Labor Supply Program*, p. 201.

all farmers for a surplus labor supply. However, actual involvement of the United States in hostilities transformed this annual ritual into a glaring reality. The United States farmer was faced with the possibility that much of his 1942 crop would go unharvested if he were forced to depend wholly on the labor of his countrymen.[7] If such a situation developed, the farmer would not be the only one to suffer; the entire war effort would be hampered.

World War II placed great demands on all sectors of society. Any weak link in the chain of aggregate action could have proved damaging to the cause of victory. One of the most vital links was agricultural production. The United States farmer was asked to produce more and more as the war progressed. Accomplishing his assigned task would have been sufficiently difficult with an adequate labor supply. Without it he could not possibly meet the quota, and the war effort would have been seriously impaired. Farmers and their spokesmen were not long in emphasizing the value of imported labor to national defense.

The contents of the telegram sent by California Governor Culbert Olson to the secretaries of agriculture, state, and labor are highly reflective of the strategy adopted by western growers in their drive to secure Mexican nationals. The appeal was not personal in nature. It was designed primarily to lobby the public in behalf of national defense. The plight of farmers themselves was recognizable by implication only. "Without a substantial number of Mexicans," the telegram read in part, "the situation is certain to be disastrous to the entire victory program, despite our united efforts in the mobilization of youth and city dwellers for emergency farm work."[8] It was not long before an inescapable fact became apparent: Individual farmers might be denied their appeals for braceros, but not the Allied defense effort.

In April, 1942, under pressure from California beet growers, the

[7] That the farmer's perpetual fantasy over labor had become a reality by 1942 may be seen in the following: *New York Times*, February 1, 1942; February 24, 1942; March 25, 1942; March 26, 1942; June 10, 1942; and June 16, 1942.

[8] *New York Times*, June 16, 1942. Similarly, see *New York Times*, March 25, 1942, and March 26, 1942.

Immigration Service formed an interagency committee to study the question of agricultural labor. Composed of representatives from the War Manpower Commission and the Departments of Labor, State, Justice, and Agriculture, the committee produced a plan for recruiting Mexican labor. Approved in May, 1942, the committee's work read like a model group composite. It reflected, as did the subsequent intergovernmental agreement, the views of the four principal groups concerned with the question of bracero labor. "The plan," observes Scruggs, "reflected the committee's efforts to resolve the conflicting demands of farmers, organized labor, and the United States and Mexican governments."[9] Thus, even before formal negotiations began, pressure from the four groups most directly affected by imported Mexican labor had made itself felt. The relative power of any one of the groups would change intermittently during the life span of the agreement; composition of the bracero program's inner four would not.

On June 1, 1942, Mexico declared war on the Axis powers. Immediately thereafter Attorney General Francis Biddle requested the State Department to approach Mexico officially on the bracero matter.[10] State was none too rapid in acceding to the request. Discussion on the diplomatic ramifications of such an undertaking had revealed a skeptical departmental outlook. The State Department's primary concern was the possibility that the fledgling Good Neighbor Policy might suffer a severe setback if Mexican nationals were exploited or discriminated against during their stay in this country. However, a growing labor shortage, the attorney general's request, and the vastly improved interagency committee proposal combined to convince even the skeptics. On June 15, Ambassador George Messersmith met with Mexican Foreign Minister Ezequiel Padilla and urged, in the name of the war effort, Mexican approval of such a program.[11]

Ambassador Messersmith's request came as no surprise to the Mexicans. President Avila Camacho had sensed the growing prob-

9 Scruggs, "Mexican Farm Labor Agreement of 1942," p. 144.
10 Ibid., p. 144.
11 Ibid., p. 146.

ability of such an appeal and had, on May 4, ordered the establishment of an interdepartmental committee to study the possible ramifications of a bracero exodus.[12] Following the Padilla-Messersmith conference of June 15, the Mexican committee examined the question in detail for an entire month. Professor Scruggs, citing State Department files, suggests that a thorough debate ensued over the advantages and disadvantages for Mexico of such a program.[13]

On the negative side, four conclusions emerged. In the first place, Mexico doubted that a legitimate labor scarcity existed in United States agriculture. She regarded the anguished cries of growers as just another effort in search of cheap labor. Second, Mexican officials realized that their countrymen would never again permit the mass reverse migration of impoverished nationals that occurred during the depression years.[14] Third, the officials were also well aware that public opinion would not permit braceros to be dispatched to particular discrimination-prone southern states. Incidents of discrimination, whether individual or state inspired, might seriously damage the increasingly cordial atmosphere of United States–Mexican relations. Fourth, the exodus of several thousand braceros might endanger Mexico's accelerating drive toward economic development.

On the positive side, members of the Mexican committee had been assured of a government-to-government program, one in which Mexico was guaranteed a strong voice. Second, Mexican agriculture stood to benefit from the knowledge acquired by braceros during their stay in the United States.[15] Third, Mexican officials saw in the suggested program a chance to contribute meaningfully to the Allied war effort. Finally, members of the Mexican committee did not wish to deny substantial earnings to individuals and the

[12] Ernesto Galarza, *Merchants of Labor: The Mexican Bracero Story; An Account of the Managed Migration of Mexican Farmworkers in California 1942–1960*, p. 47.

[13] Scruggs, "Mexican Farm Labor Agreement of 1942," p. 146.

[14] For a thorough analysis of the emigré phenomenon, see Gloria R. Vargas y Campos, "El problema del bracero mexicano," pp. 15–28; and John H. Burma, *Spanish-Speaking Groups in the United States*, pp. 42–43.

[15] Nathan L. Whetten, *Rural Mexico*, p. 270.

nation or to antagonize the consumer of a potentially large amount of Mexican raw materials during the war. From an economic perspective, the bracero program made good business sense.

In July, 1942, Secretary of Agriculture Claude Wickard, as head of the United States delegation attending the Inter-American Conference on Agriculture in Mexico City, conferred with Mexican officials on the bracero program. Foreign Minister Padilla assumed a reluctant stance. He recalled exploitation of and discrimination against Mexican citizens who had previously worked on United States farms. He described Mexican distress over the impoverished returnees during the 1930's and insisted that a number of governmentally sponsored guarantees for the braceros be included in any agreement. Other Mexican officials informed Secretary Wickard that they would support such a program, despite strong personal misgivings, as a contribution to the war effort.[16] The United States had apparently chosen as a negotiator a man well equipped with diplomatic as well as agricultural talent. The Mexicans consented to a limited trial run, and formal negotiations were scheduled to begin July 13, 1942, in Mexico City.

The 1942 Bracero Agreement. Considering the importance of the original agreement, United States and Mexican representatives produced a finished product in a brief ten-day period.[17] The accord was signed July 23 and made effective by an exchange of diplomatic notes on August 4, 1942. Though revised in 1943 and amended several times during its five-year history, the 1942 agreement served as the cornerstone of Mexican labor importation from 1942 to 1947.

Administration under the wartime program was binational. In the United States the Department of Agriculture was allotted primary responsibility. Recruitment began with certification from the United States Employment Service that a given number of braceros would be needed at a future date. In Mexico a bureau of migrant labor within the Ministry of Foreign Affairs was charged with pri-

[16] Scruggs, "Mexican Farm Labor Agreement of 1942," p. 146; Rasmussen, *Farm Labor Supply Program,* pp. 201–202.

[17] Scruggs, "Mexican Farm Labor Agreement of 1942," p. 147.

mary responsibility for the bracero program. The bureau, in cooperation with the Mexican Departments of Interior and Labor, assigned bracero quotas to various states. Prospective workers were
ultimately screened by Mexican and United States officials at the
recruitment center in Mexico City. As the wartime program ex-
panded and the recruitment situation in Mexico City grew chaotic,
other centers were added. Those chosen were then transported to
the United States and placed on farms throughout the country.
Upon completion of their contract period the braceros were again
returned to the original recruitment center in Mexico.[18]

In its statement of fundamental principles, the 1942 agreement
established four standards that were to serve as general guidelines
to the bracero program throughout its twenty-two–year history.[19]
First, Mexican contract workers would not engage in any United
States military service. Second, Mexicans entering the United
States under provisions of the agreement would not be subjected to
discriminatory acts of any kind. Third, they would be guaranteed
transportation, living expenses, and repatriation along the lines
established under Article 29 of the Mexican federal labor law.
Fourth, Mexicans entering under the agreement would not be employed either to displace domestics or to reduce their wages.

In order to implement the general principles of the agreement,
specific detailed clauses were included. Almost without exception,
each clause reflected the relative power of the groups involved.
Mexico scored a clear victory in contracts. Individual contracts
were made between bracero and employer and supervised by the
Mexican government. Crucial to Mexico was that the term "employer" signified the United States government as represented by
the Farm Security Administration. Subcontracting was conducted
between individual employers and the United States government.
Thus, the Mexican goal of a program negotiated and backed by the

[18] Jones, *Los braceros mexicanos*, pp. 2–8; and Galarza, *Merchants of Labor*,
pp. 51–52.
[19] For the text of the agreement, see U.S., 56 *Stat.* 1759. Perhaps the most
thorough analysis of the pact is contained in Jones, *Los braceros mexicanos*, pp.
3–28.

United States was achieved. Unlike previous arrangements, Mexico was no longer forced to deal in a cumbersome diplomatic manner with individual farmers or their representatives. In the case of bracero grievances, Mexico went straight to the "employer."[20]

The bracero's transportation and living expenses from the place of origin to destination and return were borne by the employer (the United States government), who was in turn reimbursed by bracero-using growers.[21] Such a stipulation was again the result of Mexican insistence. Under Article 29 of Mexico's federal labor law the employer was expected to pay for the transportation and subsistence of his agricultural employees.[22]

Perhaps the most crucial clauses of the agreement related to wages and employment. Braceros received the prevailing area wage paid natives performing similar tasks. In no case, however, was the wage to be less than thirty cents an hour.[23] Piece rates were included and were set so as to permit the average worker to earn at least the prevailing hourly wage. Braceros were guaranteed employment for at least 75 percent of the contract period (Sundays excluded) or subsistence payments of three dollars per day in lieu thereof. For periods of unemployment during the remaining 25 percent of the contract, the worker received subsistence on the same basis as that paid domestic workers. Mexican naiveté showed

---

[20] As an example of the importance that Mexico attached to this aspect of the agreement, note Vargas y Campos, "El problema del bracero," p. 25.

[21] This particular provision was altered early in 1943 as a result of pressure from bracero users. They claimed that the number of deserters, or "skips" as they came to be called, rendered the transportation clause unbearable. As a result, the government assumed the transportation cost from Mexico to the United States and from the United States to Mexico when the bracero returned (Scruggs, "Mexican Labor Agreement of 1942," p. 148).

[22] Rasmussen, *Farm Labor Supply Program*, p. 203.

[23] The only exception to the stipulation pertained to members of the bracero's family and then only on the basis of prior authorization from the Mexican government. However, no family members were ever imported under the 1942 agreement (U.S., Congress, House, Committee on the Judiciary, *Study of Population and Immigration Problems, Administrative Presentations [III], Admission of Aliens into the United States for Temporary Employment, and "Commuter Workers": Hearing before Subcommittee*, 88th Cong., 1st sess., June 24, 1963, p. 28; hereafter cited as House Judiciary Committee Hearings, 1963)

clearly in insisting on the latter guarantee, for there existed nothing resembling subsistence guarantees for native farmworkers. The provision was included, nonetheless, because subsistence payments were furnished by employers under Mexico's labor law.[24]

Provisions on housing and medical care for braceros were included and again reflected the lack of Mexican knowledge concerning agricultural conditions in the United States. Workers were assured housing facilities equal to those enjoyed by domestic farmworkers in the area. Braceros were given the same guarantees against occupational diseases and accidents as those enjoyed by natives under United States legislation. This stipulation was particularly meaningless because domestic farm labor enjoyed nothing resembling workmen's compensation at the time. It was included, however, at Mexico's insistence.

A final bow to Mexican pressure was a savings fund provision. Ten percent of each bracero's wage was deducted, placed in a rural savings fund, and subsequently transferred to Mexico's Agricultural Credit Bank.[25] If he chose, the bracero could purchase agricultural equipment from his deductions with the aid of the Farm Security Administration.

The original bracero agreement was operationalized almost immediately after it became effective on August 4, 1942. More than 4,000 Mexicans were admitted during the waning months of 1942, and a high of 62,000 was imported in 1944. Mexicans constituted by far the largest group of foreign laborers imported during the wartime emergency. In addition to Mexico, other sources of imported labor included the Bahamas, Barbados, Canada, Jamaica, and Newfoundland. Of the total of 309,538 wartime (1942–1947) importees in agriculture, 219,546, or more than 70 percent, were

[24] Farmers were particularly resentful of this provision, which, in effect, represented a guaranteed wage for their unemployed workers (George O. Coalson, "Mexican Contract Labor in American Agriculture," *Southwestern Social Science Quarterly* 33 (September 1952):231.

[25] After 1948 Mexico never again insisted on such a provision. Apparently the money reached its first destination in the Mexican agricultural bank, but it seemed somehow never to reach those for whom it was originally intended.

Mexicans.[26] During the period 1943–1947, braceros were said by a Mexican study to have earned $205 million.[27]

Group Processes and the Wartime Bracero Program

From the perspective of interest groups and the political process, the first five years of internationally sanctioned bracero importation are especially noteworthy. Of the two domestic forces involved, agricultural interests appear to have benefited substantially vis-à-vis their labor counterparts. Many crops in the Southwest would have gone uncultivated and unharvested had growers not acquired the Mexicans they so urgently demanded. In fact, many thousands of acres would have lain fallow without the bracero. However, in addition to the obvious fact that obtaining Mexican nationals was itself a clear indication of the strength of agriculture in United States politics, events during the five years of the program bore further witness to the political power base enjoyed by agrarian interests.

One clear indicator of this power was agriculture's displeasure with particular portions of the program and its successful efforts to alter them or render them meaningless. Dissatisfied from the beginning with a government-to-government program (most growers preferred the World War I agreement, whereby they did their own recruiting with little government interference on either side of the border), employers set out first to render impotent the government agency charged with administering the program.

The Farm Security Administration had been a primary target of many farm groups from its very inception during the early years of the New Deal. As administrator of the bracero program, the FSA became an even clearer target for agriculture's big guns. "Employers objected to 'government men' concerning themselves with issues that previously had been left to the discretion of the employer. The Farm Security Administration already had a reputation as

26 Rasmussen, *Farm Labor Supply Program*, p. 199.

27 Report of the Combined Mexican Working Party, *The Economic Development of Mexico*, p. 379.

a 'social reform' agency, and employers and congressmen from farm states feared that it was going to use the war period to further F.S.A. ideas of social reform in the farm labor field."[28]

Above all, agraria saw in the FSA-administered labor program the potential danger of a government-regulated domestic farm labor force and all that it implied. As the pressure increased, it became apparent that the FSA and the bracero program would soon part company. In June, 1943, control of the program passed from the FSA to the War Manpower Commission.[29]

Particular clauses in the 1942 agreement were another object of successful farm-interest pressure. With the exception of the aforementioned change on cost of bracero transportation, farm interests were often able to avoid provisions of the program that they deemed especially objectionable. In such areas as housing, wages, food, standards of transportation, and unemployment and subsistence payments, farmers did not necessarily violate provisions of the agreement; they either ignored them or fulfilled them in a manner more to their liking. Growers did not like the "bureaucratic obstructionism" entailed in the program, but they learned to live with it on their own terms in order to secure the braceros.[30]

A final example of farm-bloc influence is evidenced by the duration of the wartime program. As an emergency measure, the 1942 accord was scheduled to expire with the end of hostilities. It did not. Instead, the "wartime" bracero program was extended until December 31, 1947. To contend that the extension was wholly the result of demands from farm groups would be an overstatement.[31] The war-torn world's urgent demand for food contributed undeniably to prolongation.[32] Likewise, Mexico's acquiescence to continu-

[28] Walter W. Wilcox, "The Wartime Use of Manpower on Farms," *Journal of Farm Economics* 28(August 1946):729.

[29] Galarza, *Merchants of Labor*, p. 51.

[30] Rasmussen, *Farm Labor Supply Program*, pp. 228–232; and Burma, *Spanish-Speaking Groups*, p. 122.

[31] Galarza seems to have assumed this line of reasoning (*Merchants of Labor*, p. 48).

[32] Such a rationale is employed by Rasmussen, *Farm Labor Supply Program*, pp. 233–234.

ation must be considered an important contributing factor. Viewed comparatively, however, the voice of agriculture was the primary impetus behind extension of the wartime program through 1947.

The forces of organized labor fared a poor second behind their agricultural counterparts. However, surface appearances are often deceptive. Judged exclusively on a short-term basis, the wartime accord was somewhat of a setback to the labor sector, despite its rather nebulous stipulation on employment opportunities and wages of domestics. Many anti-braceroists felt that Mexican nationals were not absolutely necessary during the combat years. Still, they acquiesced in the face of overwhelming odds and in behalf of the defense effort. Such was not the case once hostilities ceased. The bracero program's postwar longevity was clearly a defeat for the labor sector.

From a long-term perspective, the 1942 agreement may not have been so detrimental to the labor cause. An optimist may even consider it a boon. The many government-supported guarantees granted foreign labor were denied domestics. Yet the very fact that such a program was established provided an important precedent. As a result of the original bracero accord, organized labor secured an invaluable rallying point for its future efforts in agriculture. The question was posed time and time again throughout the postwar years as to why foreign labor received government-sponsored guarantees that were not accorded domestics, and more and more Americans came to listen. Subsequently defeated in 1964, the once maligned bracero program may, in the long run, prove a blessing in disguise to organized labor and the supporters of domestic farmworkers.

From the viewpoint of the United States government, the wartime program was indeed a success. The United States needed the Mexican laborers as part of the war effort, and she got them. What is more, even the critics of the agreement, be they Mexican or American, readily admitted to its success as an instrument of diplomacy. The wartime bracero pact was, in a word, a boon to United States–Mexican relations, even though problems did arise at the international level as a result of the program.[33] Taken in its entirety, however, the wartime agreement must be considered a beneficial milestone in United States–Mexican relations.[34]

Much the same can be said of Mexico and the 1942 accord. Whereas the benefits accruing to the United States under the program were essentially intangible in nature, they were considerably more material for Mexico. Diplomatically, Mexico benefited from the agreement in much the same manner as her northern neighbor. Not only were her relations with the United States more cordial as a result of the bracero exchange, but Mexico's sincerely felt contribution to the war effort was also substantially augmented by it.[35] In addition to contributing a limited number of combat personnel, Mexico granted the United States an air base in Yucatán, supplied crucial raw materials, and helped to cultivate and harvest sorely needed crops with her nationals.

Mexico as a nation and a people benefited financially and socially from the program. Braceros earned some $205 million from 1943 to 1947.[36] Nationally, these earnings were an important source of foreign exchange. Individually, the money was far more important, because it was earned by members of Mexico's subsistence agricultural sector. Thus, like the bracero program of later years, the wartime accord funneled sorely needed funds directly into the homes of Mexico's *campesinos*.[37] Experience gained by the braceros during their stay on United States farms must also be considered beneficial to Mexico. Whether the worker did or did not return with farm implements, he acquired through experience a substan-

---

[33] Ibid., pp. 228–232.

[34] As examples of the diplomatic esteem in which the program was held, note the following: Woodrow Moore, "El problema de la emigración de los braceros," pp. 13–14; Vargas y Campos, "El problema del bracero," pp 25–26; Rasmussen, *Farm Labor Supply Program*, p. 233; Scruggs, "Mexican Labor Agreement of 1942," p. 149; and Galarza, in Jones, *Los braceros mexicanos*, preface.

[35] Note the remarks of Foreign Minister Ezequiel Padilla, as cited in Galarza, *Merchants of Labor*, p. 48.

[36] Combined Working Party, *The Economic Development of Mexico*, p. 379.

[37] Whetten, *Rural Mexico*, p. 271.

tial amount of agricultural technique. Finally, the individual worker broadened considerably his cultural horizon during his stay and thus further enhanced the mutual understanding between citizens and governments alike.[38]

For the Mexicans, the precedents that the 1942 agreement established for Mexican workers in the United States overshadowed all other salutary effects. The welfare of its citizens, whether at home or abroad, is important to every nation. Mexico's past experience with exported labor had not been a pleasant one. She demanded and got, as the price for her citizens' toil and sweat, a government-ensured agreement. Although it contained its share of imprecision, the accord consisted in the main of a series of definite guarantees for the bracero.[39] A Mexican scholar observes that the 1942 agreement proved a landmark to Mexico "because it afforded the Mexican government the opportunity to put forth the conditions which it considered pertinent in attempting to . . . secure protection for its workers."[40] Never again would Mexican contract labor enter the United States without the sanction of an international agreement. (The term "contract labor" does not include, of course, the many thousands of wetbacks who entered the United States surreptitiously.)

Summary

From 1942 to 1947 more than 200,000 braceros entered the United States as agricultural workers under the provisions of an international agreement.[41] They worked on farms in twenty-four states, with the vast majority being employed in California. Be-

---

[38] Galarza, *Merchants of Labor*, p. 48; and Rasmussen, *Farm Labor Supply Program*, pp. 228–232.

[39] Galarza, *Merchants of Labor*, p. 48.

[40] Vargas y Campos, "El problema del bracero," p. 25.

[41] The modifiers *agricultural* and *farm* have been utilized for a definite reason throughout this analysis of the World War II agreement. From May, 1943, through 1946 more than 130,000 Mexicans were admitted as railroad workers under a 1943 agreement closely resembling its agricultural counterpart. For the text of the accord, see U.S. 57 *Stat.* 1353.

cause of discrimination within Texas, that state received no braceros under contract.[42]

The wartime program was seminal as well as unique. It was indeed an "unprecedented experiment in inter-American labor migration."[43] It marked the first time that Mexican workers had entered the United States under the auspices of an intergovernmental accord. The program was unique for many reasons, two of which are especially worthy of note. In practice, it presented the strange anomaly of foreign workers receiving benefits and guarantees denied citizens of the host country.[44] Second, it presented the two governments involved with unusual collective bargaining tasks. "Because the workers were from Mexico and the employers from the United States, in a very practical sense the Government of the United States has had to assume the functions of an employer's [*sic*] representative, while the Government of Mexico has assumed the functions one generally associates with a labor union representative."[45]

Theoretically, three insights can be gained from observing the wartime bracero program. First, the group struggle among domestic interests becomes more muted as the result of overwhelming circumstances in the international environment—in this case, the war—but the struggle does not disappear entirely. Both labor and farm interests found fault with the program, but both accepted it as necessary under the circumstances. Nonetheless, pressure in behalf of group interests continued throughout the period. The politi-

[42] Report of the President's Commission on Migratory Labor, *Migratory Labor in American Agriculture*, pp. 39–40; hereafter cited as Report of the President's Commission.

[43] Carey McWilliams, "They Saved the Crops," *The Inter-American* 2(August 1943):10.

[44] On analyzing the lament voiced by native Americans over this paradoxical situation, one is struck by the similarity of the complaints raised by many contemporary West Germans against the working conditions in Germany afforded imported laborers from various European countries.

[45] John C. Elac, "The Employment of Mexican Workers in United States Agriculture, 1900–1960: A Binational Economic Analysis," p. 36. Similarly, see Report of the President's Commission, pp. 41 and 50.

cal efficacy of the agricultural sector substantiates the traditionally held belief that to the highly organized, politically articulate go the spoils. Such a conclusion is clearly evidenced by the extension of the program beyond the war's end.

From the diplomatic perspective it can be concluded that crisis situations in the international environment may permit weaker nations to diplomatically achieve victories in a short period, which in noncrisis intervals would have been obtainable only over a long period of time, if at all. The war enhanced Mexico's bargaining position considerably. It left the United States with only one alternative: meet the Mexican demands or do without the labor. Once achieved, such diplomatic gains are not easily lost with the passing of the international crisis. Mexico's good will was so important to United States Latin American policy that the guarantees afforded Mexican labor during a traumatic period became permanent fixtures, despite domestic interest group opposition to them in subsequent years.

Finally, the wartime bracero program illustrates that domestic interest-group conflict and foreign policy in democratic states need not be incompatible. In fact, the two may become congruent if the groups involved are willing to sacrifice a degree of self-interest for the national good. The 1942 bracero accord represented an excellent example of group interaction and compromise within the political process. "Given the diverse, often conflicting interests," writes Scruggs, "the agreement was as good if not better than could have reasonably been expected."[46] The wartime program was illustrative of a relatively balanced group milieu. Its immediate successor was the product of a noncrisis environment. As such, the group balance born of crisis was soon dissolved.

THE BRACERO PROGRAM, 1948–1951

Bridging the gap between the original bracero agreement and the 1951 accord was the Mexican labor program from 1948 to 1951. Wartime recruitment was entirely a government-to-government

---

[46] Scruggs, "Mexican Labor Agreement of 1942," p. 149.

proposition, with employers and employees being only intermediaries. Statutory authority for the wartime program was found, as was the case in World War I, under the ninth proviso of Section 3 of the 1917 immigration act. Supplementary legislation had been essential in order to operationalize and finance wartime recruitment. Of these acts, Public Law 45 was by far the most important.[47] Following a six-month extension in mid-1947, Public Law 45 expired December 31, 1947. With it the World War II bracero program came to an end.

From January, 1948, until the passage of Public Law 78 in July, 1951, Section 3 of the 1917 immigration act was the only statutory authority for the legal recruitment of Mexican nationals. The immediate postwar bracero program had as its international basis the agreements dated March 25, and April 2, 1947;[48] February 21, 1948;[49] and August 1, 1949.[50]

The immediate postwar accords were quite similar to their wartime predecessors in general principles. They differed fundamentally, however, in other respects.[51] On the international level the contractor was no longer the United States government, but the individual farmer or his representative. No longer was the government legally responsible for contract fulfillment. The responsibility lay with the farmer. Previously, the two governments had served as recruiting agents. From 1948 to 1951, United States farmers, in cooperation with Mexican and United States authorities, performed this task. Before he was allowed to recruit, the grower had first to secure certification from the Labor Department that a genuine shortage of domestic labor existed in his area. The fact that certification had to come from the Department of Labor

[47] A review of the legislation that financed the bracero program from 1943–1947 is found in Spencer A. Rich, *United States Agricultural Policy in the Post-war Years, 1945–1963*, p. 83; and *House Judiciary Committee Hearings, 1963*, pp. 30–31.

[48] U.S., Department of State, TIAS 2260, *United States Treaties and Other International Agreements*, pp. 3738–3744; hereafter cited as TIAS.

[49] U.S., 62 *Stat.* 3887.

[50] TIAS 2260, pp. 1048–1108.

[51] U.S., 62 *Stat.* 3387.

and not from the Department of Agriculture illustrates the most fundamental domestic change in the 1948–1951 program. During these years, responsibility for all farm placements, including foreigners, reverted to the United States Employment Service of the Department of Labor, where it had resided prior to the wartime emergency. December 31, 1947, marked the termination of Department of Agriculture responsibility in the area of Mexican labor. Finally, having secured certification from the USES, and recruited the worker in Mexico, the employer, and not the government, bore the entire cost of transportation from the point of contract to the United States farm and back to Mexico.

Work contracts between bracero and employer also differed substantially from their wartime predecessors. In this respect, the following 1948 contract stipulations are notable: First, a minimum hourly wage for braceros was not specified, as it had been under the wartime accord. Second, there was no minimum piece-rate guarantee, which had existed previously. Third, no formal compliance mechanism was established, although the United States Employment Service was granted undefined power in this area. Fourth, an employer bond was required prior to contract in order to guarantee the bracero's cost-free return to Mexico. No such bond had been required previously. Fifth, the former unemployment payment of three dollars per day was not included. Instead, a stipulation on prospective earnings was utilized. Finally, employers utilizing wetbacks were declared ineligible for bracero contracting.

Still other changes were contained in the agreements of 1949 and 1950, but with two exceptions[52] they differed little from the 1948 provisions. If they evidence little else, the above-mentioned differences do reveal one paramount fact to the student of interest-group politics: the balanced interest-group milieu of the wartime bracero program became unbalanced by the political weight of agriculture during the immediate postwar period. In fact, the neutral observer

[52] The 1949 and 1950 agreements permitted the contracting of illegal entrants, while the 10 percent savings provisions were dropped by the 1949 agreement (House Judiciary Committee Hearings, 1963, pp. 34–35).

might well consider the 1948–1951 program tailor-made to the demands of employers. It was, in many respects, similar to the World War I program, which growers looked back to so fondly in their critique of the wartime agreements.

To surmise from the content of the postwar accords that employers benefited more than the other three groups involved is not to say that the agricultural sector was totally content with the program during these three years. Nor does it imply that pressure from both governments and from organized labor did not make itself felt.

Grower interests had long sought a more direct system of recruitment under the wartime accords. Under terms of the revised agreements of March and April, 1947, they all but accomplished it in practice, when contracting of wetbacks already in the country was permitted.[53] When in February of 1948 they finally achieved a direct recruitment system, growers were not about to criticize it vis-à-vis the wartime program. Still, they were not entirely satisfied. In general, agriculture accused the State Department of being out-negotiated by its Mexican counterpart.[54] Many growers felt the contract was "absolutely one-sided, only protection for the worker and no protection whatever for the employer."[55]

Particularly criticized was the provision requiring employers to post a twenty-five–dollar bond for each bracero. Farmers contended that many braceros failed to fulfill their entire contract obligation. They would work a short while, then "skip" to another job in agriculture or industry or return to Mexico on their own. The employer would then be forced to forfeit his bond, being virtually powerless on his own to locate the bracero and force him to return. If by chance the bracero were apprehended, the grower was obligated to pay the costs involved in apprehension and return.[56] Farm-

[53] U.S., 61 *Stat.* 3738.

[54] Report of the President's Commission, p. 50.

[55] Ibid., p. 45.

[56] Senate Report No. 214, "Importation of Foreign Agricultural Workers," 82d Cong., April 11, 1951, p. 2; hereafter cited as Senate Report No. 214.

ers contended that the contract desertion rate was so high that it presented them with a financial hardship.[57] Therefore, while it is true that employers were relatively content with the immediate postwar bracero program, it was surely no "grower's paradise."

Organized labor in the United States suffered a defeat in the postwar prolongation of Mexican labor importation. Labor had unsuccessfully opposed extension of the wartime accords once hostilities came to an end. The same may be said of the mid-1947 extension of Public Law 45, which prolonged the wartime program another six months. The accords of 1948 and 1949, however, must be considered the low point in labor's long struggle against imported Mexican farm labor. Never again would the forces of organized labor appear as impotent alongside their agricultural counterparts.

Although the proviso forbidding the use of braceros to depress wages and working conditions of domestics was still intact during these three years, labor came to view the whole concept of protection as diplomatic window dressing and nonexistent in practice. For organized labor and the supporters of legislation in behalf of domestic migrants, the Mexican national, whether bracero or wetback, became a strikebreaker, a "scab," and a highly manipulable cheap-labor tool in the hands of agribusiness.[58] During the period 1948–1951, labor ceased to compromise on the question of foreign agricultural labor. The imported Mexican became an anathema to the union cause.

Whereas the stance and the power of the domestic farm and labor interests on the postwar program were clear, the positions of

[57] Such a contention seems, in part, to have been borne out by the president's commission, which listed desertion rates for one region during 1948 and 1949 at from 4 to an astounding 50 percent (Report of the President's Commission, p. 46).

[58] For the opinions of labor, note the following: *New York Times*, October 18, 1947, December 16 and 17, 1949, August 13, 1950, March 3, 1951; and U.S., Congress, Senate, Committee on Agriculture and Forestry, *Farm Labor, Hearings on S. 949, S. 984, and S. 1106*, 82d Cong., 1st sess., March 13–16, 1951, pp. 13–16, 123–135; hereafter cited as Senate Agriculture Committee Hearings, 1951.

both governments were somewhat nebulous. The years 1948–1951, perhaps more than any other period in the program's history, were particularly illustrative of the dilemma posed to Mexico by the legal and illegal exodus of thousands of her citizens. Furthermore, these years witnessed a long-delayed decision by some Mexicans to face the crux issue of why so many of their countrymen were eager to desert their homeland. Throughout the bracero program's history, official Mexico and much of the Mexican press clung tenaciously to the myth that Mexican rural conditions were not the true cause of the bracero-wetback exodus.[59] Every other conceivable reason was used as a rationale.[60] The root cause was, however, indigenous. If the uncomfortable years from 1948–1951 did nothing else, they did stir some Mexicans to seek the source of the problem in their own backyard, instead of seeking a scapegoat north of the border.[61]

Despite numerous misgivings and official utterances to the contrary, Mexico wanted the contracting of her citizens to continue after December 31, 1947. If she had not so desired, the bracero program would have ended whenever Mexico chose. Mexico continued, however, to act as the source country, except for the period from October, 1948, when Mexico abrogated the agreement, to August, 1949, when another accord was reached.

Why did Mexico agree to a system of non-government-supported, direct employer recruitment, when she had on numerous occasions vowed never again to do so? Why, in short, did Mexico acquiesce to a program that was abuse laden and nationally unpopular to an extreme during its three-year existence? The answer

[59] This tendency was particularly prevalent during the late 1940's and early 1950's. For examples, note the following: editorial in *Excelsior*, June 10, 1950; editorials in *El Universal*, June 7, 1951, and July 19, 1951; and *Excelsior*, January 21, 1954.

[60] Of all the reasons for becoming a farmworker in the United States, the favorite of Mexican apologists was "the urge for adventure." It is amazing that the Mexican press, in the face of such factors as poverty and wages, continued time and again to harp upon this rationale.

[61] Note, for example, the editorial in *Excelsior*, March 6, 1950; Bernard Ponce writing in *Excelsior*, April 11, 1950; and editorial in *El Universal*, May 26, 1951.

lies in a combination of factors that, together, explain the relationship between Mexico and the bracero program.

For Mexico the most important factor was the wetback phenomenon. Illegal Mexican entrants had been a problem long before 1948. In fact, the history of wetbackism is as old as United States immigration statutes. However, whereas the illegal stream had long been an acknowledged reality, it became a perplexing and dangerous torrent during the late 1940's and early 1950's.[62] Such variables as soil, weather, geographic proximity, the urge for adventure, salaries, credit, political bossism, and hunger combined to exacerbate extremely a problem that had long been neglected or underestimated.[63]

Faced with an embarassing exodus of her citizenry, Mexico believed that a continuation of the legal bracero program would possibly reduce the tide of illegal wetbacks. The other three groups in the bracero drama seemed, in varying degrees, to agree on this point. For Mexico, any program, even one involving direct recruitment, must have loomed superior to no program as a means of combating the ever-increasing illegal exodus. With an interna-

[62] From 1949 to 1954, the annual number of wetbacks located exceeded the number of braceros. In 1949 there were 107,000 braceros and 278,538 wetbacks; in 1950 the ratio was 67,500 to 458,215; in 1951 it was 192,000 to 500,628; in 1952, 197,100 to 543,538; in 1953, 201,380 to 875,318; in 1954, 309,033 to 1,075,168! From 1955 until the end of the bracero program the number of located wetbacks never exceeded the number of legally contracted braceros. ("Long-Term Trends in Foreign-Worker Employment: Table 3, Foreign Workers Admitted for Temporary Employment in U.S. Agriculture," *Farm Labor Developments*, February, 1968, p. 10; hereinafter cited as "Foreign Workers Admitted for Temporary Employment"; and U.S. Department of Justice, Immigration and Naturalization Service, "Mexican Agricultural Laborers Admitted and Mexican Aliens Located in Illegal Status, Years Ended June 30, 1949–1967"). The reader should be alerted to discrepancies between figures on the number of legally contracted braceros published by the Departments of Justice and Labor. For this reason, all bracero figures cited are those of the Bureau of Employment Security of the Department of Labor, while wetback figures are those of the Department of Justice.

[63] Mexico's concern over the flight of her citizens was acute. In fact, it was easily Mexico's primary news topic during these years. As examples, note the following: *Excelsior*, January 8, 1950, February 24, 1950, April 10, 1950, and April 15, 1950; *El Universal*, April 1, 1951, April 9, 1951, and April 15, 1951.

tional accord in effect, it was possible to arrange for the legalization of wetbacks already in the United States.[64] It was also possible to claim that, although not under contract, wetbacks employed on United States farms merited wages and working conditions similar to legally contracted braceros. Their illegal status, so the Mexicans reasoned, constituted in no way an open invitation to employer exploitation.[65] Therefore, since a wetback problem existed, Mexico apparently acquiesced to a system of direct grower recruitment as the lesser of two evils. If, because of the many all-but-uncontrollable "push" factors, Mexicans were bent on leaving the country despite the risks and hardships involved, the legal bracero program could serve as a diplomatic lever in the case of wetbacks. It could, in addition, prove useful should the international environment again render bracero labor invaluable to the United States even on Mexican terms.

Closely related to the wetback exodus as a causal factor in Mexican acceptance of the 1948 and 1949 bracero agreements was a two-sided economic variable. The money earned by Mexican migrants, whether legal or illegal, continued to constitute an important source of foreign exchange.[66] More important, however, was its continued individual impact. Even the lowly wetback was paid substantially more than he could earn at home.[67] As before, the

[64] Report of the President's Commission, pp. 52–53.

[65] This oft-repeated Mexican position was given legal sanction by the Mexican Supreme Court in December, 1949. The Court ruled that all Mexicans working in foreign lands, whether they were legal or illegal entrants, could not be deprived of their rights under article 29 of the Federal Labor Law (*Excelsior*, January 1, 1950).

[66] Mexican figures, which invariably understated the actual earnings, listed bracero remittances at $21.6 million in 1948, $17.6 million in 1949, $19.5 million in 1950, and $29.5 million in 1951. It should be noted, in addition, that these figures do not include wetback remittances, which may have exceeded bracero earnings (*Compendido Estadistico, 1951*, p. 285, and *1952*, p. 221).

[67] This was undoubtedly true despite protestations from Mexican and United States circles over the poverty wages paid wetbacks. Even if, as critics claimed, the wetback received as little as 30 cents an hour, he would still have earned considerably more than in Mexico, *if* he had found work there. For comparative earning figures on United States and Mexican farm labor, see Elac, "Employment of Mexican Workers," pp. 168–172. For the feeling of a typical *campesino*

dollars earned by Mexican labor went directly into the homes and local economies of rural Mexico. From this factor emerged a third reason for Mexico's continued acceptance of the direct recruitment system.

Rural Mexico was particularly restless during the late 1940's and early 1950's. Drought, tight agricultural credit, national priority to industrial development, and other factors combined to render much of Mexico's traditionally poor rural sector poverty stricken. This situation led to massive unemployment and general discontent within rural areas. Faced with a choice of either remaining in Mexico while he and his family lived on the verge of starvation or going north as a bracero, the *campesino* obviously chose the latter alternative, despite its drawbacks.

There were, unfortunately, thousands of rural Mexicans who made the same decision simultaneously, with the result that bracero quotas were filled instantly. Many thousands were turned away, and the results were invariably the same. Towns in which recruiting depots were located became scenes of teeming, hungry masses. Frustrated to an extreme by their predicament, these *campesinos* became a politically explosive force.[68] Their potential was, however, seldom realized. Instead, they became wetbacks as a last resort. Politically and socially the exodus of discontented, hungry *campesinos* served as a safety valve throughout the bracero program's history. Seldom, however, was this effect more evident than during the 1948–1951 era. One needs little imagination to visualize the extent of rural discontent that Mexico was spared as a result of the legal and clandestine northern flow during these years. Mexico was obviously unhappy with direct recruitment. However, no recruitment at all would have been far worse for Mexico's political, economic, and social well-being.

---

about why he would desert his country to seek even the lowly wetback's wages, see the interviews with ex-wetbacks in *El Universal*, May 30, 1951.

[68] The rush for bracero positions was frantic during the program's entire history. For descriptions of the chaotic conditions created by such human deluges during the immediate postwar period, see *Excelsior*, March 2, 1950; and *El Universal*, April 9, 1951, April 15, 1951, and May 3, 1951.

Group theory posits that political outputs invariably reflect the relative strength and desires of important societal groups. In the case of the Mexican government the group model was borne out during the years of direct recruitment despite surface appearances to the contrary. As was true during the entire history of the bracero program, most organized Mexican interest groups and opposition political parties were outwardly opposed to the exodus of their countrymen.[69] Much of this opposition, however, was not because they felt a direct threat to their interest, but was instead *pro forma* and based on national pride and ideology. Furthermore, the Mexican government was actually under considerable pressure of an indirect and sporadic nature from the peasant sector. As the symbol of the Mexican revolution, peasants have long comprised a potentially powerful force within the Mexican polity. Though not well organized, they have been feared and respected by other sectors of the population. At no time during the twenty-two–year history of bracero contracting did a lack of formal organization limit their access to and impact upon Mexico's omnipotent president and his immediate executive family. The support rendered the bracero program by Mexico's powerful chief executive more than offset the *pro forma* pressures for termination.

Like Mexico, the United States appears to have acquiesced to the immediate postwar program as the lesser of two evils. With rural conditions in Mexico so desperate, with more than two thousand miles of frontier to be policed by an extremely small force, and with employers obviously bent on acquiring Mexican labor in one form or another, it was a foregone conclusion that the *campesino* would cross over with or without a contract. Therefore, direct grower recruitment may not have been ideal, but in the eyes of United States officials it was superior to no legal recruitment program at all.

[69] Virtually all Mexican interest groups were formally opposed to any type of labor exodus. As examples of the opposition from labor, business, agricultural, and patriotic groups, see *El Universal*, May 24, 1951, May 31, 1951, June 3, 1951; and editorial in *El Universal*, July 19, 1951. Also note David G. Pfeiffer, "The Mexican Farm Labor Supply Program—Its Friends and Foes," pp. 98–112.

A second cause of United States acceptance of such an arrangement lay in the reality of pressure politics. The forces of agriculture were then, as they are now, a powerful political unit.[70] Their claim that braceros were necessary to avoid crop losses was trumpeted again and again during the 1948–1951 period. Congressionally, the advocates of imported Mexican labor maintained sufficient numerical strength to sustain the bracero program financially. Pressure on the State Department brought a reluctant diplomatic acquiescence.[71] State was obviously uncomfortable with a system of direct recruitment because of its diplomatic risk potential.[72] But faced with farm-bloc demands and the reality that Congress would not act at that time to formally authorize a government-to-government program, the State Department was forced to accept political reality.

Discomfort over the growing number of illegal entrants was apparent within the State Department.[73] Had there been no bracero agreement during the 1948–1951 period, the wetback problem would surely have been exacerbated. As it was, several incidents involving wetbacks occurred during these years, all of which

[70] Pressure for continuation of the program was particularly strong from large grower organizations and their spokesmen (Report of the President's Commission, pp. 7–8; and Galarza, *Merchants of Labor*, p. 48).

[71] Daniel Goott, "Employment of Foreign Workers in United States Agriculture," *Department of State Bulletin*, July 18, 1949, pp. 43–46; and Department of Justice, *Annual Report of the Immigration and Naturalization Service, 1949*, p. 38.

[72] Note the remarks of Assistant Secretary of State Ernest Gross before a Senate judiciary subcommittee (*New York Times*, July 13, 1949).

[73] Indicative of the stress placed upon the State Department by the wetback tide was the remark before the Senate Committee on Labor and Labor-Management Relations by Roy R. Rubottom, deputy director of the Office of Middle American Affairs: "The ramifications of the wetback problem are perhaps one of the most difficult problems in foreign affairs and domestic affairs that the agencies of this Government have ever been up against. It is something you live with constantly. You cannot get away from it. It is just like fighting a windmill" (U.S., Congress, Senate, Committee on Labor and Labor-Management Relations, *Migratory Labor Part I: Hearing before Subcommittee*, 82d Cong., 2d sess., February 5, 6, 7, 11, 14, 15, 27, 28, 29, and March 28, 29, 1952, pp. 129–130).

proved damaging to United States–Mexican relations.[74] With no bracero program whatsoever, the State Department might well have had to rationalize the use of force in an effort to check the wetback tide. The diplomatic risk of such potential encounters must have caused great concern within the State Department. A program of direct grower recruitment may have seemed diplomatically risky during these years. No program might have proved diplomatically disastrous.

Summary

From 1948 through 1950 more than 200,000 legally contracted braceros were imported for work on United States farms. During the same years more than twice that many wetbacks were located. The combined earnings of legal and illegal entrants were crucial to Mexico's rural sector.

In contrast to the preceding period, braceros were contracted directly by United States employers with the aid of government officials from both nations. Fulfillment of contract provisions was not guaranteed by the host government. In this and in many other respects the postwar bracero program was the responsibility of United States employers and their representatives. Government interference was held to a minimum. The years 1948–1951 constituted the *"laissez faire* era in Mexican migratory labor policy."[75] As a result, it was an unpopular program from the viewpoint of three of the four principal groups involved. Only agriculture was comparatively pleased.

Such a result should not prove surprising to the student of political interest groups. Farm interests demanded a system of direct recruitment, and they got it. Labor obviously wanted an end to all foreign labor importation. For labor and the supporters of legislation in behalf of domestic migrants, it was simply a case of having

[74] The most notable was the "El Paso Incident" of October, 1948, over which Mexico abrogated the 1948 agreement (*New York Times*, October 17, 19, and 25, 1948).

[75] Nelson G. Copp, " 'Wetbacks' and Braceros: Mexican Migrant Laborers and American Immigration Policy, 1930–1960," p. 189.

too little political power in contrast to their agricultural counterparts. It was to be several years before they could muster the group
alliance and public support needed to combat the forces of agribusiness.

The Mexican and United States governments were placed in an
uncomfortable position by the postwar bracero program. Both
would have preferred a government-to-government system. Both
realized, however, that the United States Congress would not enact
at the time the necessary enabling legislation required by such a
program. Perhaps most important, they knew that a system of
direct recruitment was far superior to no system at all. With a
program the mutually embarrassing and exasperating wetback
phenomenon could at least be combated on diplomatically acceptable terms. With no program it is doubtful whether severe stress
on the Mexican political system and harmful diplomatic effects on
United States–Mexican relations could have been avoided.

The political power of agriculture plus Mexico's inordinate rural
poverty and resultant wetback exodus combined to shape the postwar bracero system. Missing was an intervening variable originat-
ing in the international environment. World War II had proved
crucial in muting domestic interest-group conflict and had thereby
rendered possible a program better suited to diplomatic harmony.
Without this variable the most powerful domestic pressures were
able to dominate a diplomatically sensitive program. The end result was damaging to United States–Mexican relations. With the
return of this important extranational variable the bracero program again became a credit instead of a debit to United States
foreign policy.

CHAPTER 3

Group Processes and the Institutionalization of Imported Mexican Labor: The Bracero Program, 1951–1952

PRIOR TO August, 1951, the contracting of Mexican labor for work on United States farms was viewed as a temporary phenomenon. With the passage of Public Law 78 and negotiation of the bracero agreement of 1951, the program's temporary nature was threatened. By June, 1952, the bracero system became a "permanent"[1] component of United States farm labor and United

[1] "Permanent" is obviously a relative term, since the bracero program expired in 1964. It is utilized only for emphasis and as a means of comparing the program's nature during the pre- and post-1951 years. For conflicting opinions on whether the 1951 program was meant to be more than simply an emergency measure, see House Report No. 772, "One Year Extension of the Mexican Farm Labor Program," 88th Cong., 1st sess., September 6, 1963, pp. 10 and 21.

States–Mexican relations. The present chapter examines the domestic and international group struggle surrounding this institutionalization and evaluates it in terms of United States foreign policy.

INTEREST GROUPS AND THE ENACTMENT OF PUBLIC LAW 78

The years 1948–1951 were perhaps the most tumultuous in the history of imported Mexican labor. Three of the four groups most deeply concerned were openly critical of the program, while the fourth was none too enthusiastic. Several factors contributed to the demise of direct recruitment, but none was more fundamental than its diplomatic liability. Mexican opposition, when coupled with the international crisis brought on by the Korean War, rendered an employer-dominated system diplomatically unfeasible. In its place was reinstituted a program designed to promote diplomatic harmony but destined to accelerate domestic group conflict.

The most damning critique of direct employer recruitment came from neither a farm nor a labor source. In March, 1951, the findings and recommendations of the President's Commission on Migratory Labor were published.[2] Although it focused primarily on the general topic of farm labor in the United States, the commission devoted considerable time to the Mexican labor system and its domestic ramifications. It noted criticism of the program from all the principal domestic interest groups and the Mexican government.

On the diplomatic dimensions of the program, the committee was critical of a situation in which United States and Mexican authorities did not begin negotiations with equal bargaining positions. Such was said to be the case, because the State Department, in contrast to the Mexican Foreign Ministry, could not hope to negotiate in behalf of the United States as a whole when all interested groups (farm labor organizations in particular) did not possess relatively equal access to the department.

The inherent conflicts in this situation are quite apparent. If the

[2] The commission was appointed in June, 1950, to investigate the question of migratory labor in the United States agriculture. Composed of Noble Clark, William Leisenson, Robert Lucey, Peter Odegard, and Maurice von Hecke, it held twelve public hearings throughout the country during 1950.

Department of State negotiates with respect to the general interests of the Nation and of amicable international relations, it can scarcely be expected that the private interests of farm employers will, at the same time, be fully satisfied. Conversely, if the State Department, in these negotiations, were to represent farm employer interests exclusively, the general interest of the Nation and of amicable international relations might well be neglected or jeopardized.[3]

A second diplomatic dimension of the 1948–1951 program, wetback legalization, came under criticism. The commission's report pointed out that during a three-year period, 1947–1949, approximately 74,000 braceros were contracted from the interior of Mexico, while some 142,000 wetbacks were legalized by being put under contract. Such a process had the effect of rewarding the lawbreaker. Rather than go through the cumbersome process of recruitment in Mexico, the *campesino* entered clandestinely and was then given a "quickie" legalization. This process, in turn, increased the flow of illegal entrants.[4]

On the domestic impact of imported Mexican labor, the president's commission leveled three charges against the program's administration. It had first proved detrimental to the wages and working conditions of domestics. Second, braceros were, as required, paid the "prevailing wage." However, such a wage was not governmentally determined. Instead, the prevailing wage was, de facto, what employers said it was. In many cases such a rate was so low that domestic labor refused to apply. Third, and closely connected with point two, was the commission's critique of the process whereby a need for foreign labor was certified. If growers offered a prevailing wage low enough to discourage locals, a labor shortage did result, which allowed the employer to legitimately request bracero labor.[5] In sum, the commission contended that the administration of the 1948–1951 program favored employers and imported laborers at the expense of native farmworkers.

---

[3] Report of the President's Commission on Migratory Labor, *Migratory Labor in American Agriculture*, pp. 50–51; hereafter cited as Report of the President's Commission.

[4] Ibid., pp. 52–54.

[5] Ibid., pp. 56–64.

To the student of interest-group politics the commission's findings on the power of agricultural employers vis-à-vis farmworkers came as no surprise. It was but a reiteration of the oft-acknowledged political access enjoyed by United States agricultural interests. Such findings alone, no matter what their factual content and import was, would not have caused the termination of a direct recruitment system and the maladministration it engendered. What was needed was another interest group possessed of similar political prowess. No such counterweight existed on the domestic scene in the early 1950's. It was from the international environment that pressure powerful enough to end the postwar bracero program emanated.

Mexico was never happy with the bracero program during the 1948–1951 period. As the wetback flow with its inevitable employer abuses increased, the Mexican attitude became progressively more negative. Although Mexican officials were well aware of the legitimate distinction between legal and illegal migrants, the press and citizens of Mexico saw them only as fellow countrymen. In their eyes, exploitation of a *campesino*, be he wetback or legally contracted bracero, amounted to exploitation of a Mexican.[6]

The Mexican government was particularly distressed with some United States employers who, it was claimed, were not living up to various contract provisions.[7] Similar complaints had long been heard from Mexican circles. Alone, they would not have produced a more determined effort by official Mexico demanding that the United States either legislate an improved government-sponsored system or receive no Mexican labor whatsoever. In the final analysis it was the wetback situation and the individual and na-

[6] Mexican press reaction to real and imagined exploitation of braceros and wetbacks bordered on the paranoid during the late 1940's and the early 1950's. From the many possible examples, note the following: *Excelsior*, January 8, 1950, April 1, 1950; and editorial in *Excelsior*, March 6, 1950.

[7] U.S. President, "Recommendations Supplementing the Provisions of S. 984, an Act Relating to the Recruitment and Employment of Agricultural Workers from Mexico," House Document No. 192, 82d Cong., 1st sess., July 13, 1951; hereafter cited as President's 1951 Message; and U.S., Department of Labor, *Farm Labor Fact Book*, p. 163.

tional humiliation that it engendered that fostered a more adamant Mexican attitude. Although several diplomatically embarrassing instances involving wetbacks occurred during the four years of direct contracting, none so riled the Mexican and his leaders as did the "El Paso Incident."[8]

In October, 1948, a large group of Mexicans gathered in Juarez, Mexico, in hopes of becoming braceros. When it was apparent that Mexican officials would not permit them to enter the United States, the situation became extremely tense. Across the border stood Texas employers ready to transport the men to fully opening cotton fields. Apparently under pressure from Texas employers, the Immigration and Naturalization Service ceased trying to block frantic efforts by the Mexicans to gain entrance and opened the gates on October 13. Three days and four thousand illegal entrants later the gates were again closed.

Don Larin, head of the Farm Placement Bureau, blamed Mexico for the incident. He claimed Mexican officials had violated the 1948 agreement by demanding three dollars per hundred pounds of cotton picked instead of accepting the agreed-to "prevailing wage" standard. In any event, the diplomatic damage had been done, as Texas cotton growers simultaneously acquired the pickers they needed. On October 18, 1948, Mexico abrogated the 1948 agreement. In a diplomatic face-saving effort, Washington denied having sanctioned the action and apologized for the entire incident. Mexico accepted the apology but did not sign another agreement until August, 1949.

Such incidents as the El Paso fiasco must have convinced Mexican officials of the political power base enjoyed by United States growers. For the next three years Mexico never ceased criticizing the direct recruitment program and opting for a return to the government-sponsored system. Such a goal proved illusory, however, as long as it was a case of Mexican pressure versus the political strength of United States agriculture. What Mexico needed to

[8] For an account of the incident, see *New York Times*, October 17, 18, 19, 21, and 26, 1948.

tip the scales of power in her direction was an intervening variable, something that would again render a reliable flow of bracero labor necessary, even on Mexican terms. In June, 1950, forces from North Korea invaded South Korea. War in Korea meant an accelerated demand for farm labor in the United States. It proved to be the leverage needed by Mexico. The game of imported labor was soon to be played on Mexican terms or not played at all.

Faced with grower demands for more labor to meet increased wartime quotas, United States delegates met with Mexican representatives during January and February, 1951.[9] The stated aim of the Mexico City conference was to examine conditions governing the contracting of Mexican labor. It was apparent from the start, however, that the results would be more than just another extension or revision of the postwar agreements. Evidence to this effect was manifest in the composition of the United States delegation. In addition to Carl J. Storm, United States consul general in Mexico, who headed the delegation, two members of Congress vitally concerned with Mexican labor were noticeable by their presence: Allen J. Ellender, chairman of the Senate Committee on Agriculture and Forestry, and Congressman W. R. Poage of the House Agriculture Committee.

Pursuant to a formal request by the Mexican delegation that a United States government agency assume responsibility for bracero contracting, both delegations reached the following conclusions: (1) In response to Mexico's repeatedly stated desire for contracting by government agency, it was concluded that a bill authorizing such a bureau would be introduced in Congress. (2) If Congress refused to enact a government-operated program, the Mexican delegation stated that the international accord of August, 1949,

[9] Indicative of the growing demands of agriculture was the following statement: "Leaders of farm groups who met recently in Washington estimate that from 300,000 to 400,000 Mexicans would be needed this year to produce crops sufficient for defense requirements. The National Cotton Council, meeting in Biloxi, Mississippi, this week, reported at least 500,000 workers would have to be imported from Mexico, Puerto Rico, and Hawaii to enable plantations to produce 16,000,000 bales of cotton in 1951" (*New York Times*, January 27, 1951).

would be terminated. (3) Since no legislation existed at that time permitting contracting by governmental agency, Mexico agreed to extend the then current agreement until July 1, 1951. (4) Both delegations pledged a redoubling of efforts on the part of their respective immigration authorities to prevent illegal entry. Further, it was agreed that any employer hiring wetbacks would be forbidden the use of braceros. (5) Employers failing to comply with a joint determination by representatives of both nations regarding employer contract violations would be denied the use of braceros. (6) Mexico reiterated its demand that any future bracero program be consistent with the nation's own agricultural needs. Contracting, therefore, would be authorized only for those whose services were not required in Mexico.[10]

On February 27, 1951, Senator Ellender introduced S. 984 as an amendment (Title V) to the Agriculture Act of 1949. Its specified purpose was to implement many of the points agreed on during the Mexico City talks. Above all, S. 984 was designed to enable an agency of the United States government to recruit Mexican braceros, and to make the United States government guarantor of individual work contracts. In short, S. 984, which subsequently became Public Law 78 in an amended form, represented an effort by the supporters of a new bracero program to combine Mexican demands with the reality of United States politics and the Korean War.

Hearings on S. 984 and other Senate and House bills dealing with imported labor were conducted during subsequent months. Testimony was received from officials of the Departments of Labor, State, and Agriculture, farm groups, employer organizations, labor-union officials, and other interested individuals. Congressional debate on S. 984 and related bills extended over a two-month period. Amended several times during debate and conference, the Ellender bill was sent to the White House on July 2, 1951. Signed by a somewhat reluctant President Truman on July 13, S. 984

[10] "U.S. and Mexico Reach Agreement on Agricultural Workers," *Department of State Bulletin*, February 19, 1951, p. 300.

became P.L. 78.[11] From the welter of pressures emanating from a foreign state, from an international confrontation, and from domestic agricultural and labor interests, the supporters of a new bracero program accomplished something that even the pressures of World War II had not achieved: a specific commitment by the United States government to guarantee the provisions of an agreement on migratory labor subsequently negotiated with the government of Mexico. The bracero program had been codified. The most difficult step toward institutionalization had been taken.

Group Conflict and Public Law 78

If one analyzes the major provisions of P.L. 78, one finds that they are highly reflective of the group conflict that took place during its enactment.[12] They reflect, in addition, the power possessed by the four principal groups involved.

For the purpose of assisting in the production of farm products, the secretary of labor, pursuant to an agreement with Mexico, was authorized the following powers: First, he was empowered to recruit Mexican workers, including illegal entrants who had resided in the United States for the preceding five years, or who had entered originally under legal contract and remained after it expired. Heated debate arose over this provision. Opponents contended that, as originally worded, S. 984 would have permitted further "instant legalization" of wetbacks. Senator Ellender had apparently not intended for the provision to be so interpreted. He pointed out Mexican opposition to any such scheme and reworded the provision so that it clearly precluded legalization of any wetback unless he met the five-year standard.[13] Mexican pressure may have been largely responsible for the provision. Although they did not favor legaliza-

[11] Perhaps the most detailed account of the legislative struggle over P.L. 78 is contained in Richard M. Lyon's study, "The Legal Status of American and Mexican Migratory Farm Labor: An Analysis of United States Farm Labor Legislation, Policy, and Administration."

[12] This analysis is based upon P.L. 78 as it was originally enacted. Though subsequently amended, it remained the domestic foundation for bracero recruitment until termination in 1964 (U.S., 65 *Stat.* 119).

[13] *Congressional Record*, 87:4420.

tion of wetbacks per se, Mexican authorities had long decried the loss of manpower resulting from wetbacks and braceros who went to the United States and never returned. Many nationals had stayed in the United States because they feared punishment by the Mexican authorities had they returned.[14] Under this provision of P.L. 78, both the Mexican authorities and the illegal migrants could save face.

Second, the secretary of labor was authorized to establish and operate reception centers near the Mexican border in order to receive and house braceros while arrangements were made for their employment in, or departure from, the United States. Third, he was empowered to provide transportation, subsistence, and medical care for braceros from recruiting depots in Mexico to United States reception centers. Fourth, the secretary was authorized to assist employers and workers in negotiating individual work contracts. During contracting, workers were free to choose the employer and employment that best suited them; employers could offer work to braceros of their choosing, as long as they were not already under contract. Fifth, and most crucial from the Mexican perspective, the secretary was authorized to guarantee employer adherence to contract provisions that related to wages or transportation.

Further obligations were imposed on employers under provisions of P.L. 78. In order to acquire braceros, farmers had to agree (1) to indemnify the United States, since it was the guarantor, for any losses; (2) to reimburse the government for essential expenses of the program, not to exceed fifteen dollars per worker; and (3) to pay the government a sum determined by the secretary of labor in cases where workers were not returned to the reception center as provided by contract. The fifteen dollars reimbursement requirement was hotly contested by proponents and opponents of imported labor, with the former viewing the sum as excessive and the latter deeming it unrealistically small.[15] As with other provisions of P.L. 78, the sum constituted a compromise.

In an effort to protect native workers from any detrimental ef-

[14] *Excelsior*, April 11, 1950; and *El Universal*, June 16 and 18, 1951.
[15] *Congressional Record*, 97:7264–7265.

fects of imported Mexican labor, P.L. 78 held that braceros could not be made available unless the secretary of labor determined and certified that (1) sufficient able, willing, and qualified domestic workers were not available to perform a particular type of work when they were needed; (2) employment of braceros did not adversely affect working conditions and wages of domestics employed in similar tasks; and (3) reasonable efforts had been made by employers to attract domestics for such employment at wages and standard hours of work comparable to those offered braceros.

The above provisions were very similar to those contained in previous bracero agreements. For supporters of the law they represented a serious effort to protect domestic workers. Those favoring more detailed and stringent protective measures felt that, while the three requirements were fine in theory, they would not prove any more effective in practice than had their predecessors.[16] Phrases such as "adversely affect" and "reasonable effort" were somewhat controversial during the bracero program's first nine years. During its last thirteen years they became two of the most serious points of contention between friend and foe of imported Mexican farm labor.

According to the provisions of P.L. 78, no penalty bond for departure was required of employers. Such a stipulation was in obvious deference to the long-standing complaint by employers against provisions of bonds under the 1948–1951 system. In an effort to reduce the wetback traffic, P.L. 78 denied employers of illegal aliens the right to contract braceros. Such provisions followed a recommendation made earlier in Mexico City. It was, however, deemed a relatively meaningless provision by opponents of the bracero program. Foes of the statute were equally critical of a Mexican-inspired proviso exempting braceros from social security, income, and head taxes.[17] Finally, in deference to East Coast farmers, it was specifically stipulated that nothing in the act

16 Senate Report No. 214, "Importation of Foreign Agricultural Workers," 82nd Cong., 1st sess., April 11, 1951; hereafter cited as Senate Report No. 214.
17 Ibid.

could be construed as limiting the authority of the attorney general to permit importation of non-Mexican labor.

From an interest-group perspective, P.L. 78 is equally interesting for what it did not include. Opponents of the statute generally summed up their critique by observing that the act omitted many of the key recommendations made by the President's Commission on Migratory Labor.[18] In particular, the opposition claimed that P.L. 78 was a poor statute for four reasons.[19] First, it did not contain sufficient protection for domestic farmworkers. Especially lacking was a more thorough system for determining whether domestic labor shortages did in truth exist. Second, the statute did not assure that either employer or employee would meet provisions of the contract. Third, it would cost the government too much money. Fourth, and perhaps most crucial, it was contended that P.L. 78 failed to constitute a true wetback deterrent. It did not contain meaningful penalties against wetback employers.[20] Mexico had insisted on such provisions during the February conference in Mexico City. The Mexican government, press, and citizen had long contended that the wetback exodus could be stopped only when employers were penalized for hiring them.[21] In this instance, however, Mexican pressure did not prevail. Critics also deemed the act a poor anti-wetback instrument, because it did not contain authority for immigration officials to enter and search without a warrant the premises of those thought to be employing or harboring wetbacks.[22] Such provisions, stated the critics, would have

[18] For a summary of these recommendations, see Report of the President's Commission, pp. 66–67.

[19] Senate Report No. 214.

[20] The Douglas amendment to S. 984 would have provided such penalties, but it was dropped in conference in an effort to save the bill (*Congressional Record,* 97:7519–7526). Strangely enough, many Mexican-Americans opposed a penalty proviso. They reasoned that if it were enacted and enforced many of their people would be unable to show proper identification and, therefore, would not be hired by wary employers. Note the impassioned attack on the Douglas amendment by Congressman Antonio Fernandez of New Mexico (*Congressional Record*, 97: 7163).

[21] *El Universal*, April 10 and 13, 1951.

[22] An amendment to that effect was introduced by Senator Hubert Humphrey

halted the wetback tide by penalizing its primary contributing agent—wetback employers.

Their initial legislative struggle concluded, the combatants continued to seek their goals at the executive level. S. 984 was sent to the White House on July 2, 1951. It did not become law until July 13. During the interim, proponents and opponents of the bill applied intense pressure in an effort to influence President Truman's decision. Hardly a day passed that the chief executive was not visited, telegraphed, or telephoned by one or more of the group combatants, urging him either to sign or to veto the measure.[23] After considerable delay, President Truman reluctantly signed S. 984. In so doing, however, he went out of his way to criticize its shortcomings.

In his message to Congress, President Truman concluded that, although it was essentially a sound piece of legislation under the circumstances, P.L. 78 failed to deal specifically with two fundamental problems: wetback traffic and the plight of domestic farm labor. He recommended that Congress act swiftly to remedy these two crucial defects by taking the following steps: First, legislation was needed to punish individuals harboring or concealing wetbacks. It is notable that the president omitted the term "employing." He apparently realized that the use of such a term would have rendered the provision unenforceable in the courts.

Second, legislation was considered necessary to authorize immigration officials to inspect, without a warrant, places of employment where they believed wetbacks were working or quartered. It is notable that, although the chief executive likened agricultural places of employment to mines and factories because of their public nature, he did not include the farmer's dwelling as such. To say that farm buildings should be equally as subject to governmental inspection as mines and factories was one thing, to include an individual's home was another.

---

of Minnesota, but was later defeated (*Congressional Record*, 97:4956, 4961, and 4965).

[23] *New York Times*, July 6, 10, 1951; and *El Universal*, July 8, 11, 12, 1951.

Third, additional funds were said to be urgently needed by the Immigration and Naturalization Service to expand its personnel and operations in order to further combat the growing number of illegal entrants. Finally, the president contended that legislation was sorely needed to encourage the utilization of domestic farmworkers and reduce drastically our dependence on foreign laborers.[24]

INTEREST GROUPS AND THE MEXICAN LABOR AGREEMENT OF 1951

Immediately following passage of P.L. 78, negotiations were resumed with Mexico for a new international agreement.[25] Talks opened July 17, 1951, in Mexico City. The negotiating parties included representatives of the United States Departments of Labor, Justice, Agriculture, State, and Health Education, and Welfare; and the Mexican Departments of Labor, State, Public Health, and Interior.[26]

Negotiations progressed smoothly from the beginning within an atmosphere of cooperation and friendship seldom equalled in the history of United States–Mexican relations.[27] Mexico seemed impressed with the high caliber of the United States delegation and took this to be indicative of the seriousness with which that nation approached the problem. Receiving particular praise were Carl Storm, United States consul general in Mexico, and Senator Ellender, who was looked upon as a particular friend of Mexico and a "defender of wetbacks."[28]

After one week of negotiations it became apparent that full agreement would soon be reached. Only the question of penalty

[24] President's 1951 Message.

[25] The term *immediately* is most apropos. With the fall harvests rapidly approaching and recruitment being conducted on a restricted and temporary basis, United States officials asked Mexico for new negotiations just fifteen minutes after President Truman signed S. 984 into law (*New York Times*, July 13, 1951).

[26] *Farm Labor Fact Book*, p. 163.

[27] As examples of the good-neighbor atmosphere that pervaded the talks, see *Excelsior*, July 18, 20, 21, 1951; and *El Universal*, July 20, 21, 1951.

[28] *Excelsior*, July 19, 1951.

legislation for employers of wetbacks proved a stumbling block. However, this too was quickly ironed out. The Mexican delegates appeared to place great faith in the future possibility of such legislation following President Truman's message to Congress on July 13.[29]

On August 2, 1951, the United States and Mexico signed a new bracero agreement. Although international friction arose over the program in subsequent years, the 1951 agreement was a boon to United States–Mexican relations by any standard. The Mexico City talks were extremely cordial and saturated with a tone of good neighborliness. At every public appearance and press conference during the negotiations, Mexican and United States representatives sought to outpraise one another. Alfonso Guerra, leader of the Mexican delegation and a high-ranking official in the Department of Foreign Affairs, considered the negotiations an excellent piece of diplomacy on the part of the United States, diplomacy that would dispel once and for all any charges of Yankee imperialism. Carl Storm answered Guerra's praise by lauding the Mexican attitude as an example of international good will.[30] He went on to describe the negotiations as a "practical demonstration of the effectiveness of democratic methods in resolving problems between nations."[31] Undersecretary of Labor Robert Creasey, who signed the final agreement, summed up the amicable nature of the negotiations: "We came as friends, worked as friends, and parted as friends."[32]

The 1951 Bracero Agreement

Despite the sincere friendship that prevailed during the negotiation and signing of the 1951 accord, Mexico was not yet ready for a long-term project. Activated August 11, 1951, the agreement was

[29] The Mexican press followed the entire legislative struggle perhaps more closely than did its United States counterpart. For example, the full text of President Truman's message to Congress when he signed P.L. 78 was carried in at least one Mexican daily (*Excelsior*, July 14, 1951).

[30] *El Universal*, July 21, 1951.

[31] *Excelsior*, July 21, 1951.

[32] *El Universal*, August 3, 1951.

first given a six-month trial run. Mexico felt that such a period would provide an indication of the new program's worth and simultaneously give Congress adequate time to legislate penalties for employers of wetbacks.[33]

In content, the 1951 agreement and accompanying standard work contract were similar to their 1942 predecessors. The three prerequisites for bracero recruitment contained in P.L. 78 were included, as were a variety of worker guarantees. The 1951 accord was, however, far more detailed and, though subsequently amended, was to remain the foundation of imported Mexican labor for thirteen years.[34] It began with a detailed analysis of terms and listed the location of five recruitment depots in the interior of Mexico and three United States reception centers, the number and location of which varied during subsequent years.

Recruitment procedures were spelled out in detail. Mexico was given at least a thirty-day notice about how many workers were needed. She, in turn, allocated quotas to particular areas.[35] At the recruitment depots, qualified candidates were chosen by representatives of the United States Labor Department. Examination by representatives of the Mexican Public Health Service and Interior Department and successful completion of physical and security examinations administered by officials of the United States Public Health Service and the Department of Justice preceded selection. Only candidates who had complied with Mexico's military service

[33] The initial period was rather brief, which indicates that a degree of collusion appears to have taken place between executive officials in both countries. President Truman made known through Representative Emanuel Cellar, on July 18, that he favored a six-month period to allow Congress time to act on his recommendations. For the president's position, see *Excelsior*, July 19, 1951. For the Mexican position, see *New York Times*, July 21, 1951.

[34] The description of the agreement and work contract contained in this chapter is drawn from the original 1951 document (U.S., Department of State, TIAS 2331, *United States Treaties and Other International Agreements*, pp. 1940–1996; hereafter cited as TIAS.

[35] Richard H. Hancock contends that quota allotments and individual assignments were monopolized by the PRI, with nonmembers having little chance to become administrators or braceros (*The Role of the Bracero in the Economic and Cultural Dynamics of Mexico: A Case Study of Chihuahua*, p. 66).

law were eligible. Once he passed this hurdle, the prospective bracero was transported to one of three United States reception centers
at the expense of the United States government, which was later
reimbursed by employers for the bracero's transportation and subsistence. At the reception center contracting began with employers
or their representatives.

Particular classes of employers were declared ineligible to contract braceros. Employers were ineligible who (1) had failed to
honor previous contract obligations, (2) employed wetbacks once
a given area was declared eligible for braceros, (3) attempted to
hire workers for blacklisted employers, or (4) owned premises that
were determined unsanitary or unsafe according to prescribed conditions. Once an eligible contractor and worker reached an agreement, a contract was signed by them and countersigned by officials
of both governments.

Once contracted, the bracero was furnished transportation and
subsistence at employer expense from the reception center to his
place of work and back to the center at the end of the contract
period. Not all areas were ipso facto eligible for braceros. Under
the new agreement the Mexican Foreign Ministry was granted
authority to submit to the United States Department of Labor a
list of communities in which discrimination was felt to exist. If the
secretary of labor concurred, these areas were blacklisted. A system
of arbitration and joint determination was established in cases
where the secretary and the Foreign Ministry did not concur.

In addition to free transportation and subsistence en route, braceros received a substantial number of additional guarantees under
terms of the 1951 agreement. In the area of *wages*, employers
agreed to pay either a stipulated amount or the prevailing area
wage paid domestics for performing similar tasks, whichever was
greater. Standards for those working on a piece-rate basis were also
established. Braceros were given a *work* guarantee. Under its conditions Mexican nationals were assured employment for three-
fourths of the work days of their contract period or subsistence for
the time not meeting this guarantee. It was stipulated that braceros
could not be utilized to fill vacancies occurring in the event of

strikes or lockouts. *Insurance* guarantees were included in the accord. In the absence of state laws covering personal injuries or
occupational diseases, employers were required either to carry
insurance policies or to post indemnity bonds sufficient to cover
the payment of benefits. Furthermore, work contracts contained a
list of payments in cases of injury or death. In the event of serious
illness, injury, death, or refusal by the bracero to complete his
contract, employers were required to notify the Labor Department
and the Mexican consul. *Housing* guarantees were defined. Employers agreed to furnish, at no cost to the bracero, adequate,
hygienic lodging. Also included were beds, blankets, and cooking
facilities, the latter being assured only in cases where employers
did not offer prepared meals. In signing a work contract, the employer agreed to permit representatives of both governments to
inspect the facilities furnished braceros. Refusal by an employer
to allow such inspections constituted a violation of the agreement.
Tools and equipment required for the bracero to perform his assigned duties were also supplied by the employer. Finally, Mexican
nationals were assured the right to *elect their own representative* to
act in a liaison capacity with employers. Such a provision, in effect,
granted braceros the right to join United States labor unions.

Fundamental as they were, these guarantees did not loom paramount to Mexican officials. More important was the performance
guarantee assumed by the host nation. The United States government ensured employer compliance with the decisive transportation and wage provisions of the work contract. By definition,
"wages" was broadly interpreted to include remuneration for subsistence, insurance, and related benefits. Responsibility in cases of
defaulting employers was thus assumed by official Washington.

Group Processes and the 1951 Accord

The 1951 agreement reflected, as did P.L. 78, the power of the
principal groups involved. Labor, agricultural employers, Mexico,
and the United States each had a vital stake in the diplomatic
game that produced the accord. Each gained something, yet none
was completely satisfied with its contents. As in the case with most

interest-group conflicts, there was no clear winner or complete loser. The 1951 accord reflected only the relative power of a particular group over other participants. It was a compromise document.

Of the four principal groups, Mexico benefited most from the accord. Mexico achieved, first, a government-sponsored agreement. Of the many guarantees afforded braceros, the two most important were made the direct responsibility of the United States government. In addition to this paramount victory, Mexican demands were reflected in other provisions of the pact. The provision on determining discriminatory practices and subsequent blacklisting constituted an important concession to the sensitive Mexican psyche. Even though the determination was concurrent, the power to deny particular areas the use of braceros placed substantial discretionary power in Mexican hands.

Deference to Mexican demands was apparent in the location of recruiting depots. Southwestern growers had long sought border locations for such stations. It would have rendered cheaper and more convenient the entire process of securing braceros. Mexico, however, objected to locating the depots near the border for several reasons. First, border centers would encourage illegal entry. With thousands of *campesinos* seeking a limited number of positions, many would not qualify. The remainder, invariably restless and hungry, would be sorely tempted by the proximity of Yankee cottonfields and dollars. Second, such positioning would reduce the labor supply in northern Mexico during a period when Mexican growers needed the workers. Third, a scarcity of labor would precipitate higher wages. Therefore, it was obvious that Mexican growers did not want recruiting stations located on the border.[36]

Mexican pressure was also apparent in the provisions denying braceros to employers involved in the wetback traffic. Mexico was especially sensitive to the plight of illegal entrants and sought

[36] As an example of opposition to border recruitment by Mexican growers, see *El Universal*, May 24, June 3, 1951; and Galarza, *Merchants of Labor: The Mexican Bracero Story; An Account of the Managed Migration of Mexican Farmworkers in California 1942–1960*, p. 77.

punishment of their employers. Mexicans reasoned that only by punishing the user could the clandestine movement be curtailed. When it became apparent that Congress would not enact punitive legislation, Mexican pressure achieved the next best thing. In any event, with the agreement scheduled for only six months, many Mexicans reasoned that penalty provisions would soon be legislated in Washington.

Mexico proved a shrewd, hard bargainer during both the exploratory talks in January and the actual negotiation of the agreement in July. She apparently realized that war in Korea could prove an invaluable means to a national end. The result was an all-or-nothing stance. As a consequence United States supporters of a new government-based program continually argued for passage on the grounds that (1) braceros were urgently needed due to the manpower shortage precipitated by the war, and that (2) the only possible way to secure them was to grant Mexico what she demanded: a program negotiated with and supported by the United States government.[37] The 1951 bracero agreement did not grant all of Mexico's demands,[38] but it remedied many of the worst ills engendered by a system of direct recruitment.

As a group participant, the United States fared well under the 1951 accord. Official Washington accepted the thesis that imported farm labor was necessary as a result of the Korean crisis. After the United States acquiesced to such a premise, an outward congruence developed between Washington and Mexico City. Both governments had been diplomatically uncomfortable with the 1948–1951 system because of its high risk potential. Mexican demands, when coupled with the stress of military confrontation, placed Washington in a position whereby she could actively support a government-to-government program in the name of national

[37] *Congressional Record*, 97:4417, 4479, and 7151; and U.S., Congress, Senate, Committee on Agriculture and Forestry, *Farm Labor: Hearings on S. 949, S. 984, and S. 1106*, 82d Cong., 1st sess., March 13–16, pp. 7–10, 39, and 42; hereafter cited as Senate Agriculture Committee Hearings, 1951.

[38] In addition to punishment for wetback employers, Mexico failed to gain an equal role in wage determination. United States delegates were successful in placing this function in the Department of Labor.

defense. Thus, as an intervening variable, Korea indirectly proved a diplomatic asset to United States relations with Mexico.

Washington was, however, disappointed by the anti-wetback potential of the 1951 agreement. While it did contain provisions aimed at those trafficking in illegal immigrants, the accord, like its domestic legislative companion, left too many loopholes. From an anti-wetback perspective, the agreement was a vast improvement over its immediate predecessor, but it failed to live up to its true potential.

From the viewpoint of both governments, the 1951 bracero agreement was, therefore, not without its faults. Under pressure from labor and growers against any bracero exodus, Mexico still chose to continue exporting her nationals. Economic, social, and political reality dictated such a course. Pressured in opposite directions by farm and labor forces and faced with the systemic stress of war, the United States also accepted a diplomatically less than perfect accord. For Washington and Mexico City the 1951 agreement was a favorable compromise resulting from the domestic and international realities of the period. In the case of the two principal domestic interest groups, compromise was also mandatory. Yet the balance that characterized the international dimension of the 1951 agreement was noticeably lacking.

The agreement clearly reflected the political access and power of United States farm interests. This power is evidenced most clearly by the fact that an agreement to import Mexican labor was negotiated. Had the power of labor prevailed, there would have been no such agreement. Ideally, grower interests would have preferred a simple crossing card system entailing a minimum of governmental supervision. Realistically, however, agraria realized that Mexico was earnest in its pledge to end the migrant flow unless a government-sponsored program was established. Employers were also aware of the diplomatic and public relations risk potential that an unmitigated wetback flow would have entailed. Such an event would have afforded growers an unlimited short-term supply of cheap labor, but it would have hastened the day that Mexico terminated cooperation. Given these facts, employers chose to settle for less than their ideal. In doing so they gave sustenance to the very phenomenon they had so long considered an anathema: a greater role for government in the field of agricultural labor.

It was obvious to growers that no agreement would result in a complete end to the wetback flow. Without punitive legislation, farmers could continue a cautious use of illegals as a supplement to bracero and domestic labor. Above these considerations, however, there loomed a long-range calculation. Agribusiness apparently sensed the potentially beneficial aspects of a highly regulated flow of legally imported labor. Southwestern agriculture was rapidly expanding. It required an ever-growing supply of skilled, dependable stoop labor. In raising perishable crops the dependability of one's labor supply is a prime determinant of profit and loss. More than any other quality, their dependability most endeared braceros to employers.[39] As it subsequently evolved, the 1951 bracero program became dependability personified.

As written, the 1951 agreement contained several objectionable features from the point of view of employers. Most important, there was a high degree of government involvement in the entire program. As guarantor of the crucial wage and transportation provisions, Washington was sure to become more of a "bureaucratic meddler" than ever before. The second objection concerned the interior location of recruiting depots. Third, growers objected to the provision permitting workers to choose persons outside their group to represent them. In this instance pressure from Mexican and United States labor unions prevailed over that of farm groups. A fourth objection centered on the increased amount of bookkeeping chores assigned employers. Under the agreement, bracero users were burdened with an increased amount of red tape. Fifth, growers objected to the prohibition against braceros being used during

---

[39] Opponents of the program argued that the Mexican was popular because he was cheap, and, in the long run, this may have been true. When, however, one calculates the wages and benefits given the bracero, he was more expensive than the domestic. It was his dependability, his willingness to work under virtually any condition, and his skill that made the bracero such a valuable asset to southwestern agriculture.

strikes or lockouts. Despite a narrowing of this provision to a point requiring that any such dispute must seriously affect an operation in which braceros were engaged, employers were obviously aware of its potential. A final stipulation to which employers objected dealt with determination of prevailing wages. Ultimate authority in this area was assigned, on a national basis, to the Department of Labor and not to regional officials as growers had desired.

When one adds to the above stipulations the three important provisions designed to protect domestic labor from any possible adverse effect of imported braceros, it appears that farm groups emerged second best to Mexico and domestic labor interests. However, two crucial caveats must be added, which, in combination, reveal a clearer picture of the power of farm interests. In the first place, growers secured the Mexican labor they needed. Second, and perhaps equally important, the 1951 agreement, while highly objectionable in form, was one with which agraria could live. Farm interest realized that enforcement of specific contract guarantees and rather nebulous general provisions would constitute a difficult task. Laws and international accords are truly effective only to the degree that their provisions are enforced. Enforcement power under the agreement lay ultimately in Washington. Given the power base enjoyed by farm interests in the nation's capital, the distance from Washington to the principal bracero-using states could have become hyperextended. Such was the case until the power structure of imported Mexican labor underwent alteration.

Of the four principal actors in the bracero drama, only organized labor suffered a defeat as a result of the 1951 accord. Labor interests lacked effective access to particularly powerful governmental bodies and crucial individuals at the national and international level and were thus unable to avoid the worst feature of the agreement—its existence. The fundamental premise from which labor and those groups supporting legislation on behalf of domestic migrants operated was simply that the Mexican workers were not needed. Anti-braceroists felt that enough domestics were already available. They contended that predicted labor shortages resulting from the war effort were at best highly dubious and generally a blatant falsification of the facts. Instead of importing foreign workers at taxpayers' expense, labor suggested spending the money to improve the lot of native migrants. What was needed, claimed the anti-braceroists, was not more Mexicans, but improved wages and working conditions for domestics.[40] In August, 1951, domestic and international politics came forth with a reply to labor's demands: more Mexicans.

To conclude that domestic labor interests suffered a setback with enactment of the 1951 accord is not to say that their voice was not heard. The bracero agreement was dotted with many concessions to labor demands. Far more important than any one provision, however, was that the program was government sponsored. If the importation of alien farm labor was a reality that labor simply could not avoid, then far better it be under strict government auspices than controlled by employers. Government-sponsored importation was bad; compared to the 1948–1951 system it was a decided improvement. Under such an agreement labor interests would at least be able to demand strict enforcement of crucial provisions. They would, in short, be in a far better position to exert political pressure and to act as a watchdog under a government-to-government system.

Particular provisions of the 1951 accord clearly reflected the views of labor. These have been previously mentioned in other contexts and included (1) the three fundamental articles dealing with adverse effect of Mexican labor on domestic wages and working conditions, (2) exclusion of particular employers from bracero contracting, (3) permission for braceros to choose their own representatives, (4) prohibition against using Mexican nationals as strikebreakers, and (5) determination of prevailing wages by a national official.

Despite these and other stipulations, the power of labor was blunted in several crucial areas. Unable to avoid the inevitable, labor interests sought, as they did with P.L. 78, to make the 1951 agreement a more palatable document. In this respect the agree-

[40] Senate Agriculture Committee Hearings, 1951, pp. 64–72, 73, and 123; and *Congressional Record*, 97:4419, 4479, and 4591.

ment was a great blow to labor because of what it did not include. Missing were strict penalty provisions against wetback employers. In this instance, labor agreed with Mexico on the root cause of illegal migration. Anti-braceroists were especially disappointed by the wording of the prevailing-wage provision. They wanted the power of final determination located at the national level, but they feared that employers would ultimately determine the wage. Labor interests would have preferred a system of joint determination by representatives of labor, employers, and government. Instead, a system was evolved under which growers offered a particular wage, and a regional official in the Employment Service division of the Labor Department passed judgment on its credibility. This system was fine in theory. Labor contended, however, that, as a result of grower power within the United States Employment Service, the wage offered by employers would invariably become the "prevailing wage."[41] Many years later, anti-bracero forces were still making the same claim and attempting to substantiate it with facts and figures.

Similarly, labor was disappointed by the omission of a third element: a detailed elaboration of the clauses relating to protection of domestics from any debilitating effects of bracero importation. Before sanctioning the use of Mexican nationals, the secretary of labor was required by provisions of P.L. 78 and the 1951 accord to certify the existence of three conditions. First, it was necessary that not enough able, willing, and qualified domestics be available. In this instance, labor called for the inclusion of a more detailed joint determination procedure to ensure, to the satisfaction of employers, growers, and labor, that a verified shortage did exist.[42] Second, the

---

[41] Report of the President's Commission, pp. 59–61; and U.S., Congress, Senate, *Committee on Labor, Part I; Hearing before Subcommittee*, 82d Cong., 2d sess., February 5, 6, 7, 11, 14, 15, 27, 28, 29, and March 28–29, 1952, pp. 250–251; hereafter cited as Senate Labor Committee Hearings, 1952.

[42] Note the remark of Senator Dennis Chavez of New Mexico in deriding Labor Department efforts to recruit domestics: "They are doing everything they can. Perhaps saying the Lord's Prayer, doing good deeds, meaning to do the right thing, but not getting the labor they could get" (*Congressional Record*, 97:4601).

secretary was required to certify that the use of braceros would not adversely affect wages and working conditions of domestics. Anti-braceroists claimed that the importation of Mexican nationals did produce an adverse effect. They recommended that the agreement include a detailed system of joint determination to verify whether an adverse effect did result.[43] Third, the labor secretary had to certify that "reasonable effort" had been made to recruit native workers under wages and working conditions comparable to those offered braceros. Labor interests denied that such an effort had been made in the past. Again they opted for more elaborate joint processes to determine whether employers had put forth a reasonable effort.[44] In the case of these three crucial provisions and in other articles throughout the 1951 agreement, anti-braceroists sought to add flesh and blood to otherwise skeletal stipulations. They were unsuccessful. The forces of ambiguity proved more powerful than those of explicitness.

Summary

On July 12, 1951, the first crucial step toward institutionalization of imported Mexican labor was taken. Congress established a precedent by granting specific legislative authority for contracting foreign labor on a government-to-government basis. The second step toward permanency occurred on August 2, when the 1951 bracero agreement was concluded. Mexico was, however, not yet prepared to make the final move. From the Mexican viewpoint, institutionalization was still risky. The 1951 accord was given only a six-month life span. Renewal, and, by it, permanency, would depend on action by the United States Congress.

Taken as a whole, P.L. 78, the 1951 agreement, and the standard work contract came to be known as the bracero program. Though subsequently amended, these three documents served as the foundation of imported Mexican labor for thirteen years. To the student of interest groups and the political process, the struggle over enact-

[43] Senate Labor Committee Hearings, 1952, pp. 250–256, and 268; and Report of the President's Commission, p. 59.
[44] Senate Labor Committee Hearings, 1952, pp. 244–250, 268.

ment as well as the content of the program raise several interesting points.

If one focuses on the domestic group participants, one obvious conclusion appears: the power of agricultural interests to affect the outcome and content of P.L. 78 and its accompanying international accord was disproportionate to that of labor. Several factors account for the impotence of anti-bracero forces. Of the indigenous factors, congressional location of the group struggle was paramount. Despite contrary opinion,[45] the importation of Mexican farmworkers was deemed an agricultural question. S. 984 was introduced as an amendment to the Agriculture Act of 1949. Decisive hearings were conducted by agriculture committees in both houses. These committees were chaired by known supporters of the bracero program. Witnesses testifying in behalf of bracero importation were treated with utmost courtesy, opponents with sharp cross-examination.[46] Representatives to the conference committee that finalized S. 984 were disproportionately pro-braceroists. In short, the importation question was from the beginning the personal property of pro-bracero interests in Congress.

Organization and tactics constituted a second factor in the legislative success of the supporters of Mexican labor. Witnesses testifying in support of the program were generally well prepared and businesslike in their presentations. They came equipped with facts and figures to substantiate their case.[47] Particularly telling was the line of reasoning utilized by supporters of the program. Whether they were politicians or laymen, pro-braceroists employed time and again with great effectiveness three rationalizations for supporting the program. It was said to be mandatory because (1) the defense effort required it, (2) it would substantially reduce the wetback tide, and (3) it would be a boon to United States–Mexican rela-

---

[45] As an example note the effort by Senator Wayne Morse of Oregon (*Congressional Record*, 97:4484–4585).

[46] Senate Agriculture Committee Hearings, 1951; and U.S., Congress, House, Committee on Agriculture, *Farm Labor: Hearings on H.R. 2955, H.R. 3048*, 82d Cong., 1st sess., 1951, March 8–14, 1951.

[47] Senate Agriculture Committee Hearings, 1951, pp. 56–61, and 78–123.

tions. Supporters of imported labor seldom missed an opportunity to lobby the public.[48]

In contrast, opponents of the program were poorly organized and tactically awkward. Anti-braceroists came off a poor second when they appeared before somewhat hostile committee members. Their arguments were often emotional and not statistically supported.[49] Perhaps most damaging was the failure of either the AFL or the CIO to come forward with a fully coordinated condemnation of importation. With labor unionism in agriculture still at the embryonic stage and with the odds against their cause, the leaders of United States unionism presented little more than token opposition to the bracero program.[50] More often than not the only unmitigated opposition came from the National Farmers Union of the AFL. During congressional debate, only Senator Dennis Chavez of New Mexico and Representatives Eugene McCarthy of Minnesota and Emanuel Celler of New York contested the proposal.[51] In contrast, the forces of big agriculture presented an all-out support effort. Of the major farm groups, only the Farmers Union, traditionally supportive of the small farmer, demurred.

A final factor in the legislative failure of anti-bracero forces was their inability to swing uncommitted legislators to their cause. In many respects the struggle over P.L. 78 presented a classic example of pork barreling among uncommitted legislators, especially among congressmen from midwestern and northwestern states. If one theme characterized their attitude toward imported Mexican labor it was: "What's in it for me and my constituents?"[52] In the final analysis they apparently found more in the presence of braceros than in their absence.

The same lack of access to crucial individuals and official bodies

[48] Ibid., pp. 10–12, 19, 39, 44, and 45.

[49] Ibid., pp. 72–77 and 155–159.

[50] As an example note the statement of Walter J. Mason, representing the AFL (Ibid., pp. 123–135).

[51] *Congressional Record*, 95:4479, 4494, 4520, 4591, 4601, 7154, and 7254.

[52] In particular, note the remarks of Senators Wayne Morse, Guy Cordon, William Langer, and Representative H. R. Gross (Ibid., pp. 4590, 4677, 4969, 7167).

that hampered the anti-bracero cause at the domestic level also blunted its efforts internationally. Perhaps the best example of this was evidenced in the preliminary talks held during January and February, 1951, in Mexico City. While United States proponents of continued bracero importation were obvious by their presence, opposition delegates were noticeable by their absence. One labor source contends that unions were not even aware until the last moment that the conference had been scheduled. Representatives of the National Farm Labor Union and the Railway Labor Executives' Association, on belatedly requesting consultant or observer status, were turned down by the State Department.[53] A similar blackout of domestic farm-labor sympathizers occurred during actual negotiation of the 1951 agreement. If access to important international consultative and negotiating bodies was any criterion for gauging effectiveness in the group struggle over bracero importation in 1951, one would expect to have seen it evidenced in the final product, as it was.

Shifting attention to the international participants provides further insights to the student of group processes. Of particular interest was the enormous impact of a phenomenon from outside the international environment of the bracero question—the Korean War. Even had there been no such intervening variable, importation would likely have continued. Mexico's great rural poverty in conjunction with the political power of United States farm interests rendered some type of labor flow inevitable. A government-sponsored program could have emerged, but given the distaste of grower interests for such a system, it would have necessitated an extended struggle. More likely a system of direct recruitment would have continued. A third possibility could have been no legal system of importation, accompanied by a still greater wetback influx. The second possibility would have been harmful to United States–Mexican relations, the third disastrous.

The Korean conflagration was crucial, therefore, not only to the bracero program's development, but to United States–Mexican re-

[53] Ibid., pp. 4713; and *Hispano Americano*, February 23, 1951, pp. 3–4.

lations as well. Primarily because of the war's impact, rapid negotiation of a diplomatically salutary arrangement was possible. In
contrast to the 1948–1951 situation, the 1951 group struggle over
imported Mexican farm labor spawned a program that became a
major asset to United States diplomacy. Such a successful program
might not have been devised had it not been for a factor totally un-
related to Mexican braceros. Nine years after its inception the bracero program had all but become a permanent fixture of United
States–Mexican relations. It had changed in some respects, but not
in others. In its sensitivity to forces outside its own milieu, the 1951
version differed little from the 1942 model.

INSTITUTIONALIZATION OF THE BRACERO PROGRAM

Importation of bracero labor did not assume permanency in
1951. Executive officials in both nations denied the program their
final blessing by agreeing that the accord of August 11, 1951,
would be in effect only until February 11, 1952. They made it clear
that extension or renegotiation was totally dependent upon congressional action against United States citizens trafficking in wetbacks. Public Law 78 was scheduled to remain in effect until December 31, 1953, but there would be no braceros if Congress failed
to act by February, 1952. Thus, both governmental groups applied
pressure to Congress on behalf of a single objective. The result was
preordained; so too was a sharp struggle among domestic interests
and their representatives.

Administration officials realized the delicate nature of such sanctions and produced a compromise document. They chose an especially shrewd legislative route by which to reach their goal. The
proposal was designed with two things in mind. First, it had to
prove acceptable to Mexico as well as to the Departments of Agriculture, Labor, and Justice. Second, the measure had to be drafted
so that it would withstand the constitutionally based attack of congressional critics. In particular, a bill was required that would simultaneously mollify the Mexicans and survive the onslaught of
southwestern representatives in the House. Such a measure was
Senate Bill 1851.

President Truman, in signing a joint resolution to fund the bracero program on August 16, 1951, expressed once more the hope that Congress would comply with his recommendations for strengthening the program's penalty provisions so that renewal would be possible.[54] The president thus aligned himself with the Mexican position: either punitive legislation aimed at halting the wetback flow would be enacted by Congress, or there would be no bracero program. From the time of the chief executive's remarks, the only question became one of degree. Just how punitive would the legislation be?

Mexico sought legislation similar to the amendment introduced by Senator Paul Douglas of Illinois, which the Senate rejected in 1951. It would have made it a felony to employ an alien suspected of having entered the country illegally. Defeat of the amendment in conference obviously alerted Mexico to the fact that, while some form of punitive legislation was possible, it would be a difficult chore. No sooner had the 1951 agreement been signed than the Mexican press began calling for anti-wetback measures as the price for renewal. The United States ambassador to Mexico, William O'Dwyer, sensed apparently that Mexico was again about to demand the unfeasible and cautioned his hosts. In the course of an interview, the ambassador expressed serious doubts about Congress ever making the employment of wetbacks a felony.[55]

Despite such warnings, Mexico continued to press for strict sanctions as the price for renewal.[56] The United States press appeared to buoy Mexican hopes by editorially supporting such legislation.[57] At his press conference of January 3, 1952, President Truman supported the Mexican position by warning Congress that the price for inaction would be the loss of Mexican labor.[58] Congress was thus under pressure from international as well as national interests to

54 *Excelsior*, August 17, 1951.
55 *El Universal*, September 15, 1951.
56 Ibid., December 24, 1951.
57 *New York Times*, November 4, 1951.
58 *El Universal*, January 4, 1952.

act or face the consequences. On February 5, 1952, Senate debate began on S. 1851, a bill that would eventually constitute the third step in the institutionalization of imported Mexican farm labor.[59]

Punitive measures aimed at employers dealing in the wetback traffic were defeated when they were offered as amendments to P.L. 78. That the administration had chosen another legislative route to the same issue became apparent when S. 1851 was introduced not as an agricultural or a labor measure but as an amendment to the 1917 immigration act. Termed the "wetback bill," the measure as originally worded would have made it a felony punishable by a fine not exceeding two thousand dollars or by imprisonment for not more than five years, or both, to aid anyone entering the country illegally or harboring or concealing an illegal entrant. It would have allowed federal officials without a warrant to search private property, excluding homes, within twenty-five miles of the border for illegal entrants. Under its provisions, administrative search warrants could be issued in cases when there was "reasonable probability" of illegal entrants being harbored on particular lands. Finally, under S. 1851, employing such individuals was not deemed harboring.[60] The latter stipulation was vitally important. It constituted a clear indication that the administration had already compromised on the issue prior to introduction.

Unlike the debate over P.L. 78, congressional consideration of S. 1851 was not a case of proponents of imported labor versus opponents. With the bracero program an accomplished fact of 1952, debate on the wetback bill centered on the question of whether harboring wetbacks should be made a felony, and, if so, how said felons should be apprehended and punished. Consideration resulted in a strange anomaly. The original anti-braceroists opposed S. 1851 on the grounds that the bill would not stop the wetback flow due to its

[59] S. 1851 was originally introduced during the 1st session of the 82d Congress by Senator Harley Kilgore of Texas.

[60] For the contents of the bill as it was introduced in 1952, see Senate Report No. 1145, "Assisting in Preventing Aliens from Entering or Remaining in the United States Illegally," 82d Cong., 2d sess., February 4, 1952.

nebulous wording and its failure to make employment as well as harboring a crime.[61] Some proponents of imported labor also opposed the bill, saying that it would not deter wetbacks. They argued, however, that the measure was too stringent and violated the Fourth Amendment to the Constitution, which forbids illegal search and seizure. For them, solution to the wetback problem was simple. What was needed was not stringent measures against those harboring wetbacks, but the abolition of a cumbersome agreement and the return to a simple crossing card system.[62]

Debate in both houses of Congress was structured around two principal themes: (1) Mexican demands for punitive sanctions, which was the price for renewal of the bracero pact, and (2) the constitutionality of S. 1851. The element of time was emphasized by supporters of the measure, especially those in the Senate, where debate on this vitally important measure was surprisingly limited.[63] Senate proponents continually stressed the February 11 deadline and Mexican intentions not to renew unless Congress acted. While resentment against such foreign pressure was voiced by some senators,[64] S. 1851 emerged unscathed and was sent to the House on February 6, 1952.

House consideration of the wetback bill did not begin until February 25, some fourteen days beyond the expiration date of the bracero agreement. In the interim, Mexico apparently decided that half a loaf was better than none. Senate passage of S. 1851 had, in effect, reversed the power position of the two international group combatants. It enabled the United States to prevail upon Mexico to temporarily extend the 1951 accord. The latter obviously did not want the program to expire. Therefore, despite its displeasure over

[61] *Congressional Record*, 98:793–795, 797–798, and 1413–1414.

[62] Ibid., pp. 1340–1341, 1344–1345, and 1352–1355.

[63] The bill was considered by the Senate on February 5 and 6. Since no hearings were held on the measure, the brevity of debate is even more surprising. For the entire Senate debate on S. 1851, see *Congressional Record*, 98:791–813.

[64] Senators Allen Ellender, John Connally, and William Knowland were obviously perturbed. Senator Ellender seemed especially resentful of Mexican pressure, since Mexico appeared to be unloading the entire wetback burden, while doing virtually nothing herself about the problem (Ibid., pp. 795–796).

the Senate's failure to deem wetback employment a crime, Mexico agreed on February 9 to a ninety-day extension.[65]

Mexican officials utilized the Senate's action as their principal rationalization for extension. Although the Mexican secretaries of foreign relations and interior were not ecstatic with S. 1851, they did consider it a step in the right direction. They noted that the wetback exodus had decreased during the first six months of the 1951 program and that termination would create a chaotic situation for braceros and employers alike. Furthermore, Congress would have sufficient time to complete action on the wetback bill during the ninety-day period.[66] With this action, the position of the participants in the game of international pressure politics was again reversed. Mexico had seized the offensive. The House of Representatives was placed in the unenviable position of having to act or face the consequences.

During Senate debate, opponents of S. 1851 had attempted to amend the measure by expanding its scope. House opponents attacked it from the opposite direction and, unlike the senators, were somewhat successful. House opposition consisted primarily of southwestern representatives, and it struck hard at three aspects of the bill. First, the opponents attacked its constitutionality, particularly its provision for administrative warrants. Second, opponents assailed the measure for its lack of universality. The measure was, to their way of thinking, aimed at only one particular section of the country and not at the entire nation. It would punish southwestern farmers severely, while scarcely affecting citizens in other parts of the country. Third, the opposition severely criticized the atmosphere of foreign coercion and threat surrounding consideration of the measure. To approve the bill, its critics reasoned, would be to legislate under Mexican duress.[67]

Representative Francis Walter of Pennsylvania, who had origi-

---

[65] As an example of Mexican displeasure with S. 1851, see *New York Times*, February 9, 1952. On the extension itself, see TIAS 2531.

[66] "U.S., Mexico to Extend Migratory Labor Agreement," *Department of State Bulletin*, March 3, 1952, p. 359; and *El Universal*, February 10, 1952.

[67] *Congressional Record*, 98:1335–1359.

nally authored S. 1851, responded to the second criticism by defending the measure as one applicable and beneficial to all United States citizens.[68] By making it a felony to transport or harbor an illegal entrant, S. 1851 would fill a void created by the Supreme Court's ruling in the Evans[69] case of 1948. In its decision the Court ruled unenforceable various punitive provisions of the 1917 immigration act, holding that Congress had never supplemented the act by enacting appropriate penalty measures. In response to the first critique, Representative Walter defended the bill's overall constitutionality. He acquiesced, however, to specific criticism of its administrative warrant provision by offering an amendment that was subsequently approved by the House. Under its terms, only a "court of competent jurisdiction" could issue warrants for the privilege of entering private lands in search of illegal entrants.[70]

The House, after it had defeated further opposition efforts to amend or delete the provision permitting search without a warrant within twenty-five miles of the border, approved S. 1851 in its amended form on February 26, and sent it to the Senate. A conference was called, since neither chamber accepted the other's version. The conference report, which accepted the Walter Amendment, was approved March 13. On March 20, 1952, S. 1851 became Public Law 283 when President Truman signed the measure.[71] In an effort to reduce the wetback tide, Washington had finally legislated against those who would willfully import, transport, or harbor illegal aliens. By its action the United States again assumed the offensive. The final move in the institutionalization of imported Mexican labor would be up to the source country.

Passage of the wetback bill did not, however, mean instant renegotiation of the 1951 bracero agreement. Preliminary talks between representatives of the two nations were held in Miami Beach

[68] Ibid., pp. 1345–1346.
[69] 33 U.S. 483, 1948.
[70] *Congressional Record*, 98:1415.
[71] For the complete text of P.L. 283, see U.S., 66 *Stat.* 26.

during mid-April. Conducted behind closed doors, the talks consisted essentially of discussions of possible means to improve operation of the program.[72] Subsequently unable to reach a mutually acceptable solution, the two countries agreed to a second three-month extension. The principal stumbling block appeared to be Mexico's insistence on guarantees for wetbacks.[73] Despite disagreements, neither country desired an end to the agreement. Facing a June 30 expiration date, delegates from the United States and Mexico finally succeeded in renegotiating the agreement of August 11, 1951. It was announced on June 12 that agreement on a new accord had been reached. The revised agreement was extended for an eighteen-month period. Its termination date was scheduled to coincide with that of P.L. 78. Both were set at December 31, 1953.

Although it contained minor amendments reflecting pressure from the principal groups involved, the agreement of June, 1952, is notable not so much for its contents but for the precedent that it established.[74] The revised accord of 1952 represented the final step toward permanency. In July, 1951, Congress codified the bracero program by enacting P.L. 78 and by placing ultimate authority for its administration in the hands of the secretary of labor. One month later Mexico and the United States concluded the migrant labor agreement of 1951. On March 20, 1952, P.L. 283, which made the harboring of wetbacks a felony, was enacted. On May 19, an eighteen-month extension of the 1951 migrant labor agreement

---

[72] *New York Times*, April 17, 1952.

[73] Ibid., May 10, 1952. On the extension itself, see TIAS 2531.

[74] Among the notable changes included in the revised agreement were the following: first, the secretary of labor was the sole party responsible for determining the prevailing wage rate. Second, both nations would determine eligibility for braceros. Third, provisions relating to employer record-keeping were tightened and spelled out in greater detail. Finally, changes were made in the location of recruitment depots and reception centers (U.S., Department of State, "Mexico, Mexican Agricultural Workers, Agreement Extending and Amending the Agreement of August 11, 1951. Effected by Exchange of Notes Signed in Mexico May 19, 1952; Entered into Force May 19, 1952," TIAS 2586, pp. 4341–4393).

was concluded. In the interim, Mexico had created the Bureau of Migratory Farm Labor Affairs within the Department of Foreign Relations and charged it with internal responsibility for the bracero program. The importation of Mexican farm labor had become a permanent fixture of United States–Mexican relations.

CHAPTER 4

Group Processes and the Era of Stabilization: The Bracero Program, 1952–1959

WITH THE PASSAGE OF THE wetback bill and the extension of the migrant-labor agreement early in 1952, the bracero program entered a seven-year period of growth and stabilization. After the program survived the hectic period of unilateral recruitment early in 1954, a system of labor importation designed originally as an emergency measure rapidly assumed a characteristic of permanency. With but a single exception, the period 1952–1959 was one of muted interest-group conflict at national and international levels. It was not, however, a period void of group activity. Domestic proponents of Mexican labor were solidifying their ranks and contemplating the benefits of a liberal import policy. Antibraceroists, those individuals and interest groups who favored either an end to or substantial modification of P.L. 78, were increasing in number, gaining in political access, and preparing for an all-out attack on imported labor at a later date.

This chapter discusses (1) the group conflict surrounding unilateral recruitment early in 1954, (2) the wetback's demise, (3) the bracero program at its zenith, and (4) the domestic interest-group milieu surrounding bracero importation during the era of stabilization.

THE 1954 GROUP STRUGGLE OVER UNILATERAL RECRUITMENT

A seven-year period of unprecedented bracero importation followed amicable negotiation of the migrant labor agreements in 1951 and 1952. From 1952 to 1959 more than 2.5 million Mexican nationals, or a yearly average of more than 335,000, were employed on United States farms.[1] During most of this period the bracero program acted as a catalyst to improved United States–Mexican relations. There was, however, one very notable exception. Faced with a recalcitrant Mexican bargaining stance as well as demands from indigenous governmental and private circles calling for a firmer position, the United States inaugurated early in 1954 an abortive unilateral recruitment system. As a result, United States–Mexican relations sank to their lowest point since the late 1930's. Only the presence of thoughtful executive leadership in both nations avoided what might have become a seriously damaging international incident.

The unilateral program of 1954 presents a unique example of simultaneous group conflict at the national and international levels. Never during the entire twenty-two–year history of the bracero program did the United States assume a more adamant and diplomatically daring position. Never was the political power and access of agricultural interest more clearly evident in the bargaining stance of United States negotiators.

Hardly had the revised agreement of June, 1952, gone into effect

---

[1] "Long-Term Trends in Foreign-Worker Employment: Table 3, Foreign Workers Admitted for Temporary Employment in U.S. Agriculture," *Farm Labor Developments*, February, 1968, p. 10; hereafter cited as "Foreign Workers Admitted for Temporary Employment."

when a more determined and skeptical Mexican attitude toward the emigration of her nationals became apparent. Late in July, Mexico threatened to withdraw several thousand braceros engaged in cotton picking because of the low wages being offered.[2] Numerous accounts from Mexico City told of a growing anti-bracero attitude. These accounts were coupled with unofficial reports that the new administration of President Ruiz Cortines would reduce the number of migrants, although continuing to honor the agreement of its predecessor.[3] Reaction from United States growers to such a possibility appeared in two forms. First, they threatened to hire Asian and West Indian laborers in the event that Mexico did restrict the flow of braceros.[4] Second, agricultural interests began vociferously to support a hard line on the part of United States negotiators. Such a stance became increasingly evident during congressional hearings on extension of P.L. 78 held in March, 1953.[5]

Not only did these hearings reveal a more adamant grower stance, but they also clearly indicated a general stiffening of United States congressional and administrative attitudes toward Mexican demands. In lead-off appearances before Senate and House agriculture committees, Under Secretary of Labor Lloyd Mashburn set the more militant tone that would carry over into 1954. He called for only a one-year extension of P.L. 78, reasoning that the Labor Department could use such an abbreviated extension as a lever in its negotiations with Mexico. Long-term renewal would only buttress the Mexican attitude of "You need the people; you are coming with your hands out. We are going to be pretty hard to get along with."[6]

[2] *New York Times*, July 23, 1952.

[3] Ibid., July 24 and 25, 1953.

[4] Ibid., January 11, November 23, 29, 1953; and *Excelsior*, January 1, 1954.

[5] U.S., Congress, Senate, Committee on Agriculture and Forestry, *Extension of the Mexican Farm Labor Program: Hearings on S. 1207*, 83d Cong., 1st sess., March 23 and 24, 1953; hereafter cited as Senate Agriculture Committee Hearings, 1953. U.S., Congress, House, Committee on Agriculture, *Extension of Mexican Farm Labor Program: Hearings on H.R. 3480*, 83d Cong., 1st sess., March 24, 25, and 26, 1953; hereafter cited as House Agriculture Committee Hearings, 1953.

[6] Senate Agriculture Committee Hearings, 1953, p. 23.

Such a declaration appeared to unearth a growing frustration among United States congressmen toward the increasing demands of the Mexican government. Senator Ellender, one of the original architects of the bracero program, observed, "If we do not get any help from the Mexican Government . . ., I would be almost willing to abandon this method."[7] Senator Bourke Hickenlooper of Iowa asked how the Mexican government would react if the United States assumed a more steadfast position and declared that we would not be "suckers" any longer. He posed the possibility of abandoning the whole program and saying to the Mexicans, "Come on boys, there is work here, come in under your own power and go back under your own power."[8]

Grower representatives echoed similar sentiments and augmented them with specific demands. They called for either long-term—and in some instances permanent—extension of P.L. 78, or a return to straight grower recruitment.[9] Second, they called on United States negotiators to press Mexico on the subject of border recruitment. Texas growers were particularly upset over the cost and inconvenience of recruiting braceros from deep in the Mexican interior when there were so many Mexicans right across the border seeking work on Texas farms.[10] Third, employers argued against the increasing red tape and administrative meddling from both governments, which were increasingly becoming a part of the bracero system. Why, they questioned, could the entire procedure not be simplified?[11]

Following conference committee consideration, P.L. 78 was ex-

[7] Ibid., p. 24.

[8] Ibid., pp. 24 and 26.

[9] The Farm Bureau and the National Grange called for a three-year extension; the National Council of Farmer Cooperatives and the National Farm Labor Users Committee opted for permanency (Senate Agriculture Committee Hearings, 1953, pp. 56, 64, 72; and House Agriculture Committee Hearings, 1953, p. 36).

[10] In his statement, Austin Anson, executive manager of the Texas Citrus and Vegetable Growers and Shippers Association, stressed this point (Senate Agriculture Committee Hearings, 1953, pp. 41–56).

[11] Particularly reflective of this sentiment was the letter from John Schmidt (House Agriculture Committee Hearings, 1953, pp. 10–14).

tended without amendment for two years and scheduled to expire December 31, 1955. During congressional debate, only Representative Eugene McCarthy of Minnesota spoke out strongly in behalf of the critics of bracero recruitment.[12] For all practical purposes, his was a lonely voice. At this stage in the bracero program's history, the central theme was not criticism of imported labor but how to make it more compatible to the wishes of employers. Compatibility in this instance would have to come from Mexican concessions at the international bargaining table. Such concessions had been few in the past. Achieving them in the future was to prove equally difficult.

Formal negotiations on the migrant-labor agreement, scheduled to expire December 31, 1953, began in September of that year. From their inception, three facts became apparent. It was obvious, first, that the new Eisenhower administration had followed through on hard-line recommendations from farm groups, legislators, and administrators. Second, the Mexicans were equally adamant in their demands relating to protection of individual braceros as well as the Mexican economy. Third, and as a result of this stand-off, the United States appeared prepared to inaugurate a diplomatically explosive, go-it-alone policy of unilateral recruitment at a most inopportune moment.

It was not long after negotiations got under way in Mexico City that a deadlock developed. The United States delegation presented its Mexican hosts with a novel bargaining approach: a list of six negotiable items it deemed crucial to any renewal of the agreement.[13] There was first the matter of the location of recruitment depots. United States negotiators wanted the center at Monterrey, which Mexico had closed, to be reopened. Mexico refused. Second, and most important to official Washington, were wages. Friction

[12] *Congressional Record*, 99:3148–3150, and 3157.

[13] Unless otherwise noted, the analysis of the United States position is based upon the testimony of Assistant Secretary of Labor Rocco Siciliano before the House Agriculture Committee (U.S., Congress, House, Committee on Agriculture, *Mexican Farm Labor: Hearings H. J. Res. 355*, 83d Cong., 2d sess., February 3, 5, 8, 9, 10, and 11, 1954, pp. 2–17; hereafter cited as House Agriculture Committee Hearings, 1954.

between the two nations over determining wages had been apparent for several months before the talks began.[14] In an appearance before the House Committee on Agriculture, Assistant Secretary of Labor Rocco Siciliano summed up the impasse in these words: "The Mexican Government wants the Department of Labor to set wages, not find a prevailing wage. They want us to set the wages in advance."[15]

Third on the list of negotiables was the question of subsistence payments. As with wages, Mexican officials had disagreed with United States administrators concerning the amount of subsistence braceros should receive. Since they had timed their demands to coincide with harvest seasons and had remained steadfast in their position, Mexican consuls had forced growers to acquiesce to Mexican demands. Employers had, in turn, complained vociferously to Department of Labor officials on the matter. Fourth was the question of nonoccupational insurance for braceros. Mexico insisted that such protection, heretofore optional, be made mandatory under the international agreement, and that she be allowed to name the United States firms responsible for these policies.

Fifth was the problem of worker responsibility. The Labor Department had received numerous complaints about "skips" from employers, who demanded that braceros be made more responsible. United States negotiators hoped to end the problem with an enlarged system of wage holdings. A final question that the United States delegates deemed essential to extension of the agreement concerned the practice of blacklisting. On several occasions Mexico had unilaterally blacklisted individual employers and counties, thus depriving them of braceros. Such action was said to directly violate the bracero agreement, which called for joint determination in cases of alleged violations. As a whole, the overriding theme of the United States position was opposition to unilateral action on the part of Mexico.

Faced with stubborn Mexican resistance, the United States soon made it evident through unofficial sources that, should Mexico re-

[14] *New York Times*, July 23, 1952.
[15] House Agriculture Committee Hearings, 1954, p. 6.

fuse to compromise, the possibility of unilateral recruitment was indeed real.[16] Washington was apparently very serious in its desire to alter the migrant-labor pact fundamentally and, in so doing, halt the growing Mexican propensity for unilateral action. The question was soon posed: If Mexico refused to negotiate on this crux issue, would the United States follow through on its threatened go-it-alone policy?

As the months of October, November, and December passed, the moribund negotiations came to represent a rare example of interest-group activity at the international level. The United States continued to demand negotiations on six fundamental issues. The Mexicans refused to negotiate. Mexico was aware of the unofficial threats of unilateral action emanating from Washington circles.[17] Still, she would not compromise.

Three factors appear to have dictated the Mexican position. Mexico must have reasoned that the United States would not, despite its threats, dare invoke a policy of unilateral recruitment, so great was the diplomatic risk. At a time when United States Latin American policy, particularly United States–Mexican relations, was deteriorating, the new administration in Washington surely would not adopt a go-it-alone attitude in such a sensitive area.[18] A second factor contributing to Mexico's intransigent stance was pride. Facing the Yankee colossus, Mexico apparently felt she could not compromise when it came to the welfare of her citizens.[19] A final factor was Mexico's keen sense of timing and its relevance to pressure politics.[20]

[16] *New York Times*, October 8, 1953.

[17] It was reported during November that the Justice Department was considering opening the border to braceros, "even at the risk of an international incident" if a new agreement were not negotiated (*New York Times*, November 8, 1953).

[18] In addition to the bracero program, other factors contributing to a deterioration of United States–Mexican relations included (1) border closing over the problem of hoof-and-mouth disease, (2) alleged violations by United States fishing boats of Mexico's territorial waters, and (3) increased tariffs on Mexican mining products (*Hispanic American Report* 6 [August 1953]:9).

[19] *Excelsior*, January 15–22, 1954.

[20] House Agriculture Committee Hearings, 1954, p. 10.

United States farmers employed some braceros during the spring and summer months, but the paramount need for Mexican nationals came during the harvest season in the fall. The bracero agreement had been temporarily extended on several previous occasions. Mexico may well have opted for a simple six-month extension late in 1953. If it could have been arranged, Mexico would have placed herself in a far stronger bargaining position. The farmers' need for field hands was all but nil in December.[21] In late June the situation would have been different. Many things might have been different if the above calculations had proved correct. They did not.

As the talks wore on through December, 1953, with no new agreement in sight, Mexico began to apply the tactic of delay. Mexican officials assured their United States counterparts that as long as negotiations continued there would be no termination of the bracero flow, even if the agreement should expire in the interim.[22] Mexican officials realized, however, that the United States was serious in its efforts to end the practice of unilateralism. It was obvious that Washington had assumed its strongest bargaining stance since the inauguration of the program. If Mexico insisted on exercising a unilateral veto in the areas of wages, working conditions, and blacklisting, there would be no new agreement. There were always the thousands of Mexicans more than willing to work on United States farms, with or without the auspices of an international accord.

Less than a week before the expiration deadline, an announcement from the Mexican Foreign Ministry buoyed hopes for a settlement. The two countries were said to have agreed "in principle" to the contents of a new bracero contract. A spokesman confirmed that talks were progressing well and that bracero contracting would continue after December 31.[23] In this atmosphere the two countries agreed to a fifteen-day extension of the agreement. The negotiators had until January 15, 1954, to resolve the crux issue of Mexican

---

[21] Mr. Siciliano made it clear that the United States was equally aware of the time element (House Agriculture Committee Hearings, 1954, p. 10).

[22] *New York Times*, December 22, 1953.

[23] Ibid., December 27, 1953.

control over braceros and their working conditions once they entered the United States.[24]

Although both sides continued negotiations, it was clear that no real progress was being made. Mexico simply refused to compromise on crucial United States demands. By the second week in January three things became apparent: (1) The United States was obviously not interested in any limited extension, during which time talks might progress while Mexico gained a more favorable bargaining position. Instead, United States delegates sought major concessions or no agreement at all. (2) Such a stance was buttressed by the resolve of the Departments of Labor, Justice, and State to pursue demands of farm groups and continue recruitment with or without Mexican approval.[25] (3) Any form of unilateral recruitment was certain to exacerbate rapidly deteriorating United States–Mexican relations.[26]

On January 15, 1954, the event occurred that Mexico felt would not happen and that students of United States–Mexican relations hoped would not happen. Talks were suspended, and, in a joint communique, the Departments of Labor, Justice, and State announced the launching of an interim program of unilateral recruitment to become effective January 18.[27] The dispatch noted that three months of earnest negotiations had failed to produce a mutually agreeable accord and reiterated United States readiness to resume talks with Mexico in search of a mutually satisfactory agreement. In the interim a unilateral system would be inaugurated that, in many respects, would be identical to its predecessor.[28] However, in two crucial respects the new system would differ radically from its forerunner: (1) it was unilateral, and (2) it

[24] Ibid., January 1, 1954; and U.S., Department of State, TIAS 2928, *United States Treaties and Other International Agreements*; hereafter cited as TIAS.

[25] *New York Times*, January 12, 1954.

[26] Editorial in *Excelsior*, January 14, 1954.

[27] *New York Times*, January 16, 1954.

[28] For an elaboration of the unilateral program as well as the rationale behind it, see House Report No. 1199, "Mexican Agricultural Workers," 83d Cong., 2d sess., February 12, 1954, pp. 1–5 (hereafter cited as House Report No. 1199).

placed complete control over braceros in the hands of United States officials.

Initial Mexican reaction to Washington's bold new policy was quick and sharp. As the press depicted the new policy in banner headlines, the Mexican secretaries of foreign affairs and interior denounced the move. They termed it a program to which Mexico would never acquiesce and announced on January 16 that braceros could no longer be legally contracted.[29] In expectation of the Mexican announcement, unofficial State Department sources quickly let it be known that unilateralism would be pursued despite Mexican protestations. Washington sources also reacted skeptically to Mexico's professed intention to halt the northward flow of her citizens. Mexico had long been urged to curtail the wetback traffic, only to reply that it was physically impossible. Why would it now become feasible?[30] Representative Ken Regan of Texas summed up this feeling of skepticism when he observed: "I am sorry that a disagreement exists between the two republics, but I doubt if the closing of the frontier is going to be very effective. The Mexicans need North American dollars and we need their labor. It is an aid to the Mexican economy and to ours."[31]

United States officials were thus prepared for a sharp Mexican reaction to the go-it-alone policy. Testimony by a top Labor Department official subsequently revealed that Washington was also cognizant of the diplomatic risks it entailed.[32] What the United States was not aware of, however, was the solidifying consequence such a policy would have on the Mexican populace. Its effect was to unite the Mexicans more firmly than had been the case in years.

All political parties, warring labor groups, the press, farmers and farm workers' organizations, government workers, and the proverbial man-in-the-street have joined in the battle. They are almost unani-

[29] *Excelsior*, January 16, 1954. It is noteworthy that, while denouncing the program, *Excelsior* listed publicly for the first time the major obstacles to agreement as well as the United States position on crucial issues.

[30] *New York Times*, January 17, 1954.

[31] *Excelsior*, January 17, 1954.

[32] When questioned by Congressman Cooley of North Carolina about the policy's impact on United States–Mexican relations, Mr. Siciliano responded:

mous in condemning a United States proposal to continue hiring braceros for work on American farms, despite the absence of a new agreement protecting them.

Conservative newspapers found themselves in mild agreement with the Communist press on this subject. No major public figure or organization has come out in defense of the American position.[33]

Actual recruitment and the chaos it created did not begin until January 22, 1954. In the meantime a thaw appeared to develop in the ever-cooling relations between Washington and Mexico City. During a January 19 press conference, Secretary of State John Foster Dulles stated that the United States regreted the discontinuance of talks and was prepared to reopen negotiations. He commented that Mexico could be assured that the United States would seek to conduct the talks on a mutually satisfying and cordial basis.[34] In his opinion, the problem was more transitory than fundamental. Mexico's first official reaction to the secretary's remarks was none too encouraging. Mexico's ambassador to Washington, Manuel Tello, observed that a resumption of talks under current circumstances was impossible. Negotiations would be resumed only when the United States abandoned its "open door" plan.[35] Unofficially, however, Mexico City's response was heartening. Editorial comment revealed a warm reaction to Secretary Dulles's use of the term "transitory" and a willingness to admit that Mexican officials had perhaps been a bit overzealous in seeking to protect their countrymen. While it would be no easy task, given the attitude of Secretary Dulles a mutually acceptable system could certainly be worked out.[36]

A second giant stride toward rapprochement was taken on January 20. In a Mexico City address before the National Confederation of Farm Workers, President Ruiz Cortines went out of his way to

---

"I agree that it may have a very grave effect . . ." (House Agriculture Committee Hearings, 1954, p. 6).

[33] *New York Times*, January 18, 1954. In a similar vein, see *Excelsior*, January 19–21, 1954.

[34] *Excelsior*, January 20, 1954.

[35] Ibid.

[36] Editorial, and Bernardo Ponce, "Perspectiva," in *Excelsior*, Ibid.

emphasize that the current bracero situation should not be blown out of proportion. It certainly did not, to the president's way of thinking, constitute an international crisis. "It is not a problem," he observed, "only an incident that should be resolved under the norms of good neighborliness."[37] Responsible Mexican press reaction was again highly supportive of the chief executive's remarks. One daily commented that, compared to the questions of true hemispheric import, the bracero problem was indeed a "mere incident."[38] Once actual unilateral recruitment began, the statements of Messrs. Ruiz and Dulles shone like beacons in a stormy sea of United States–Mexican ill will.

When it became known that beginning January 22 braceros were to be unilaterally contracted at El Centro, California, the mad rush was on. Despite threats and pleadings from Mexican officials, *campesinos* flocked into the region. Mexico's initial reaction was one of force. When seven hundred braceros ignored warnings and swarmed across the border, Mexico posted armed guards.[39] In what was to become an oft-repeated pattern during the short-lived period of unilateral contracting, United States officials, after initially refusing to process the illegal entrants, acceded to a process of instant legalization. The *campesino* would enter clandestinely, run back to the official border crossing point, put one foot on the Mexican side, and dart back to be legally processed.[40]

The mixture of armed guards and desperate, hungry men soon proved explosive. From January 23 to February 5, a series of bloody clashes and riots between Mexican guards and aspiring braceros erupted at several cities along the border.[41] In virtually each instance the pattern was the same. When the desperate Mexicans rushed the border, guards repelled them with clubs, fists, water hoses, and guns. For those who crossed illegally, the process of

[37] Ibid., January 21, 1954.

[38] Editorial in *Excelsior*, January 21, 1954.

[39] Ibid., January 23, 1954.

[40] It is obvious that not all or even a majority of these men were so recruited, but a great many were (*New York Times*, January 23, 1954).

[41] Ibid., January 24, 27, 28, 29, and February 2, 1954; and *Excelsior*, January 24, 28, 29, and February 3 and 4, 1954.

instant legalization also became precarious. As he attempted to touch Mexican soil and dart away, the bracero was often grabbed and beaten by guards from his own country. Perhaps the epitome of absurdity was depicted by a photograph showing a hapless bracero being pulled south by a Mexican border official and north by a United States officer.[42]

The bulk of actual recruitment under the ill-fated unilateral system was completed in a very brief period. Although suspended February 5, 1954, processing was only minor and sporadic after January 28. Nevertheless, thousands of Mexicans waited hopefully for the call that a given number of braceros was needed. Each time it came there would ensue a mass crush at the gates, from which only a few hundred would be processed.[43] Once Mexico abandoned its original closed-door policy, Mexican and United States border officials had more than they could handle trying to curtail illegal entrants and control the frantic mob rushes that accompanied each sporadic recruitment announcement.

On February 2, 1954, the Department of Labor was advised by the comptroller general that under the terms of P.L. 78 federal funds could no longer be spent on a unilateral program.[44] February 5 witnessed the system's official demise.[45] However, United States proponents of such a policy did not cease their struggle on this date. In fact, they had just begun to fight.

House Joint Resolution 355

One of the most vociferous spokesmen for southwestern grower interests during the 1950's was Kansas Representative Clifford Hope, chairman of the House Committee on Agriculture. Congressman Hope was aware that the United States would launch a program of unilateral recruitment and apparently sensed that such a

[42] *Hispanic American Report* 7 (February 1954):1.

[43] *New York Times*, January 27 and February 2, 1954.

[44] Letter to the secretary of labor from Lindsay C. Warren, comptroller general of the United States (House Agriculture Committee Hearings, 1954, pp. 125–127).

[45] *New York Times*, February 6, 1954.

course might eventually necessitate firm statutory support. He therefore introduced on January 20, 1954, H.J.R. 355.[46] Clearly designed to provide legal foundation for one-sided bracero recruitment, the resolution called for a minor, but very important, amendment to Article V of the Agriculture Act of 1949 (P.L. 78). Section 501 of the act would be altered by striking out the parenthetical clause "pursuant to arrangements between the United States and the Republic of Mexico" and inserting in its place "pursuant to arrangements between the United States and the Republic of Mexico *or after every practicable effort has been made by the United States to negotiate and reach agreement on such arrangements.*"[47] The comptroller general labeled the go-it-alone policy illegal on February 2, 1954. On February 3, hearings began on H.J.R. 355.

Lead-off testimony of Assistant Secretary of Labor Rocco Siciliano and the retorts of Representative Harold Cooley of North Carolina established the ground rules around which six days of testimony and subsequent congressional debate would be structured.[48] Siciliano asked that the resolution be enacted because it would substantially aid United States negotiators in their talks with the stubborn Mexicans, who had steadfastly refused to compromise on any of the six major issues.[49] If the measure were enacted, it would probably never be implemented. With the measure as a lever, the Mexicans would begin to negotiate in earnest. However, should they prove as stubborn as before, the resolution would provide statutory authority for a unilateral program.

Representative Cooley's interrogation of the secretary was pointed and focused (1) on the questionable rationale lying behind the original go-it-alone endeavor, and (2) on the past and future impact of such a venture on our Latin American policy, especially on

---

[46] *Congressional Record*, 100:561.

[47] Italics added.

[48] House Agriculture Committee Hearings, 1954, pp. 2–17.

[49] This line of reasoning was also emphasized in the strongest terms by the director of the Bureau of Employment Security, Robert Goodwin (Ibid., p. 198).

our relations with Mexico. Siciliano hedged on the initial inquiry, but in subsequent testimony Albert Misler, Department of Labor legal advisor, stated that the departments involved felt the language of P.L. 78 was "sufficiently ambiguous" for them to proceed. "We operated," he explained, "until we got an opinion from the Comptroller General telling us that it was illegal."[50]

On the possible impact of unilateralism on United States–Mexican relations, Siciliano admitted the possibility of a diplomatically adverse reaction.[51] Yet the secretary, subsequent witnesses, and congressmen supporting the unilateral program did not appear overly concerned about this aspect. In their minds, it was time to show some concern about the United States and its citizens. Mexico had long been unyielding in her position without seeming to worry about our reaction. Now it was our turn to negotiate from a position of strength. In any case, they reasoned, with this resolution as a lever, the United States could achieve a more reasonable agreement and, thus, not be forced to resort to a go-it-alone policy. With their economic situation what it was, they argued, all we had to do was show the Mexicans that we did not need their cooperation on the matter, and they would come around.[52] The key to negotiating successfully with the Mexicans was to show them you had "trumps in your hand."[53]

Such reasoning was not shared by all those offering testimony or by many members of Congress. Representative Cooley led the fight against H.J.R. 355, but he was not alone. As might have been expected, traditional anti-bracero interest groups spoke out against

---

[50] Ibid., p. 202.

[51] Ibid., p. 6.

[52] Typical of this reasoning was the remark of Representative Poage of Texas. When told by Congressman Cooley, "You will not get an agreement with a pistol in their backs," Poage replied, "They have been pretty successful in getting an agreement with a pistol in our backs" (Ibid., p. 12). Similarly, ibid., pp. 35, 36, 135, 190, 198; and *Congressional Record*, 100:2487, 2488, 2495, and 2498.

[53] Statement by Representative Poage (House Agriculture Committee Hearings, 1954, p. 10).

unilateralism on diplomatic grounds. In their minds, a multilateral bracero program was bad enough; a unilateral system was worse.[54] More significant, however, were the opinions of numerous members of Congress, many of whom were not necessarily anti-bracero-ists. For them, such a policy was diplomatically ill conceived and launched at a most inopportune moment for United States–Latin American relations.

> Throughout the years we have in the Republic of Mexico cultivated the sweet flower of friendship. Let us not now ruthlessly pull the petals from the lovely flower which should flourish throughout the years to come.[55]

> I feel that at a time when our world relationships and particularly those in Latin America seem to be deteriorating, we should not take action which will give offense to the very proud countries in Central and South America.[56]

> By this legislation we are going out of our way to affront our neighbor to the South, and when you affront any Central or South American country, you affront all nations in South America . . . I hope the Government of Mexico, and the press of Mexico, and the people of Mexico will not hold its passage and its affront to them against all Americans. To me it is one of the strangest situations to see . . . at this time with the Secretary of State in Venezuela at a meeting, at a conference of South American and North American nations calling for unity and amity . . . the House of Representatives of America considering and passing this bill. . . . The only construction that can be placed upon it by the people of Mexico is that we are putting a club over their head . . . This bill is not conducive to better relationships with our neighbor to the South, but is conducive to increasing tensions, at the disadvantage of both countries.[57]

> We have sent our Secretary of State to Caracas, to breathe good will. The President has sent his distinguished brother, Dr. Milton Eisenhower, to South America to breathe good will. Yet the Congress of the

---

[54] Note in particular the statement of CIO President Walter P. Reuther; ibid., pp. 73–79, and the statements of Walter J. Mason and Ernest Galarza of the AFL; ibid., pp. 102–117.

[55] Remarks of Representative Page Belcher of Oklahoma (*Congressional Record*, 100:2494).

[56] Remarks of Representative Robert Condon of California. Ibid., 2497.

[57] Remarks of Representative John McCormack of Massachusetts. Ibid., 2502.

United States, in utter disregard of the wishes of the Mexican Government—the Government of a free and sovereign state, and a partner in the Rio pact—completely flouts the will of the Mexican Government, and is willing to authorize the entry of Mexican contract labor, despite the desire of the Mexican Government to negotiate a fair and equitable agreement . . . [It] is a way to lose friends and make enemies.[58]

Whether the policy of unilateral recruitment was sound or ill advised was thus highly debatable and dependent upon what one sought to accomplish by it. Its opponents were correct in viewing such a scheme as risky diplomatic arm-twisting. However, its supporters proved equally astute in their assessment. Hearings on H.J.R. 355 were not yet completed when Mexico began to "come around."

While conflicting testimony was being heard before the House Committee on Agriculture, President Eisenhower announced during a February 10 press conference that following talks with Mexican Ambassador Manuel Tello, at the request of Mexico, formal negotiations on a new agreement would resume immediately.[59] The announcement came as a surprise to all but the most knowledgeable.[60] President Eisenhower revealed that he had met with the Mexican ambassador a week prior to the announcement. Asked whether Mr. Tello had mentioned the diplomatic harm being done by Washington's go-it-alone policy, the president averted the query and replied simply that the ambassador had requested a resumption of friendly talks, and that he had agreed.

While the Mexican press greeted the president's announcement with optimism,[61] United States proponents of unilateralism continued to seek legal sanction, just in case it was needed. With serious talks now again under way, the time was deemed ripe to further strengthen the hand of our negotiators. In their report to

[58] Remarks of Senator Hubert Humphrey of Minnesota. Ibid., 2558–2560.

[59] *Excelsior*, February 11, 1954.

[60] Subsequent testimony by Robert Goodwin of the Bureau of Employment Security revealed that informal contacts between the two nations over the bracero problem had occurred sporadically during the January 15–February 10 interim (House Agriculture Committee Hearings, 1954, pp. 201, 202).

[61] Bernardo Ponce, "Perspectiva," in *Excelsior*. February 11, 1954.

Congress on February 12, members of the House Committee on Agriculture summed up this line of reasoning: "It is the committee's belief, which is strongly concurred in by the Department of State, that the passage of this legislation, enabling the Department of Labor to carry on the placement program in the absence of a formal agreement if it is impracticable to reach such agreement will substantially assist and strengthen our efforts to negotiate a new agreement."[62] When, during the first week in March, 1954, both houses of Congress approved H.J.R. 355 by sizable margins and sent the resolution to the president, it became obvious that the great majority of United States congressmen agreed with the committee.[63]

The Mexican Response to Unilateralism

Mexican reaction to the entire unilateral recruitment episode was one of bitterness, humiliation, and soul-searching. No postwar United States policy has so incensed and humiliated the Mexican public as did the foray into unilateral bracero contracting in 1954. When it became apparent that the United States would launch such a program, literally thousands of Mexicans inundated border communities in search of jobs on United States farms. That their countrymen were so desperate as to trek hundreds of miles, suffer hunger, humiliation, beatings, and even death just to contract for the most menial of tasks was a shock to many Mexicans. Their reaction to this phenomenon took two forms. First, the Mexicans blamed the United States and its go-it-alone policy. Second, and perhaps of greater importance to Mexico's long-term development, the Mexicans began to seriously question the indigenous causes of such desperation.

There can be no doubt that Mexico resented bitterly the one-

[62] House Report No. 1199, p. 2. Additional examples of this line of reasoning once formal talks were resumed are contained in House Agriculture Committee Hearings, 1954, p. 198; and *Congressional Record*, 100:2487, 2488, 2495, 2499, and 2568.

[63] The margin of victory in the House was 250 to 156, with 28 representatives not voting. In the Senate the vote was 59 to 22, with 15 abstentions (*Congressional Record*, 100:2510 and 2571).

sided United States recruitment program. From the Mexican perspective, it was indeed an excellent way to make enemies and lose friends. Since the program was the progeny of a new Republican administration, many saw in it the demise of good neighborliness and a return to "big stick" diplomacy. How, questioned the Mexicans, could the United States, after diligently pursuing the Good Neighbor Policy for so long, now revert to a strong-arm policy? How, in particular, could Washington follow such a diplomatically damaging course at a time when (1) Americans were being so coolly received in Caracas? (2) they were under fire for their Guatamalan policy? and (3) they were locked in a bitter ideological struggle with communism? Such a program could not but damage the image of the United States within the world community, especially among the emerging nations. From the Mexican viewpoint, the only possible answer to such diplomatic lunacy lay in the composition and outlook of the administration and the political access of growers thereto.[64]

While the Mexican was humiliated and bitter over the unilateral recruitment program and all that it engendered, he was also pensive. The colossus of the North had long been a scapegoat for Mexican neuroses, and often rightly so. Here again the Mexican knew very well that those thousands of desperate *campesinos* would not have swarmed northward had it not been for the new program. But why was the bracero, a Mexican citizen, so desperate in the first place? Why would he willingly suffer such trials and tribulations? Why indeed, unless he were so hopelessly desperate as to have no other choice. Such was the stark reality of rural Mexican poverty that the *campesino* willingly sought work on United States farms, no matter the hardships. This was a very diffi-

---

[64] Among the many illustrations of this attitude, note the following: *New York Times*, January 24 and February 2, 1954; Gualterio Douglas, "Los braceros reviven un viejo conflicto entre México y EE. UU.," in *Excelsior*, January 25, 1954; editorial in *Excelsior*, February 10, 1954; Mario Sanroman, "Máximo daño, o máximo arreglo," "Más sobre los braceros," and "¿Concluye el nuevo trato?" in *El Universal*, January 30, 1953, February 13, 1954, March 6, 1954; and José Lázaro Salinas, *La emigración de braceros: Vision objectiva de un problema mexicano*, pp. 12–13.

cult pill for the average Mexican to swallow. Many refused to do so, choosing instead the easy refuge of anti-Americanism. Others, however, met the core problem head on and posed the fundamental questions that had seldom been broached. The following passages are highly reflective of this growing tendency among the Mexican people to face up to a bleak indigenous situation.

The problem of braceros has nothing to do with racial discrimination which, it is said, is practiced against them in the United States, nor with the so-called protection braceros have when an agreement between the Governments of Mexico and the United States is in force. The problem in its crudest reality is that the great mass of campesinos of Mexico and a great part of the national proletariat, live under subhuman conditions and that, therefore, they have turned their eyes toward a possible improvement beyond our frontiers.

The real problem is that Mexican society has neglected the great majority of the population . . . The problem of the braceros is a national social problem, it is a national economic problem; it is not, fundamentally, a problem of international relations with the United States; neither is it a problem of patriotism or chauvinism as interested people try to make it appear. If at this moment Mexico City were near the border, many of the inhabitants of the proletarian slums, of the terrible suburbs of the city, would truly immigrate en masse to the United States.

It is painful to have to confess these truths, but if they are not admitted there cannot be a remedy.

The Mexican bracero who flees his country because he is denied the conditions necessary for a human and dignified life, the bracero who doesn't know the English language, no matter how badly he may be treated in the United States or how hard he may have to work, values the receipt of a wage which not only permits him to take care of his needs but which also permits him to accumulate savings which he either takes back to his country or sends to his relatives, savings which he never could have made by caring for his miserable parcel of land.[65]

They do not leave out of pleasure, but are pushed by the need to live . . . Mexicans are leaving because of a lack of remunerating work, because of a lack of housing, because of a lack of security: this is the ter-

[65] Jose Colin, "The Braceros, National Shame," in House Agriculture Committee Hearings, 1954, pp. 118–119.

rible truth. The only way to check this painful and debilitating drain is to provide them housing and their due and just security.[66]

One must come, finally, face to face with the truth: the fact before our eyes is clear: the Mexican no longer wants to live—that is, to die—in Mexico.[67]

Perhaps of all the Mexican observers, Ignacio de la Torre best summarized the national implication of the entire phenomenon. He saw in the bracero's dilemma a microcosm of the entire nation and called for decisive government action in their behalf—"because the Mexican braceros are the *campesinos*, are the workers, are the inhabitants of Mexico."[68]

The Mexican Labor Agreement of 1954

As some Mexicans felt compelled to face the reality of the bracero question, so too did the Mexican government when it came to the conference table early in 1954. Congress passed H.J.R. 355 and sent it to the president during the first week in March. President Eisenhower did not sign the bill immediately.[69] Yet, for all practical purposes, the hammer of unilateralism was cocked. The bargaining power of each nation dictated compromise on Mexico's part. The diplomatic liability of continued unilateral recruitment dictated compromise on the part of the United States. On March 10, the two nations concluded a new bracero agreement. As any student of pressure-group politics would have predicted, it was a compromise document. However, the negotiations of 1954 did not represent the typical model of international bargaining. Originally, the United States had presented a list of six items that it deemed negotiable. The Mexicans had refused to negotiate. Therefore, any compromise was ipso facto a triumph for the United States and its agricultural interest groups.

---

[66] Editorial in *Excelsior*, January 22, 1954.

[67] Rodolfo Usigli, "Los braceros y la verdad mexicana"; ibid., February 1, 1954.

[68] "La cuestion de los braceros"; ibid., February 5, 1954.

[69] President Eisenhower finally signed the bill March 16, 1954 (*New York Times*, March 17, 1954).

The accord of March 10, 1954, extended the migrant-labor program to December 31, 1955. Its expiration date coincided with that of P.L. 78. Contained in the revised document were five important provisions as well as an article calling for the creation of a binational commission that would investigate and make recommendations on the question of legal and illegal migration.[70]

The first provision dealt with wages. It reaffirmed the ultimate authority of the secretary of labor to determine prevailing wage rates and subsistence allowances, but clearly emphasized Mexico's right to request a review. In the event of disagreement between the two parties, recruitment of braceros would continue uninterrupted while disagreements were being ironed out. The Mexicans had thus yielded on this crucial point. Unilateral action on Mexico's part was all but eliminated in the areas of wage and subsistence levels.

The United States conceded to Mexican demands on nonoccupational insurance. The right of Mexico to study and institute such an insurance program was affirmed. Choice of the United States firms was to be a joint endeavor. The bracero would now have the benefit of nonoccupational as well as occupational insurance.

A third revised provision dealt with the question of blacklisting. It was emphasized that places of unacceptable employment would be determined jointly. There was to be no further blacklisting of entire counties. Thus, unilateral Mexican action in another crucial area was ended.

Provisions on the transportation of braceros who did not fulfill their entire contract period were also altered. They too reflected the demands of United States growers. Employers would not be required to pay the entire transportation and subsistence cost for skips. In such cases the employer would pay only in proportion to the services rendered by the bracero. In addition, he would be permitted to withhold three, instead of the previous two, days' wages in order to discourage premature contract termination.

A final revision dealt with the location of Mexican recruitment

[70] TIAS 2932, pp. 379–415.

depots. It too involved a Mexican concession. In addition to the stations at Durango, Irapuato, and Guadalajara, a new depot was opened at Mexicali, while those at Monterrey and Chihuahua were reactivated. Many prospective braceros living near the border would no longer have to travel great distances for contracting. Many growers would be paying reduced transportation and subsistence fees.

Summary

No event during the entire twenty-two–year history of the bracero program more clearly reflected the interplay of international and domestic pressures than did the unilateral recruitment episode of 1953–1954. Three noteworthy conclusions for the student of interest groups may be deduced from this low-level venture into brinkmanship. The first pertains to Mexico.

If the policy of unilateral recruitment accomplished little else, it forced Mexico to do some painful soul-searching. Whereas unilateralism brought to Mexico a short-term national solidarity based on anti-Americanism, it also produced a more salutary long-range effect. With the conclusion of a new agreement in 1954, the threat of unilateral recruitment receded and with it the heightened anti-Americanism. Yet the movement crystallized by the policy of a foreign nation continued to grow. Rural poverty in Mexico was not eliminated as an indirect result of United States policy early in 1954. Nevertheless, the problem was faced squarely by a large number of persons for the first time. Mexicans came to admit a painful fact: as a nation Mexico could progress only if the *campesino* progressed. Thus, it may be concluded that pressure emanating from the international environment may bring about changes in domestic policies that otherwise might not have taken place.

A second lesson for the student of pressure politics emanating from the events of 1954 relates to the factor of timing. Although it had played an important role previously, the element of timing and its impact on international pressure politics was highlighted during the period of unilateralism. On previous occasions Mexico had adroitly employed this principle to secure the bulk of her demands.

In 1954 the United States made excellent use of the time factor by refusing to provisionally extend the agreement, recruiting without Mexican sanction, and subsequently passing a measure clearly designed to legalize unilateral contracting. The conditions of Mexico's rural sector rendered the bracero program essential to that nation. The United States clearly sensed this and combined bold policy and legislation with a keen sense of timing to achieve a more favorable agreement. From this experience it may be concluded that many of the norms of domestic group politics—and in particular the timing of one's demands to coincide with the opponent's most vulnerable period—may prove equally applicable at the international level.

A third conclusion to be drawn from the events surrounding unilateralism involves the impact of domestic group pressures on the conduct of United States foreign policy. The access of domestic farm interests to key governmental officials charged with negotiating and administering the bracero program was clearly evidenced during late 1953 and early 1954. It would be a mistake, however, to see the unilateral policy as purely and simply the result of grower pressure. Employer demands were but one of several contributing factors. The previous militancy of Mexican officials and their propensity toward unilateral action in the areas of wages and blacklisting must be considered, as well as the abject poverty of the Mexican countryside. The extent of such poverty was clearly illustrated by the fact that in 1953 there were 201,380 legally contracted Mexicans[71] compared to 875,318 known wetbacks.[72] The more militant posture of the Eisenhower administration in the area of foreign policy was also reflected in the 1954 bracero policy. Unilateralism was not just a policy sanctioned by the secretary of state alone. The entire administration appears to have supported H.J.R. 355.[73]

[71] "Foreign Workers Admitted for Temporary Employment."

[72] U.S., Department of Justice, Immigration and Naturalization Service, "Mexican Agricultural Laborers Admitted and Mexican Aliens Located in Illegal Status, Years Ended June 30, 1949–1967"; hereafter cited as "Illegal Mexican Entrants."

[73] One may note, as an example, the words of House Majority Leader Charles

Agricultural groups were able to realize several of their demands, because they had substantial political access and timed their demands in a forceful manner, coinciding with the temper of the times. Thus, the ability of interest groups to influence United States foreign policy, whether favorably or detrimentally, is dependent not only upon political access but also upon the overall milieu of a particular policy at a given time. It should also be recalled that actual unilateral recruitment lasted less than two weeks. H.J.R. 355 became Public Law 309. But it was never used.

DEMISE OF THE WETBACK

In 1951, those in favor of supporting legalized bracero importation argued that it would curtail the flow of illegal entrants. In fact, supporters of H.J.R. 355 stressed the element of wetback deterrence in their drive to pass the measure. They assumed that negotiations might fail to produce agreement and contended that Mexicans were going to cross the border, with or without government consent, and that without such legislation there would be no way to curtail the flow or to protect the Mexican national once he entered the United States.[74] Critics of such reasoning retorted then, as they did on numerous occasions throughout the 1950's and 1960's, that neither P.L. 78 nor any of its derivatives would stop the stream of illegal aliens.[75] What was needed was penalty legislation against employers and increased vigilance by immigration officials. Whereas the former was never achieved, the latter became a reality in the mid-1950's.

The wetback movement, which had long existed in the Southwest, rose to alarming proportions during the early 1950's. In 1950, there were 67,500 braceros and 458,215 Mexican aliens located in

---

Halleck in support of H.J.R. 355: "So far as the administration is concerned . . . it should be understood here without any question that this legislation should proceed to enactment" (*Congressional Record*, 100:2495).

[74] House Agriculture Committee Hearings, 1954, pp. 9, 11, 35, and 36; *Congressional Record*, 100:2487, 2495, 2496, 2555, and 2569.

[75] House Agriculture Committee Hearings, 1954, pp. 57, 60, 179, and 182; *Congressional Record*, 100:2508 and 2562.

illegal status. In 1952, the comparative figures were 197,000 braceros and 543,538 wetbacks. In 1953, the figures were 201,380 and 875,318. By 1954, the figures had become fantastic: 309,033 braceros and 1,075,168 *known* wetbacks.[76]

Such a torrent of illegal entrants did present an awkward situation to virtually all concerned. It was especially embarrassing and humiliating to Mexico. The obvious fact that so many of her citizens had reached such a state of desperation as to opt for status as a lowly wetback—an individual stripped of all guarantees provided legally contracted braceros and subjected to exaggerated exploitation on both sides of the border—was a sad commentary of life in rural Mexico.[77]

The United States was also upset over the ever-rising wetback tide. In the first place, it represented an open violation of United States immigration standards. Second, it acted as a thorn in the side of United States–Mexican relations. Mexico claimed that the only solution to the problem was to punish wetback employers.[78] The United States countered by accusing Mexico of laxity in enforcing provisions designed to deal with those entering clandestinely.[79] Third, the wetback phenomenon became a somewhat embarrassing cause célèbre in the early 1950's. Journalists and congressmen bemoaned the many ills associated with wetbackism. Suffering, exploitation, filth, disease, crime, narcotics, soaring welfare costs, and subversive infiltration were all said to be by-products of the mass illegal migration.[80] There thus emerged a growing demand

[76] "Foreign Workers Admitted for Temporary Employment" and "Illegal Mexican Entrants."

[77] In his lament of the situation, the Mexican generally placed braceros and wetbacks in the same category. See notes 65–68 in this chapter.

[78] Notes 56 and 57 in Chapter 3.

[79] *Congressional Record*, 100:2570.

[80] Of the numerous journalistic treatments, note the following: "Wetbacks Swarm In," *Life*, May 21, 1951, pp. 30–37; "Wetbacks in Middle of Border War," *Business Week*, October 24, 1953, p. 66; "The Wetbacks," *Time*, April 9, 1951, p. 24; and the series by Gladwyn Hill, *New York Times*, March 25–29, 1952. Congressional critiques of the wetback phenomenon and the ills it engendered were numerous in the early 1950's. Typical examples are contained in *Congressional Record*, 100:2558–2562.

for action to end the disgraceful conditions that the wetback flood engendered. Belatedly, but effectively, the call for action was answered in 1954.

Operation Wetback

As the tide of illegal entrants rose alarmingly in the early 1950's, pressure for positive governmental action became intense. As a result, it soon became a question not of whether the mass migration would be curtailed, but how. The problem was admittedly a difficult and sensitive one. Its solution involved careful handling of an especially touchy diplomatic issue. Opposition from politically powerful southwestern growers, who had long been accustomed to utilizing wetback labor, also had to be overcome.

During August, 1953, Attorney General Herbert Brownell toured the border area of California for a firsthand look at the wetback problem. Following his expedition, which included lengthy talks with those closest to the situation, Mr. Brownell termed the entire situation "shocking," a "social, economic, political, and moral problem of the first magnitude."[81] Shortly thereafter he met with President Eisenhower to lay plans for an attack on the problem. A three-way approach to the situation was devised requiring concerted action at the state, national, and international level.[82]

Reaction of some growers to the proposed assault was similar to that of previous occasions when the government had attempted to move against the wetback problem. Certain growers had long utilized wetbacks because they were cheap labor and far more easily acquired than their legal counterparts under the bracero program. For this type of farmer the wetback had always been, and would always be, a "minor" problem.[83] As subsequent events illustrated, such opinions were not shared by the great majority of bracero employers.

---

[81] *New York Times*, August 16, 1953. A thorough discussion of Mr. Brownell's tour and the problems and opinions he encountered are contained in Willard F. Kelly, "The Wetback Issue," *I and N Reporter* 2(January 1954):37–39.

[82] *New York Times*, August 18, 1953.

[83] Ibid., September 26, 1953.

For a time it appeared that nothing more than a verbal attack would be launched. During the hectic months of controversy surrounding unilateral recruitment, the newly concocted anti-wetback plan seemed to have gone into a state of limbo. However, once the amended agreement of 1954 was concluded, it became apparent that an all-out assault would be launched.

In April, 1954, General Joseph Swing was appointed commissioner of immigration and naturalization. At the time of Attorney General Brownell's tour of California, General Swing was commander of the Sixth Army in California. The general, a one-time classmate of President Eisenhower at West Point, apparently impressed Mr. Brownell with his ideas on the wetback problem. He discouraged the attorney general from sending United States troops to the border in an effort to halt the influx. The matter, he contended, could be handled with available men and resources if proper planning and coordination were involved. Mr. Brownell took the general at his word. Soon after his retirement from active duty in February, 1954, General Swing was appointed to the commissioner's post and given full authority over "Operation Wetback."[84]

The all-out, fully coordinated drive began in California on June 17, 1954. With an enlarged border patrol, the California Highway Patrol, employees of the Department of Employment, city police, county sheriffs, and Mexican authorities, a sweeping operation was launched that netted 57,000 wetbacks during June and July. As a result of press and radio cooperation, thousands of illegals returned to Mexico on their own accord.[85] Employers were also informed of the nature of the operation and urged to rid themselves of wetbacks. The extent of cooperation from employers and their organizations was gratifying. "Employers using legally contracted Mexicans welcomed 'Operation Wetback.' It relieved them of the unfairness they had felt in adhering to the wage, housing and other regula-

[84] Ibid., July 7, 1956.

[85] Edward F. Hayes et al., " 'Operation Wetback'—Impact on the Border States," *Employment Security Review* 22 (March 1955):16–17.

tions governing the legal use of Mexicans, while neighbors using wetbacks were not subject to such regulations."[86]

A similar pattern of coordinated action at state, national, and international levels was repeated, with equal success, throughout the Southwest. Nonwestern cities too felt repercussions from the drive. More than 20,000 wetbacks were removed from industrial jobs in St. Louis, Spokane, Chicago, and Kansas City.[87] In the interim, Congress also sensed the operation's success and passed a supplementary appropriations act providing additional funds for the Immigration and Naturalization Service.[88]

Based upon coordinated action of many elements at various levels, Operation Wetback was an overwhelming success. The greater part of what it accomplished was due to cooperation from grower interests. Such complicity did not come by accident. From the operation's inception, General Swing took pains to cultivate grower cooperation. Farmers were promised assistance in securing domestics and legally contracted braceros to replace wetbacks. In return, most of them cooperated.[89]

So successful was the 1954 wetback operation that the number of illegal Mexican entrants dropped drastically in subsequent years. From more than one million in 1954, the number of Mexicans located in illegal status plummeted to less than 250,000 in 1955. By 1956, less than 73,000 wetbacks were apprehended. And by 1960, the number had dropped to less than 30,000.[90] When, on April 14, 1955, the United States and Mexico concluded an agreement relating to illegal entrants, the wetback had, for all practical purposes, ceased to exist.[91]

[86] Ibid., p. 17; and *New York Times*, June 27, 1954.

[87] U.S., Department of Justice, *Annual Report of the Immigration and Naturalization Service, 1955*, pp. 9–12.

[88] *New York Times*, June 23, 1954.

[89] Hayes et al., "Operation Wetback," pp. 17 and 21; and J. M. Swing, "A Workable Labor Program," *I and N Reporter* 4(November 1955):15–16.

[90] "Illegal Mexican Entrants."

[91] TIAS 3242. The reader is alerted to the fact that the wetback has once again become a major concern of United States and Mexican officials.

THE BRACERO PROGRAM AT ITS ZENITH: A MICROCOSM

With the wetback's demise, there ensued an era of unprecedented bracero contracting. Approximately 2.5 million Mexicans were imported during the period 1954–1959, with an all-time high of 445,197 being contracted in 1956.[92] According to conservative Mexican figures, braceros remitted more than $200 million during these six years.[93] What was the bracero program like during its apogee years? In which states did the Mexican national work? What kind of individual was he? These and other questions may best be answered by examining the program during a given year, in this instance 1959.

In 1959, 437,535 braceros were legally contracted[94] at a cost of more than $2 million to United States taxpayers.[95] A total of twenty-four states utilized these Mexican nationals. Yet, taken alone, this figure is deceptive. The states of Texas, California, Arizona, New Mexico, and Arkansas employed 94 percent of all braceros. The remainder was scattered among the other nineteen user-states. Furthermore, Texas and California alone accounted for 79 percent of the total, with the former utilizing 45 percent of all

[92] "Foreign Workers Admitted for Temporary Employment."

[93] *Revista de Estadística* 19:422, 21:112, 22:108, 23:168.

[94] "Foreign Workers Admitted for Temporary Employment." This figure does not include those braceros who were recontracted. There were 45,573 recontracts in 1959. These data, compiled by the Bureau of Employment Security of the Department of Labor, were presented to the House Committee on Agriculture by Assistant Secretary of Labor Newell Brown (U.S., Congress, House, Committee on Agriculture, *Extension of Mexican Farm Labor Program: Hearings before Subcommittee on H.R. 9869* and others, 86th Cong., 2d sess., March 22, 23, 24, 25, and 31, 1960, p. 380; hereafter cited as House Agriculture Committee Hearings, 1960).

[95] The figures were for the fiscal year 1959. Mexican labor program costs totaled $6,032,000 in that fiscal year, but $3,841,000 was paid by bracero employers from a revolving fund (Official Labor Department figures; U.S., Congress, House, Committee on the Judiciary, *Study of Population and Immigration Problems, Administrative Presentations [III], Admission of Aliens into the United States for Temporary Employment, and "Commuter Workers": Hearing before Subcommittee*, 88th Cong., 1st sess., June 24, 1963, p. 48; hereafter cited as House Judiciary Committee Hearings, 1963).

braceros contracted.[96] During 1959, Mexicans performed 1,630,950 man-months of labor; those working on Texas and California farms contributed 1,294,414 man-months of the total.[97] ("Man-month" describes the unit of work performed by one man in one month, and is used especially as a basis for wages and cost finding.) Although utilized during each month of the year, the greatest number of braceros was employed during the fall months of August, September, October, and November.[98]

Although they constituted by far the largest bloc of foreign workers used in 1959,[99] Mexicans were employed by fewer than 2 percent of all United States farms. Fifty-two percent of United States farms used no hired labor in 1959, while 46 percent used native workers only.[100] As one might expect, approximately 71 percent of all farms utilizing braceros were in the states of Texas and California. In these two states, and in Arizona and New Mexico, approximately 11 percent of the farmers used Mexicans.[101] Employed on a total of only 48,788 farms during 1959, braceros were contracted by 305 associations (composed of 38,715 members), 86 food processors, and 5,131 individuals.[102]

Since less than 2 percent of all United States farms hired braceros and since the great majority of their number worked in only two states, one might well question why such a labor system was so controversial, and why the bracero was deemed so essential by farm interests. The answer lies in where, how, and in what crops the Mexicans were used.

Particular crops and areas in the five principal user-states came to be heavily dependent upon Mexican labor. Lettuce provided the

96 Ibid., p. 44.
97 House Judiciary Committee Hearings, 1963, p. 44.
98 Ibid., p. 45.
99 Of the 455,420 foreign workers in 1959, 437,643 were Mexicans, 8,772 were West Indians, 8,600 were Canadians, and 405 were Japanese or Filipinos ("Foreign Workers Admitted for Temporary Employment").
100 U.S., Department of Labor, Bureau of Employment Security, *Hired Farm Workers in the United States*, p. 40.
101 Ibid.
102 House Judiciary Committee Hearings, 1963, p. 47.

best example. In an appearance before the House Agriculture Committee, Assistant Secretary of Labor Newell Brown testified that during the peak harvest season braceros constituted 80 percent of the workers in lettuce. Bracero-usage "virtually dominates the labor market in some crops and areas . . . In one state, in 1959, they represented more than 75 percent of the total seasonal work force." In 1959, according to the secretary, braceros in 279 major farm areas constituted approximately 20 percent of all seasonal farm labor during the peak harvest season. Furthermore, they performed more than the usual arduous stoop labor for which they were noted. Mr. Brown disclosed that some eighteen thousand Mexicans were contracted during 1959 on a year-round basis, many of them being utilized in tasks demanding specialized skills and knowledge.[103]

It would appear, therefore, that the bracero, though constituting a minute proportion of the entire United States farm labor force and utilized on less than 2 percent of the farms, had by 1959 become an essential, if not indispensable, part of the work force in particular areas and crops. His numbers may not have been large on a comparative basis, but the Mexican's skills and dependability were such as to render him most valuable to southwestern employers.

The Bracero Cycle

One means of examining any given program is to view it from an individual perspective. A case study of the process through which the average bracero passed is highly reflective of the functioning of the program as a whole. Six stages were involved in the bracero cycle of the late 1950's.

Stage One: Quota Allotments. After receiving long-range estimates from the United States Department of Labor as to how many braceros would be needed during a particular season or month, the Mexican Bureau of Migratory Farm Labor Affairs assigned quotas to the governors of certain states. The governor then allocat-

---

[103] House Agriculture Committee Hearings, 1960, p. 366.

ed the state's quota among the various municipalities.[104] The criterion generally used as a basis for quota allotments to states and municipalities was that of economic conditions, with areas of chronic unemployment being assigned larger quotas. However, in his case study of Chihuahua, Richard Hancock found that quota allotments to various municipalities were often arbitrarily determined and not necessarily based on local economic conditions. Tradition was also an important criterion, with given areas receiving the same quota year after year.[105]

Stage Two: Securing Certification. Juan Garcia lived with his family in the state of Guanajuato.[106] Work had been scarce and, when available, provided earnings of only three or four pesos (24–39¢) a day.[107] So Juan, like many of the young men in his area, decided to become a bracero.[108] His first important task was to journey to the nearest municipality and secure a permit (*certificado de aspirante a bracero*) from the mayor. The permit indicated that Juan was eligible to become a bracero applicant. It stated generally that the applicant was a resident of the area, a landless unemployed farmer, an industrious person, and a man of high moral character.[109]

[104] Ernesto Galarza, *Merchants of Labor: The Mexican Bracero Story; An Account of the Managed Migration of Mexican Farmworkers in California 1942–1960,* p. 81.

[105] Richard Hancock, *The Role of the Bracero in the Economic and Cultural Dynamics of Mexico,* pp. 71–72.

[106] Mexican data indicate that in the period 1951–1962 Guanajuato supplied more braceros than any other state. All told, six states provided approximately 65 percent of all braceros during these eleven years: Guanajuato, 13.69%; Jalisco, 11.21%; Chihuahua, 10.74%; Michoacan, 10.61%; Durango, 9.42%; and Zacatecas, 9.35% (Vargas y Campos, "El Problema del bracero," pp. 32–34).

[107] These earnings figures appear in *Farm Labor Fact Book,* p. 168; and Ernesto Galarza, *Strangers in Our Fields,* p. 2.

[108] The great majority of all braceros ranged between 18 and 25 years of age (Gloria Vargas y Campos, "El Problema del bracero mexicano," p. 31).

[109] Galarza, *Merchants of Labor,* p. 81; and Hancock, *The Role of the Bracero,* p. 64. In some of the small municipalities, a game of chance often determined who, among the eligible aspirants, received the *certificado* (S. W. Coombs, "Bracero's Journey," *Americas* 15[December 1963]:8–9).

At this stage, and elsewhere during the contracting process, Juan was likely to pay the *mordida*, a bribe assuring him the permit. The practice of *mordida* pervaded the entire bracero program in Mexico.[110] Apparently, every aspirant realized and accepted that he would have to pay the bribe. Many, unfortunately, were swindled by unscrupulous "coyotes," who posed as officials and assured the aspirant of quick, sure contracting. Still the *campesino* paid the *mordida* because it was the thing to do and seemed, somehow, to provide him with a freedom from anxiety. "There exists a fixation in the psyche of the individual, a true obsession, in the sense that his enrollment will not be accomplished successfully if a bribe is not paid to the contracting officials by an intermediary."[111]

Stage Three: Contracting. Having secured his permit, Juan Garcia journeyed, at his own expense, to the nearest recruiting center. After considerable delay, and in all likelihood another *mordida*, he was admitted to the contracting center. Once inside, he was interrogated by Mexican officials, who again checked to see if Juan was a verified *aspirante* and a registered voter, and had fulfilled his military obligations.[112] He was interviewed by a United States Department of Labor official to determine if he was truly a farmworker. Juan was then interrogated by a United States immigration official, who, after a series of questions, decided that he posed no security risk. He next received a thorough physical examination by Mexican doctors employed by the United States Public Health Service.[113]

Past this hurdle, Juan had, for all practical purposes, completed his processing. He thus became somewhat of a unique individual. Out of thousands of hopefuls he had gained admittance to the recruitment center. Once there, he became one of the 93 percent

110 So widespread and lucrative was the *mordida* trade that it was said in 1957 to involve more than $7.2 million (*Hispanic American Report* 10[November 1957]:520).

111 Lázaro Salinas, *La emigración de braceros*, p. 101.

112 Hancock contends that membership in any party other than the PRI apparently jeopardized one's chances of becoming a bracero (*The Role of the Bracero*, p. 66).

113 *Farm Labor Fact Book*, p. 170.

that, on an average, successfully completed processing.[114] Sometime prior to Juan's arrival at the recruitment depot, a California farmer had gone to the regional farm-placement office and certified that domestic farm labor was unavailable in the area. Once this shortage was verified, a representative of an association to which the farmer belonged journeyed to the border reception center that was to be Juan's next stop.

Juan Garcia was transported, at the expense of his future employer, to a United States reception center near the border. There he was again given medical and immigration clearance. Juan was then chosen by the grower association representative and in a short time signed his contract. Theoretically, he could have chosen his employer, but this seldom occured in practice. As an average bracero, our subject was contracted by an association that was responsible for the fulfillment of his contract guarantees.[115]

Stage Four: Employment. Once Juan Garcia signed the contract, he was legally employed. He was quickly transported inland by bus to an association labor camp. During the next six weeks Juan and his countrymen worked for various California farmers who were members of the contracting organization.[116] They were fortunate in having come to California where living facilities and wages were the best of all bracero-using states.[117]

During his stay, our subject worked exclusively in tomato harvesting. The work was difficult and the hours were long, which mattered little to Juan, who accepted it stoically and focused his

[114] Of the seven rejectees, four were turned down for medical reasons, two because they were not agricultural workers, and one for security reasons (Ibid.).

[115] Ibid., p. 171; and Hancock, *The Role of the Bracero*, p. 66.

[116] The duration of the average bracero contract for California farms was six weeks (Report of the Senate Committee on Labor and Welfare, *California Farm Labor Problems*, p. 88). As of 1958, the average duration of the employment contract for all braceros was 3⅓ months (Letter of June 27, 1958, from Assistant Secretary of Labor Newell Brown to Representative E. C. Gathings. U.S., Congress, House, Committee on Agriculture, *Farm Labor and Mexican Labor: Hearings before Subcommittee on H.R. 7028 and others*, 85th Cong., 2d sess., February 28, March 1 and 3, June 9–12, and July 2, 1958, p. 452; hereafter cited as House Agriculture Committee Hearings, 1958).

[117] House Judiciary Committee Hearings, 1963, p. 48.

thoughts on the wages he was earning. During his contract period Juan averaged thirty-five dollars a week. Out of this amount he paid eleven dollars for meals.[118] All told, he managed to save more than one hundred dollars in addition to purchasing some clothing and small gifts for his family. Juan was well treated during his stay. Like the great majority of his fellow braceros, he had no complaints to register with the Mexican consul who, along with a foreign-labor service representative, inspected the camp and questioned the braceros about their work, food, and general treatment.[119] Juan Garcia would have welcomed a chance to contract again at a later date, but at the end of six weeks he was homesick for Mexico and his family.

Stage Five: Return Home. Upon completion of his contract period, Juan and his *compadres* were returned at employer expense to the United States reception center through which they were originally processed. He was subsequently transported, again at employer expense, to his original contracting station in Mexico. After he had successfully finished his tour, Juan was given a laminated identification card. The card classified him as a dependable worker and proved to be invaluable when he again became a bracero.[120]

Stage Six: Reflection. Once he returned home, Juan Garcia had time to reflect on his adventure. Compared to his friends and relatives who had not been braceros, he felt much more worldly. Unlike some of his fellows, Juan did not squander his earnings foolishly. Instead, he used them to improve his lot and that of his family. Other than that, Juan had some definite thoughts on his stay in the United States.[121]

[118] *Farm Labor Fact Book*, p. 48. For additional figures on bracero earnings, see *Congressional Record*, 107:18805.

[119] An excellent analysis of the role of foreign-labor service representatives in the bracero program is contained in Gordon B. Friese, "A Day in the Life of a Foreign Labor Service Representative," *Employment Security Review* 24 (March 1957):3–6.

[120] Hancock, *The Role of the Bracero*, p. 66.

[121] The reflections of Juan Garcia are based upon interviews conducted during the late 1950's by Henry P. Anderson of Claremont, California. The interviews reflect rather accurately the opinions of the average bracero during these years (House Agriculture Committee Hearings, 1958, pp. 412–420).

Like most braceros, Juan definitely planned to contract again in the future. He would, in fact, like to return as a visaed immigrant. However, based on his short experience, Juan did not think he would like to become a United States citizen. Of the many things he recalled about his tour as a bracero, Juan's primary recollections concerned money, the great cities, and the freeways. Yes, he had been treated very well despite the hard work. Juan admitted that he really did not understand all the rights and protections granted under his contract. Still, it seemed his employers had been honest and fair in their dealings with him. His only real regret concerned the results of his isolation while a bracero. Juan never got a chance to really know the people of California. He never got a chance to dine or socialize with a United States family. In short, Juan felt that the only thing he knew about life in the United States was what he had seen from the fields and heard in the barracks. Still, all things considered, he would return again as soon as possible.

THE GROUP MILIEU OF BRACERO IMPORTATION DURING THE ERA OF STABILIZATION

After it survived the international crisis over unilateral recruitment early in 1954, the bracero program became an all-but-permanent feature of southwestern agriculture and United States–Mexican relations. On three different occasions during the period 1953–1959, P.L. 78 was extended with little difficulty.[122] The Mexican migrant labor agreement was likewise renewed on four occasions.[123] The issues debated and the domestic interest groups involved changed little during these years. Gone, however, was the intervening variable of international conflict that had proved to be crucial in the early 1940's and 1950's. Drastically reduced was the role of Mexico as a pressure group in the administration of the bracero program.

[122] Act of August 8, 1953, U.S., 67 *Stat.* 500; act of August 9, 1955, U.S., 69 *Stat.* 615; and act of August 27, 1958, U.S., 72 *Stat.* 934.

[123] Agreement of March 10, 1954, TIAS 2932; agreement of December 23, 1955, TIAS 3454; agreement of December 20, 1956, TIAS 3714; and agreement of August 31, 1959, TIAS 4310.

Following the 1954 crisis over unilateral recruitment and the subsequent enactment of legislation authorizing unilateral contracting, Mexico became a quiet partner within the bracero program's group milieu. Unilateral action by Mexican officials virtually ceased. Mexican demands were less vociferous and channeled more discretely through the United States Department of Labor. It appears that the events of 1954 brought home most vividly to the Mexicans the reality of international pressure politics. Obviously in need of bracero remittances as a crucial source of foreign exchange (they ranked no lower than third behind tourism and cotton) and fully cognizant of the program's value as an outlet for sociopolitical frustrations, Mexico decided not to risk the loss of a good thing through unreasonable demands and capricious actions.[124]

Domestic Interest Groups and the Institutionalization of Imported Mexican Labor

Interest-group conflict over bracero labor assumed a decidedly indigenous character during the mid and late 1950's. P.L. 78 was extended in 1953, 1955, and 1958. Only in 1955 were opponents of importation able to amend the law, and even then the changes were relatively minor.[125] The 1950's were years of entrenchment and solidification within the ranks of those supporting bracero importation. For them, extending the program was no obstacle. The question was merely the length of each renewal. For anti-braceroists, the period 1953–1959 must have resembled the Dark Ages. It was only toward the end of the era of stabilization that opponents of bracero importation increased in number and gained a sympathetic hearing from Congress and the public. As the 1950's drew to a close they secured as a sympathizer the one man most respon-

---

[124] Vargas y Campos, "El problema del bracero," pp. 42–43.

[125] Two amendments were added in 1955. One was a concession to employers in the area of transportation costs for "skips." The second required the secretary of labor to consult with employers *and* workers in determining the questions of availability of domestics and adverse effect. Furthermore, such information had to be posted in public places (Act of August 9, 1955, U.S., 69 *Stat.* 615).

sible for administrating the bracero program: the secretary of labor.

Forces Supporting Extension of P.L. 78. If one draws on the records of hearings and congressional debates involving P.L. 78 from 1953 to 1958, one can construct a picture of the group struggle surrounding importation of foreign labor during its apogee years.[126] The forces supporting extension were notable ones within the Eisenhower administration: the Departments of Labor, Agriculture, Justice, and State. Also advocating prolongation of P.L. 78 were the powerful voices of the American Farm Bureau Federation and the National Grange. In favor of extension for various periods of from two years to permanency were the following national and regional organizations, several of which merit annotation:

National Canners Association: nonprofit trade organization representing some 750 canners of food for human consumption and producing 75 percent of the annual volume of these commodities

National Cotton Council of America: delegate body representing the six segments of the raw cotton industry: farmers, ginners, warehousemen, merchants, seed crushers, and spinners

National Council of Farmer Cooperatives: an organization of more than 1,100 members representing bracero users in twenty-three states

Western Growers Association: nonprofit association composed of vegetable and melon growers in California and Arizona, whose members grew and shipped approximately 85 percent of the vegetables and melons grown in these two states. Forty percent

---

[126] Sources for the construction of the group milieu surrounding P.L. 78 (1953–1959) include Senate Agriculture Committee Hearings, 1953; House Agriculture Committee Hearings, 1953; House Agriculture Committee Hearings, 1954; U.S., Congress, House, Committee on Agriculture, *Mexican Farm Labor Program: Hearings before Subcommittee on H.R. 3822*, 84th Cong., 1st sess., March 16–22, 1955; House Agriculture Committee Hearings, 1958; and *Congressional Record*, 99:3144–3158; 100:2486–2510, 2555–2571; 101:10007–10024; 104:17652–17662.

of all vegetables and melons consumed in the United States were
grown in Arizona and California
United States Beet Sugar Association
National Mexican Users Committee
United Fresh Fruit and Vegetable Association
Vegetable Growers Association of America
Holly Sugar Company
Amalgamated Sugar Company
Great Western Sugar Company
National Cotton Compress and Cotton Warehouse Association
Farmers and Manufacturers Beet Sugar Association
Northwest Farm Labor Association

State and local interest groups supporting extension of the bracero program in the 1950's were also numerous:

Texas
El Paso Cotton Association
Texas Citrus and Vegetable Growers and Shippers
Texas Sheep and Goat Raisers' Association
Trans-Pecos Cotton Association
Farmers, Ranchers, and Laborers Association of Fort Stockton
Plains Cotton Growers, Inc.
Olton Co-op Producers Association
Lower Rio Grande Ginners Association
California
Cochella Valley Farmers Association
Imperial Valley Lettuce Growers Association
California Sugar Beet Growers Association
Imperial Valley Farmers Association
Imperial Farmers Association
San Joaquin Farm Production Association
California State Board of Agriculture
Grower Shipper Vegetable Association of Central California
Merit Packing Company of Salinas
San Antonio Employment Association
Corona Growers, Inc.

Lompoc Valley Agriculture Council
Yolo Growers, Inc.
Northern California Growers Association
Progressive Growers Association of San Jose
Riverside Agricultural Association
San Diego County Farmers, Inc.
Seaboard Lemon Association
Somis Lemon Association
Southern California Farmers Association
Vallies Farm Labor Association, Inc.
Los Angeles Chamber of Commerce

Arkansas

Agricultural Council of Arkansas
Crittenden Farmers Association
Lee County Farmers Association, Inc.
Monette Growers Association
Shady Lane Cotton Growers Association of Blytheville

Arizona

Phoenix Chamber of Commerce
Vegetable Growers of Arizona
Arizona Cotton Growers Association

New Mexico

Dona Ana County Farm and Livestock Bureau
New Mexico Farm and Livestock Bureau
New Mexico Independent Mexican Contracting Association

Michigan

Heinz Growers Employment Committee, Inc., of Holland

Indiana

Indiana Canners Association

In addition to a variety of interest groups and associations, many congressmen were vocal supporters of imported Mexican labor during these years:

Representatives

Texas: O. C. Fisher, Joe Kilgore, George Mahon, Ken Regan, Olin Teague

California: Charles Gubser, Leroy Johnson, John Phillips, James
    Utt, Bob Wilson
New Mexico: Antonio Fernandez, Joseph Montoya
Mississippi: Frank Smith
Arizona: John Rhodes
Michigan: Alvin Bentley
Kansas: Clifford Hope
Missouri: Paul Jones
Iowa: Charles Hoeven
Arkansas: E. C. Gathings
Utah: Henry Dixon

Senators

Louisiana: Allen Ellender
Florida: Spessard Holland
New Mexico: Clinton Anderson
Texas: Lyndon Johnson
California: William Knowland
Arizona: Carl Hayden

Forces Opposing Extension of P.L. 78. Whereas supporters of the
bracero program were all but unqualified in their endorsement, opponents of extension were, with a few notable exceptions,[127] more
qualified and reserved. In general, they were groups and individuals who, while acquiescing to the need of some imported labor,
desired substantial modification of P.L. 78, in order to protect
wages and working conditions of domestics. If one acknowledges
that the label "anti-braceroist" did not necessarily signify unmitigated opposition to Mexican labor, the following may be classified
as forces opposing extension of P.L. 78 during the 1950's:

Agricultural Organizations

National Farmers Union[128]

---

[127] Representative H. R. Cross of Iowa and George Long of Louisiana may be
classified as being in complete opposition. The same may be said of the National
Sharecroppers Fund and the National Agricultural Workers Union.

[128] There may be some debate about this classification, but it certainly was
appropriate during the late 1950's. Note the 1958 statement of the union's di-

Representatives of Organized Labor
AFL–CIO
International Brotherhood of Teamsters
National Agricultural Workers Union
United Packinghouse Workers of America
United States Section of the Joint United States–Mexico Trade
Union Committee

Religious and Social Reform Groups
National Catholic Rural Life Conference
American GI Forum of Texas
National Sharecroppers Fund
National Consumers League for Fair Labor Standards
National Catholic Welfare Committee
American Friends Service Committee

Anti-bracero congressmen were fewer in number and far less vociferous during the peak years of imported Mexican labor.

Representatives
California: Harlan Hagan, James Roosevelt, Dilip Singh Saund,
John Shelley
Tennessee: Howard Baker, Ross Bass
Minnesota: Eugene McCarthy
Indiana: Winfield Denton
New York: Victor Anfuso
South Dakota: George McGovern
Louisiana: George Long
Iowa: H. R. Gross

Senators
Illinois: Paul Douglas
Minnesota: Hubert Humphrey
New Jersey: Harrison Williams
New York: Herbert Lehman
Oregon: Wayne Morse

---

rector, John A. Baker, before the House Committee on Agriculture (House Agriculture Committee Hearings, 1958, p. 586).

Arguments Pro and Con

One might reasonably expect the arguments for and against importation to have reflected the complex nature of the 1950's bracero program. Instead, an all-too-simplistic case for or against the Mexican national became the rule. Debate generally revolved around six fundamental propositions, with neither side willing to grant much credence to the opposition's case.

One argument centered on justification for the program's existence. Opponents of imported labor contended that P.L. 78 was enacted solely as an emergency measure because of the Korean War.[129] In direct contradiction of the intentions of Congress, bracero importation had not disappeared with the passing of the international crisis. Instead, it had grown enormously. Proponents of the bracero program retorted that P.L. 78 was never intended to be merely an emergency program. Instead, Congress foresaw the long-range shortage of farmworkers and, therefore, provided a firm statutory base for long-term bracero contracting.[130]

A second point of contention concerned the question of adverse effect. Anti-braceroists produced statistics in support of their argument that increased employment of Mexicans had adversely affected the wages and working conditions of natives.[131] Those supporting P.L. 78 presented equally elaborate data indicating clearly that the bracero had, if anything, proved beneficial to the working conditions and wages of domestics.[132]

The wetback phenomenon provided a third basis for argument. Supporters of imported Mexican labor held that P.L. 78 was a primary contributing factor to the wetback's demise.[133] Without the program, the influx of illegal entrants would prove unmanageable. Anti-braceroists rebutted that efficiency, initiative, and increased

---

[129] House Agriculture Committee Hearings, 1960, pp. 389–390; and House Agriculture Committee Hearings, 1958, p. 390.

[130] House Agriculture Committee Hearings, 1960, pp. 389–390.

[131] House Agriculture Committee Hearings, 1958, pp. 438–440 and 502–507.

[132] Ibid., pp. 239 and 461.

[133] Ibid., p. 460; and *Congressional Record*, 101:10007.

funding had eradicated the wetback problem, not P.L. 78. How, they queried, could the act be seriously considered a wetback deterrent when two years after its enactment the number of illegal entrants had exceeded one million?[134]

A fourth reason for debate concerned the relationship between imported labor and the availability of domestic farmworkers. Opponents of importation asserted that sufficient native labor was available. All that was needed were decent wages, improved working conditions, and other guarantees. In sum, with the presence of high unemployment, all that was required was a program for domestic farmworkers similar to that offered braceros.[135] Supporters of the Mexican labor system replied that a package deal for domestics similar to that granted braceros would, if native workers accepted, bankrupt the United States farmer. However, even if the employer were compelled to offer such benefits, he would still not get the needed labor. No incentive, regardless of what it entailed, would entice native workers to pick tomatoes or hoe beets ten or twelve hours a day in 110-degree heat. The factory worker would not endanger his unemployment check or the healthful condition of his sacroiliac to do stoop labor, no matter what you offered him. Without the bracero, the crops simply would rot.[136]

The question of who benefited from bracero importation provided a fifth bone of contention. Anti-braceroists held that the Mexican labor program benefited only a minute number of corporation farmers in no more than five states. As a result, the small farmer, unable to compete against commodities produced by cheap foreign labor, was being systematically forced out of business.[137] Perpetual importation of Mexican workers would mean the sure demise of the small family farm. Although they did not deny the benefits accruing to large-scale farming operations as a result of the bracero program, supporters of Mexican labor argued that it also

[134] *Congressional Record*, 100:2508 and 2570.
[135] House Agriculture Committee Hearings, 1958, pp. 35, 438, and 500–502.
[136] *Congressional Record*, 104:17654 and 17658.
[137] House Agriculture Committee Hearings, 1958, pp. 495, 498, and 586.

benefited the small operator. As a member of an association, the small grower could utilize his share of braceros. Termination of the program would affect the little man much more than the big operator. Because of his capital investment, the latter could afford to mechanize if forced to pay exorbitant wages. The small farmer could afford neither to mechanize nor to pay higher wages and would thus be forced to give up farming.[138]

A final question involved the impact of bracero recruitment upon the Mexican economy, the Mexican citizen, and United States–Mexican relations. For those championing its cause, the bracero system was deemed a boon to the Mexican economy, to the *campesino*, and to United States foreign policy.[139] Critics of P.L. 78 demurred on the first two contentions; it would have been foolish to do otherwise. It was the third assumption that they challenged. In their eyes, the separation of families and exploitation of the bracero, when coupled with strong-arm governmental tactics (unilateral contracting in particular) at the behest of agribusiness, had severely damaged our relationship with Mexico and the individual Mexican citizen.[140]

The size, impact, and complexity of the bracero program was clearly reflected in each of these points. In fact, empirical evidence existed supporting the conclusions of each side of these and other issues. In one respect, P.L. 78 could have been viewed simultaneously as a temporary and a long-range program. Evidence did indicate an adverse effect trend. However, the highest wages for farmworkers were paid in California, the second-largest employer of braceros in the 1950's. Operation Wetback was the deciding factor in the elimination of the illegal immigrant. Yet, without a program for legal recruitment, the wetback drive may have proved infeasible. After all, the key to Operation Wetback was the farmers, many of whom had been assured braceros to replace the wetbacks

---

[138] Ibid., pp. 519–520; and *Congressional Record*, 106:14975 and 14988.

[139] House Agriculture Committee Hearings, 1958, pp. 296 and 460.

[140] Ibid., pp. 443–446; Galarza, *Strangers in Our Fields*, Chaps. 4–12; and *Congressional Record*, 100:2493–2494.

they had previously utilized. Sufficient numbers of native workers might have been available if better wages and working conditions had been offered. Yet, because of the arduous nature of stoop labor, the crops might have rotted without the bracero, no matter how attractive the offer made to domestics. Large corporate farms employed by far the great majority of Mexican workers. However, agribusiness would have survived without the bracero; the little man would have gone under. Finally, the bracero program was undeniably important to Mexico and the Mexican *campesino*. After it survived the unilateral recruitment episode, the program proved an asset to United States foreign policy. Still, the few verified cases of bracero exploitation, the isolation of the bracero from the mainstream of United States life, and the cloud of unilateralism were not conducive to improved United States–Mexican relations. In sum, the bracero program of the 1950's was certainly not all things to all people.

Summary

No period in the history of the Mexican labor program more clearly reflected the political power and access of pro-bracero farm interests than the years 1952–1959. Critics of the program were wholly unsuccessful in their efforts to halt the growth of imported labor during the 1950's. The almost effortless extensions of P.L. 78, coupled with the codifying of unilateral recruitment, clearly indicated the degree to which the bracero had become an integral, if not inseparable, part of agriculture in the Southwest. With the wetback's demise, it appeared as if the Mexican labor program had reached the stage of institutionalization.

Aware of the futility of attempting to abrogate the program entirely, and perhaps not wanting to do so, anti-braceroists attempted the next best thing—amendment of P.L. 78 in order to bring about better wages and working conditions for domestic farm labor. They tried to accomplish this by requiring employers wishing to use foreign labor to first offer native workers guarantees similar to those afforded braceros. In each instance such efforts failed by substantial majorities.[141] Indeed, they never had the slightest chance of being enacted.

Success of the forces supporting imported labor during these years is rather easily explained. As in 1951 and 1952, their achievement resulted from coordinated effort, political access at all levels and branches of government, detailed and logical presentation before friendly congressional committees, logical and well-publicized rebuttals to charges made against the bracero, the need by Mexico and the Mexicans for United States dollars, political logrolling, and the uncoordinated, ineffective efforts of the opposition. During this period there was no all-out, coordinated effort among anti-bracero elements aimed at terminating or substantially altering the program. In fact, unmitigated opposition to bracero importation in any form came only from the National Agricultural Workers Union, and not from its parent organization, the AFL-CIO.

Institutionalization of the Mexican labor program in the 1950's demonstrated that those groups possessing political access and utilizing coordinated tactics receive the political spoils. In addition, it was indicative of an uncomfortable reality for the student of interest groups and the political process in democratic states.

Much of the literature on interest groups in democratic states extols the virtues of pluralism. Inherent in these writings is the underlying theme of offsetting or countervailing interests. John Kenneth Gailbraith has perhaps best exemplified this school of thought in his theory of countervailing powers.[142] He argues, as do most group theorists, that over a given period of time one interest, or a bloc of interests, may dominate policy-making in a particular field, even at the expense of majority opinion. Yet, in the long run, countervailing forces will emerge and eventually off-set the seeming disproportionate power of previously dominant interests.

[141] The best example of such tactics occurred when P.L. 78 came up for renewal in 1955. Representatives Eugene McCarthy of Minnesota and Victor Anfuso of New York introduced bills that would have required farmers seeking braceros to offer domestic workers benefits similar to those required for Mexicans. Both amendments were defeated by almost 2–1 majorities (*Congressional Record*, 101:10012–10024).

[142] John Kenneth Galbraith, *American Capitalism*, chaps. 9 and 10.

In the rare event that such a cycle of countervailing powers does not come full circle, government, by virtue of the fact that it represents the public interest, may be forced to employ its power to right the situation.

As the 1950's drew to a close approximately eighteen years of decided dominance of employer interests in agriculture over the forces of domestic farm labor had been witnessed. That less than 2 percent of the nation's farms in five states could for so long dictate policy detrimental to the interests of resident workers, and perhaps to the majority of all United States citizens, was cause for serious concern to the student of democratic process. It appeared to some observers that democratic group theorists may have come across an exception to the rule of counterbalancing interest in the person of imported farm labor.[143] Yet the element of time is a crucial and essentially undefined variable in the lexicon of democratic theory. In a comparatively short time the seemingly unbalanced group milieu of imported Mexican labor was to right itself. The process by which this reversal was accomplished was a vindication for democratic group theorists. It provides the basis for the fifth chapter in this study.

[143] Robert D. Tomasek realized the dilemma that the bracero program of the late 1950's posed to democratic theory ("The Migrant Problem and Pressure Group Politics," *Journal of Politics* 23[May 1961]:318–319).

CHAPTER 5

Group Processes and the Demise of the Bracero Program: 1960–1964

Public Law 78 expired on December 31, 1964. With its expiration twenty-two years of large-scale bracero contracting came to an end. Events leading up to the demise of the bracero program constituted a fundamental reversal of the interest-group structure surrounding imported Mexican farm labor. However, the program's termination involved far more than a shift in the power and access of group participants. Other factors must be taken into account, for instance, the acceleration of agricultural mechanization, the orientation of new presidential administrations, an increasing moralization of the entire bracero question, and the mounting burdens associated with bracero contracting. All told, they brought about the termination of a labor system that had become an institutionalized aspect of southwestern agriculture.

Yet despite its demise in 1964, the bracero program displayed remarkable staying power in the face of increasingly powerful opposition. Such persistence was due, in part, to the continued access and power enjoyed by the congressional supporters of imported labor. More important, however, was Mexican pressure in support of prolongation. Had it not been for the diplomatic ramifications of the bracero program, it is doubtful whether it would have survived beyond 1961.

THE 1960 EXTENSION OF PUBLIC LAW 78

In August, 1958, Public Law 78 was extended to June 30, 1961. When in June of 1959 the Mexican labor agreement was also extended to June, 1961, it appeared that the bracero program had become a firmly entrenched part of southwestern agriculture and United States–Mexican relations. Yet on September 14, 1960, P.L. 78 was granted only a six-month renewal. A program that had appeared unassailable in the 1950's suddenly seemed in jeopardy late in 1960. The root causes of this turn of events may be found in policies emanating from the Department of Labor in the late 1950's.

With the amazing growth of bracero recruitment during the late 1950's it appeared that farm groups were content with the program, which, in fact, was not the case. While they obviously preferred the system as it existed during these years to no program at all, growers were becoming more and more uncomfortable with its administration, especially with the secretary of labor. The basis for rising grower discontent lay in new Department of Labor regulations covering the areas of housing, wages, and transportation.

In December, 1956, the Labor Department issued new regulations designed to improve bracero housing. Under terms of the revised regulations, growers seeking braceros were required to furnish dwellings with minimum twelve-foot-high ceilings, beds with springs and mattresses, hot water, and regular garbage disposal facilities.[1] That the Labor Department meant to enforce these

---

[1] *Hispanic American Report* 10(March 1957):63.

new regulations soon became apparent. By August, 1957, fifty-eight bracero camps had been closed temporarily or permanently in California and Arizona. This figure represented 10 percent of all such facilities in the two states.[2] While most employers complied with the new regulations, a total of 248 units in 1957, and 157 units in 1958, were closed after being declared substandard.[3]

Action by the secretary of labor in the area of bracero wages was a second reason for grower discontent. The question of what constituted a prevailing wage had always been difficult to determine. Upon this decision rested the rate of bracero wages in particular areas, and in many cases the wages paid domestic farmworkers. Prior to September, 1958, the prevailing wage was determined under what was termed the "two-thirds rule"; that is, the wage rate paid to two-thirds or more of the domestics was deemed the prevailing wage for an area. However, beginning in September, a new formula was adopted in an effort to narrow the range of wages paid within a particular area.[4] In effect, the new method was a "40 percent" formula, according to which the prevailing hourly wage would be that received by the greatest number of native workers if that number constituted 40 percent or more of the workers covered in a sample survey. Under such a formula it was hoped that the adverse effect often associated with bracero employment could be reduced.

In addition to the new prevailing hourly wage formula, the Department of Labor instituted in 1958 a new method for determining the earnings of braceros engaged in piece-rate activities.[5] The so-called 90-10 formula riled farm groups even more than the new regulations governing prevailing wages. Mexican and United States officials had for several years an understanding to the effect

[2] *New York Times*, August 18, 1957.

[3] U.S., Department of Labor, "Report of Operations of Mexican Farm Labor Program Made Pursuant to Conference Report No. 1449," House of Representatives, 84th Cong., 1st sess., January 1–June 30, 1959.

[4] Linwood K. Bailey and Samuel Vernoff, "Agricultural Wage Policy Developments During 1958," *Employment Security Review* 20(February 1959):12–14.

[5] *New York Times*, July 31, 1958; and Bailey and Vernoff, "Agricultural Wage Policy Developments," pp. 12–14.

that no bracero should earn less than an average of 50 cents an hour.[6] However, this minimum was often not upheld, particularly for braceros engaged in piece-work activities. The Department of Labor thus promulgated a new policy whereby competent and diligent braceros could average at least 50 cents an hour. Termed the "90-10 formula," the new regulation established a system requiring employers to increase wages in cases where 90 percent of the braceros engaged in particular piece-rate activity did not average 50 cents an hour.

Despite their consternation over administrative rulings in the areas of housing and wages, the reaction of growers was mild when compared to their bitter resentment over a ruling by Secretary of Labor James P. Mitchell in November, 1959. At that time the Department of Labor issued what was generally termed the "New Wagner-Peyser Regulations."[7] With authority under the Wagner-Peyser Act of 1933, Secretary Mitchell issued regulations that required particular prevailing wages and minimum working standards for domestic farmworkers recruited through the farm placement service of the Labor Department. The new policy forbade interstate recruitment through governmental agencies of domestics for work in states or areas providing poor wages and substandard working conditions. It was a very bold step by the man who, although he could not be properly termed an anti-braceroist, had come to be considered a friend of native farmworkers.

Adding to the growing disgust of farm groups over administration of the bracero program in the late 1950's was a consultants' report published in October of 1959.[8] In response to a growing

---

[6] U.S., Congress, House, Committee on Agriculture, *Extension of Mexican Farm Labor Program: Hearings before Subcommittee on H.R. 9869 and others,* 86th Cong., 2d sess., March 22, 23, 24, 25, and 31, 1960, p. 392, hereafter cited as House Agriculture Committee Hearings, 1960; and idem, *Farm Labor and Mexican Labor: Hearings before Subcommittee on H.R. 7028 and others,* 85th Cong., 2d sess., February 28, March 1 and 3, June 9–12, and July 2, 1958, p. 603; hereafter cited as House Agriculture Committee Hearings, 1958.

[7] House Agriculture Committee Hearings, 1960, p. 5.

[8] U.S., Department of Labor, Bureau of Employment Security, "Mexican Farm Labor Program, Consultants' Report."

uneasiness within the Labor Department over the apparent adverse effect of bracero usage on the wages and the working conditions of domestics, Secretary Mitchell appointed a distinguished group of consultants to review the problem.[9] The consultants analyzed six fundamental aspects of the bracero program and made recommendations on the basis of their findings.

It was concluded that (1) despite efforts to avoid it, adverse effect had occurred in particular cases; (2) although designed originally as an emergency measure to meet stoop-labor shortages in essential crops, braceros were being utilized increasingly in skilled and semiskilled jobs the year round; (3) shortages of domestic workers often resulted from Mexicans being offered better working conditions than natives; (4) employers often did not put forth bona fide efforts to recruit domestics; and (5) despite reservations, Mexico still favored the program because of its economic benefits.

The consultants recommended that (1) the use of braceros be confined to unskilled, nonmachine jobs in essential crops where temporary labor shortages existed; (2) the secretary of labor be given broader powers in establishing prevailing wage rates; (3) the secretary be authorized to take the action required to ensure active competition for available domestic workers; (4) he further be empowered to establish standards for judging adverse effect; (5) a tripartite group consisting of representatives of growers, workers, and the general public be established to advise the secretary on the bracero program.

It soon became apparent that the secretary of labor agreed with the findings and recommendations of the consultants and that a bill embodying many of their findings would be introduced in Congress. When P.L. 78 came up for extension in 1960, it was equally clear that grower resentment over administration of the bracero program would no longer be hidden by statistics depicting the growing number of recruited Mexican nationals.[10] The secre-

[9] Under the leadership of William Mirengoff, the group included Glenn E. Garrett, the Very Reverend Msgr. George G. Higgins, Edward J. Thye, and Dr. Rufus B. von Kleinsmid. Ibid.

[10] It should be noted that grower resentment over new housing regulations

tary of labor had become *persona non grata* to bracero employers
and their representatives in Congress.

The Six-Month Extension of 1960

In 1958, P.L. 78 had been extended to June 30, 1961. The group
struggle over further prolongation began in earnest during the
second session of the Eighty-sixth Congress. Grower resentment
over Secretary Mitchell's actions surfaced early in the session when
a group of bills aimed at sharply curtailing the secretary's authority over farm labor were introduced. These measures called for the
secretary of agriculture to become a joint administrator of the
bracero program along with the secretary of labor. Both men
would share in determining the existence or absence of adverse
effect. If adverse effect were determined, adjustment of wages or
working conditions would be a shared endeavor. A second major
feature of these bills was a direct result of Secretary Mitchell's
actions under the Wagner-Peyser Act. Public Law 78 would be
amended to state specifically that nothing in the law be construed
to confer authority upon the secretary of labor to ". . . regulate the
wages, hours, prerequisites or other conditions of employment of
domestic farm workers."[11] The objective of these measures was to
reduce substantially the authority of the secretary of labor in the
areas of imported and domestic agricultural labor.

When it became apparent that the administration would not,
despite hopes to the contrary, introduce a bill embodying the
recommendations of the 1959 consultants' report, anti-bracero
elements in Congress acted on their own.[12] Early in March, 1960,
Representative George McGovern of South Dakota introduced an
amendment to P.L. 78 that contained the bulk of the consultants'

---

and the "90-10" formula became apparent in 1958 during hearings on P.L. 78
(House Agriculture Committee Hearings, 1958, pp. 302–316, 460–469, and
593–598).

[11] House Agriculture Committee Hearings, 1960, pp. 2 and 3.

[12] Arnold Mayer contends that a Labor Department bill to this effect was
blocked within the administration by supporters of farm groups ("The Grapes
of Wrath, Vintage 1961," *The Reporter*, February 2, 1961, pp. 34–37). In this
connection, also see below, note 16.

recommendations and called for a gradual phasing out of the bracero program.[13] When hearings opened on March 22, the crux issues were clear: Would the power of the secretary of labor over imported and domestic farm labor be drastically reduced or substantially augmented? Furthermore, was it possible that there would be no bracero program after June 30, 1961?

Testimony before a subcommittee of the House Committee on Agriculture indicated a polarization of the opposing group interests. Traditional supporters of bracero importation rallied behind those measures aimed at curbing the power of Secretary Mitchell.[14] Anti-bracero organizations opposed such bills and demanded either an end to the program or passage of the McGovern amendment.[15] In this connection the 1960 hearings were reminiscent of their predecessors. Yet in one crucial respect they were different.

During the 1950's, forces of the Eisenhower administration had afforded blanket support to bills designed to extend P.L. 78, which was not the case in 1960. Faced with two widely divergent choices, the Departments of Labor, Agriculture, and State chose to assume a neutral posture.[16] While not supporting the McGovern bill, they all testified in opposition to measures designed to shift administration of the bracero program to a joint basis.[17]

The Labor Department was especially strong in its opposition to any reduction in the secretary of labor's authority over foreign and domestic farmworkers. In defense of the secretary's actions under the Wagner-Peyser Act, department spokesmen stressed the support rendered Secretary Mitchell's actions by the attorney gen-

[13] House Agriculture Committee Hearings, 1960, pp. 3–4.

[14] Ibid., pp. 4–25, 57–59, 61–66, 96, 178–182, and 264–271.

[15] Ibid., pp. 73–75, 146, 148, 153–156, 162–174, 190–242, and 289–291.

[16] It was subsequently revealed that a compromise to this effect had been reached within the administration. The secretaries of labor and agriculture had differed on what type of proposal the administration should offer, with the former supporting an amendment incorporating the recommendations of the consultants' report of 1959 and the latter opposing such a stand. As a result, the administration's position was essentially noncommittal (*New York Times,* March 31, 1960).

[17] House Agriculture Committee Hearings, 1960, pp. 352–399 and 400–402.

eral.[18] Although he did not assume a particular posture on any one measure, State Department spokesman Melville Osborne cautioned against any action that might upset the complex diplomatic nature of bracero recruitment.[19] Thus, if anything positive emerged from the testimony of administration officials, it was that the bracero program should be extended without appreciable change. It appeared that, in proposing to curtail the authority of the secretary of labor, farm groups and their loyal supporters in Congress may have overextended themselves.

As subsequent events revealed, this is exactly what happened. Late in the session, the House Committee on Agriculture ignored recommendations of its Subcommittee on Equipment, Supplies, and Manpower[20] and suggested simply that P.L. 78 be extended, without amendment, for two years.[21] The committee had initially considered a two-year extension embodying joint administration of the bracero program and sharp curtailment of the power of the secretary of labor. It then decided to eliminate the joint administration provisions, yet retain the amendments designed to curb the power of Secretary Mitchell. Finally, the committee ruled out these amendments and, on June 22, 1960, recommended a two-year, unamended extension.[22]

Congressional debate on extension of P.L. 78 began on June 28, 1960. In the interim, Senator Eugene McCarthy of Minnesota introduced a bill that resembled the McGovern amendment.[23] When a large group of prominent senators subsequently joined Senator McCarthy as cosponsors, it became apparent that anti-bracero forces in both houses of Congress had substantially augmented their ranks and were prepared, for the first time, to seriously challenge any unamended extension of P.L. 78.

---

[18] Ibid., pp. 355–365.

[19] Ibid., p. 401.

[20] The subcommittee voted to recommend a two-year extension as well as a curtailment of the labor secretary's power (*Congressional Record*, 106:14971).

[21] House Report No. 1954, "Farm Labor Program," 86th Cong., 2d sess., June 22, 1960.

[22] *Congressional Record*, 106:14068.

[23] Ibid., p. 12377.

The first task facing congressional supporters of the bracero program was to maneuver a simple two-year extension of P.L. 78 through the House. Opposition to such a move in the lower chamber was stronger than on any previous occasion. Anti-bracero representatives argued that the law should not be extended unless altered along the lines suggested by the consultants' report of October, 1959.[24] Although their arguments rang true to opponents of imported labor, the House and its committee on agriculture were still the stalwart sanctuaries of grower interests. An amendment similar to the McGovern bill, but lacking the phasing-out provision, was offered by Representative John Fogarty of Rhode Island. Congressman Alfred Santangelo of New York submitted an amendment designed to prohibit the use of braceros in cotton production by limiting their employment to cultivating and harvesting food supplies. Both amendments were defeated by almost 3–1 margins.[25] On June 29, by a voice vote, the House elected to extend P.L. 78 without amendment for two years. Pro-bracero forces had cleared their first hurdle. A more difficult barrier lay ahead.

Following action by the House, the bill calling for a simple two-year extension was referred to the Senate Committee on Agriculture and Forestry. When it was not reported out after several days, it became evident that the committee, as well as the entire Senate, was sharply divided on the issue. Finally, on August 23, 1960, a last-second compromise was reached. The committee reported out a bill calling for only a six-month, unamended extension of P.L. 78.[26] The hour was such that no time remained for thorough debate or the offering of amendments to the abbreviated extension. The Senate considered and passed the bill by acclamation on August 31. That afternoon the House concurred in the Senate version. On September 1, the final day of the session, P.L. 78 was officially

[24] The statements by Representatives James Roosevelt and John McFall of California, John Fogarty of Rhode Island, and Edith Green of Oregon reflected this sentiment (Ibid., pp. 14809–14810, 14973–14975, 14978, 14982).

[25] The Fogarty amendment was defeated by a vote of 138–51. Representative Santangelo's measure was overwhelmed 122–33 (Ibid., p. 14988).

[26] Senate Report No. 1901, "Mexican Farm Labor," 86th Cong., 2d sess., August 23, 1960.

extended for six months and scheduled to expire December 31, 1961.

Just how close the Senate came to taking no action at all on P.L. 78 during 1960 was revealed by the report of the Senate Agriculture Committee and by remarks during Senate debate. Both the debate and the committee report disclosed the extent to which the Senate and the two departments most directly concerned were divided by the issue. While the House bill was still being considered by Senator Ellender's committee, correspondence from the Departments of Labor and Agriculture revealed a wide difference of opinion on whether P.L. 78 should be extended without change.

Secretary of Labor Mitchell openly favored amendment of the law along lines recommended by the 1959 consultants' report. Since the hour was such as to preclude thorough Senate consideration of such changes, Mr. Mitchell called for no action during 1960 in deference to thorough consideration during the first session of the Eighty-seventh Congress.[27] The Department of Agriculture informed Senator Ellender that it, too, favored no action during 1960,[28] not because the Agriculture Department supported changes in P.L. 78 similar to those recommended by Secretary Mitchell, but because it favored a more thorough airing of the issues involved prior to extension. In effect both departments called for inaction but for opposite reasons.

In remarks before the Senate, Mr. Ellender disclosed the mounting opposition within the Senate Agriculture Committee to a six-month, unamended extension. He defended such a prolongation on the grounds that, if P.L. 78 were not renewed by June 30, 1961, it would work undue hardship on bracero employers. This situation would be avoided if P.L. 78 were to be terminated in late December, after the great majority of crops had been harvested.[29]

Anti-bracero senators were still skeptical over the potential inherent in a Senate-approved six-month extension. For, if the Senate

[27] Letter from the secretary of labor to Senator Allen Ellender (Ibid.).

[28] Letter from the acting secretary of agriculture to Senator Allen Ellender (Ibid.).

[29] *Congressional Record*, 106:18625.

bill differed from that of the House, a conference would be in order. And strange things happened during such sessions. "There is grave fear that if we go into a conference with the House, the Senate, as is sometimes the case, will get the short end of it, and if we seek to extend the act for two years or one and a half years, there is a probability there will be no legislation at all."[30]

Grasping the none-too-subtle threat of a filibuster, Senator Carl Hayden of Arizona was adamant in assuring his anti-bracero colleagues that there would be no last-minute capitulation on the part of the Senate conferees. "I guarantee," he stated, "either the House will accept this extension or there will be no law."[31] The Arizona senator was true to his word.

Summary

Seemingly impervious in the late 1950's, the supporters of bracero importation were dealt a substantial defeat in 1960. Although they did not halt extension of P.L. 78 entirely, anti-bracero groups and their congressional allies came very close to doing just that. In addition, and equally significant, they were successful, first, in defeating amendments designed to drastically curtail the secretary of labor's power over domestic and foreign agricultural labor and, second, in thwarting an unamended two-year extension of P.L. 78. The surprising success of anti-bracero forces emanated from a combination of two factors: clumsy tactics by pro-bracero forces, and the increasing number of groups and individuals who, as a result of Labor Department disclosures, had come to take a hard second look at imported Mexican labor.

As subsequent events illustrated, pro-bracero forces clearly overplayed their hand in attempting to emasculate the power of the secretary of labor. The effort to make administration of the bracero program a joint endeavor was doomed to failure from the start. The Agriculture Department, despite its obvious affection for grower interests, did not favor such a move.[32] Many uncommitted con-

---

30 Remarks of Senator George Aiken of Vermont (Ibid., p. 18626).
31 Ibid.
32 House Agriculture Committee Hearings, 1960, p. 353.

gressmen, who heretofore supported bracero recruitment, balked at efforts to undermine the authority of the secretary of labor. In his actions under the Wagner-Peyser Act, Secretary Mitchell may have gone a bit too far. Yet to strip him of all power to regulate wages, hours, and working conditions of domestic farmworkers was overretaliation. In their haste to strike back at Secretary Mitchell, such groups as the Farm Bureau and the Grange, with their admitted political acumen, committed a fundamental error.

A second cause for the setback suffered by pro-bracero forces in 1960 lay in the disclosures and pronouncements by the Labor Department about the mounting adverse effect inherent in bracero contracting. That the bracero had, for all practical purposes, become the property of a limited number of growers in only a few states was made known through various Labor Department sources. That imported labor was in fact adversely affecting the wages and working conditions of domestics became the dominant theme of departmental testimony before Congress.[33] Departmental surveys, the 1959 consultants' report, and testimony by affected interest groups substantiated this conclusion.[34] Therefore, when an all-out assault was launched against Secretary Mitchell, a growing number of individuals and groups reacted by rising in defense of actions that the secretary had taken in an effort to improve the status of domestic agricultural workers.

By 1960, more interest groups had joined the fight against imported Mexican labor. Augmenting the previously thin anti-bracero ranks were the following groups:

Federation of Settlements and Neighborhood Centers
National Council of Churches of Christ
Amalgamated Meat Cutters and Butcher Workmen
New Jersey Migrant Labor Board
Textile Workers Union of America
National Advisory Committee on Farm Labor
California Citizens Committee for Agricultural Labor

[33] Ibid., pp. 366 and 374–376.
[34] Ibid., *passim*.

Migrant Workers Committee of Palo Alto, California
Minnesota Council of Churches
National Child Labor Committee
Opportunity Council of Arlington Heights, Illinois
National Association for the Advancement of Colored People

The words and deeds of various members of Congress disclosed a growing number of senators and representatives who, in addition to those mentioned previously,[35] merited the title of "anti-bracero-ist" in 1960:

Senators
    Kenneth Keating and Jacob Javits of New York
    Philip Hart and Pat McNamara of Michigan
    James Murray of Montana
    William Proxmire of Wisconsin
    Joseph Clark of Pennsylvania
    Stephen Young of Ohio
    Thomas Dodd of Connecticut
    Eugene McCarthy of Minnesota[36]

Representatives
    John Fogarty of Rhode Island
    Thomas Lane of Massachusetts
    Alfred Santangelo of New York
    Edith Green of Oregon
    Frank Thompson of New Jersey
    Jeffery Cohelan of California
    Denver Hargis of Kansas
    Burr Harrison of Virginia
    Lester Johnson of Wisconsin
    Thomas Pelly of Washington[37]

The year 1960 may thus be viewed as a watershed in the history

[35] See Chap. 4, p. 143.
[36] *Congressional Record*, 106:12377–12380 and 18624–18630.
[37] Ibid., pp. 14806–14812, 14968–14991; and House Agriculture Committee Hearings, 1960.

of Mexican contract labor. It signified a turning point in the group struggle surrounding bracero importation. With the secretary of labor a confirmed ally,[38] anti-bracero forces would no longer be wholly reactive in their approach. From 1960 on, the forces supporting bracero labor were put on the defensive. However, those whom Secretary Mitchell once termed "the most powerful opposition I have ever seen" were to prove equally strong in their new role.[39] Agribusiness and its congressional supporters encountered their first test in the art of rear-guard politics in 1961.

THE 1961 EXTENSION OF PUBLIC LAW 78

With a six-month extension in September, 1960, P.L. 78 was scheduled to expire December 31, 1961. Early in the first session of the Eighty-seventh Congress, Representative E. C. Gathings of Arkansas, chairman of the crucial Subcommittee on Equipment, Supplies, and Manpower of the House Committee on Agriculture, introduced H.R. 2010. The bill called for a four-year unamended extension of P.L. 78. From that moment on, there ensued an eight-month struggle over the fate of imported Mexican labor.

For the first time, supporters of the bracero program encountered in 1961 an administration united in its opposition to any unamended extension of P.L. 78. During the Eisenhower administration, grower interests had enjoyed direct access to Secretary of Agriculture Ezra Taft Benson, himself a past president of the American Farm Bureau Federation, while only the secretary of labor had opposed the excesses inherent in large-scale bracero contracting. With the election of a man pledged to achieve the New Frontier for all United States citizens, imported Mexican labor came under fire from an entire administration. No longer would growers use the support of the secretary of agriculture as a counterweight to

[38] The feelings of Secretary Mitchell on imported farm labor and its impact on domestic farmworkers may be found in *New York Times*, February 6 and 24, 1959, April 7, 1960; *Congressional Record*, 106:3175–3176; House Agriculture Committee Hearings, 1960, pp. 394–395; and "An Interview with Secretary Mitchell," *The Reporter*, January 22, 1959, p. 20.

[39] *New York Times*, July 25, 1960.

the policies of the secretary of labor. No longer would the appeals of agribusiness ring true to the overwhelming majority of congressmen. Survival of the bracero program was to require all the political leverage and acumen of grower interests and their congressional supporters. Even this might not have proved sufficient had it not been for the program's impact on Mexico.

The new administration of President John F. Kennedy made known its position on imported farm labor early in 1961. The asking price for extension was to be substantial change in Public Law 78. Without revision, growers were informed that they might be sans braceros in 1962.[40] "The time for study has passed," said the new Secretary of Labor Arthur Goldberg, "the time for action is now."[41] The "action" to which the secretary referred was spelled out in June, 1961, before the Senate Committee on Agriculture and Forestry.

Four amendments to P.L. 78 were recommended by the new administration.[42] First, the secretary of labor should be authorized to limit the number of braceros that any one grower might employ "to the extent necessary to assure active competition for domestic workers." Second, employers seeking Mexicans should be required to offer "conditions of employment" to natives comparable to those afforded braceros. Third, the use of braceros should be prohibited ". . . in other than temporary or seasonal work or in work involving the operation of power-driven machinery." Fourth, farmers utilizing braceros should be required to pay them wages ". . . at least equivalent to the Statewide or National average rate for hourly paid farm labor, whichever is the lesser."

Secretary Goldberg's statement made it clear that he was seeking statutory authority for actions that had riled bracero employers in the past.[43] On numerous occasions, critics of Mr. Goldberg and his

40 Ibid., April 20, 1961.

41 Ibid., April 16, 1961.

42 U.S., Congress, Senate, Committee on Agriculture and Forestry, *Extension of Mexican Farm Labor Program: Hearings before Subcommittee on S. 1466, S. 1945, H.R. 2010,* 87th Cong., 1st sess., June 12 and 13, 1961, pp. 159–166 (hereafter cited as Senate Agriculture Committee Hearings, 1961).

43 Ibid., p. 166.

predecessor Mr. Mitchell had based their complaints on the contention that the secretary of labor had taken actions for which he possessed no statutory authority.[44] They had contested the secretary's actions both in and out of the courtroom, in the areas of wages, housing, and working conditions. Thus in 1961, the administration decided to clear up the entire question of authority under P.L. 78 by offering Congress a chance to act on the matter. Should it choose not to grant the secretary specified powers and he subsequently acted on his own accord to protect domestics from adverse effect, members of Congress would have only themselves to blame.

When hearings on the Mexican labor act began in March, 1961, before a subcommittee of the House Committee on Agriculture, there appeared to be three possible fates awaiting the statutory foundation of imported Mexican labor. One, P.L. 78 could be allowed to expire as a result of congressional inaction, which was the goal of a growing list of die-hard anti-bracero groups and individuals. Second, it could be extended without amendment. Considering the rapidly changing interest-group milieu of imported and indigenous farm labor early in 1961, virtually all avid proponents of the bracero program aimed for extension. Third, and in line with the administration's position, P.L. 78 could be extended, but only after it had been appreciably altered so that it afforded greater protection to domestic farmworkers. Again, as had so often been the case, a compromise appeared in order. The crux issue thus became one of degree: What type of compromise could be arrived at that would withstand the opposition of the rabid proponents and opponents of imported Mexican farm labor?

Following hearings on the Gathings bill (H.R. 2010), debate began in the House of Representatives. In its report, the House

[44] House Agriculture Committee Hearings, 1958, pp. 461–464; House Agriculture Committee Hearings, 1960, pp. 4–11; and U.S., Congress, House, Committee on Agriculture, *Extension of Mexican Farm Labor Program: Hearings before Subcommittee on H.R. 2010*, 87th Cong., 1st sess., March 6–9 and 17, 1961, pp. 37–38 (hereafter cited as House Agriculture Committee Hearings, 1961).

Committee on Agriculture suggested a simple two-year extension of P.L. 78. The committee considered but rejected the major amendments offered by Department of Labor officials, deeming them "administratively impractical," a "dictatorial" grant of power to the secretary of labor, and a "backdoor approach" to a minimum wage for agriculture. An unaltered extension of the bracero program was suggested on the following grounds: (1) It had supplied farmers with labor that was unavailable domestically. (2) It had all but ended the wetback menace. (3) It had benefited the workers, communities, and economy of Mexico. (4) It had benefited our own economy.[45]

The committee report split the House into two antagonistic camps. H.R. 2010 lacked amendments designed to improve the lot of domestic farmworkers and was, thus, anathematic to anti-bracero congressmen. Contrariwise, supporters of the Mexican labor program considered the bill highly appropriate to the task at hand. Following the presentation of pro and con arguments by various congressmen, Representative Merwin Coad of Iowa, who had originally introduced the administration-sponsored bill, offered a series of amendments to P.L. 78. The first amendments would have prohibited the use of braceros on power-driven machinery. It was defeated by a vote of 103–75. Representative Coad next suggested that bracero usage be limited strictly to seasonal, temporary work. This amendment was rejected by better than a two-to-one majority. Undaunted, the Iowan proposed that Mexican nationals be paid either the average state or national wage for performing particular tasks. Again his amendment was soundly rejected.[46]

The anti-bracero cause was next taken up by Representative Alfred Santangelo. The New Yorker proposed that braceros be prohibited from working in all crops deemed in surplus supply. Had this proposal been adopted, it would have denied braceros to their principal employer: the cotton farmer.[47] It too was rejected by

[45] House Report No. 274, "Continuation of the Mexican Farm Labor Program," 87th Cong., 1st sess., April 24, 1961.
[46] *Congressional Record*, 107:7721–7727.
[47] Ibid., pp. 7869–7870.

a two-to-one margin. A final effort at change was contained in an amendment offered by Congressman Jeffrey Cohelan of California. He called for a gradual phasing out of the bracero program over a number of years. Like its forerunners, this amendment was rejected.[48] On May 11, 1961, by a vote of 231–157, the House approved an unaltered extension of P.L. 78 for two years. The overwhelming vote made it abundantly clear that substantial alteration or defeat of P.L. 78 in 1961 would have to overcome strong opposition in the House.

Although it had not done so since 1953, the Senate held extensive hearings on P.L. 78 during mid-June, 1961. Faced with the fact that the House had ignored its recommendations for change, the Kennedy administration dispatched Secretary of Labor Arthur Goldberg to plead its case before the Senate.[49] In addition to Mr. Goldberg, witnesses appeared to support or to condemn the administration-sponsored amendments to P.L. 78.

The argument of grower interests, and thus the case against the administration-supported amendments, was succinctly stated in lead-off testimony by Matt Triggs of the Farm Bureau.[50] His arguments in favor of extension of P.L. 78 were very similar to those offered on previous occasions, namely, the lack of available domestics, the lack of adverse effect, and the program's value to the small grower and to Mexico. In addition to defending the bracero program, Mr. Triggs was emphatic in condemning the administration-sponsored amendments to P.L. 78. He stated that further enhancement of the powers of the secretary of labor under the act was wholly unwarranted. The secretary already possessed far too much authority. The Farm Bureau was equally opposed to the requirement that employers provide employment conditions to domestics equivalent to those afforded braceros. Such a requirement was deemed unnecessary, impractical, and laden with undesirable consequences.

The Senate Committee on Agriculture and Forestry had not been

[48] Ibid., pp. 7870–7871.
[49] Senate Agriculture Committee Hearings, 1961, pp. 159–166.
[50] Ibid., pp. 5–18.

as strong a supporter of imported Mexican labor as had its counterpart in the House. Following Senate hearings on P.L. 78, the committee recommended several of the administration-supported
amendments to P.L. 78. Among other recommendations, the committee suggested that braceros should not be employed unless (1)
employers had attempted to hire domestics at "wages, standard
hours of work, and working conditions" comparable to those offered
braceros; (2) they were used only in seasonal or temporary occupations; (3) they be forbidden to operate power-driven machinery,
except in cases of undue hardship; (4) they be excluded from certain food processing activities; and (5) the employer paid both
domestics and braceros in his employment no less than the prevailing area wage.[51]

Full Senate debate on extension of P.L. 78 began on September
8, 1961. It was evident from the start that anti-bracero senators
were more numerous than at any previous time, and that they
were determined that the new administration should have all of its
amendments included as the price for extension. On the opening
day of debate, Senator Eugene McCarthy of Minnesota offered an
amendment requiring that braceros be paid at least 90 percent of
the average farm wage prevailing in the state or 90 percent of
the average national agricultural wage, whichever was the lesser.[52]
Designed to raise domestic wages in such bracero-using states as
Texas and Arkansas, Senator McCarthy's amendment was the object of two days of heated debate. It was passionately defended as
the only means of rendering acceptable an otherwise unacceptable
program. It was attacked as an attempt to indirectly legislate a
minimum wage for agriculture.[53] On September 11, 1961, the
Senate placed itself in the anti-bracero camp by the thin margin
of one vote. The McCarthy amendment was approved by a vote of

---

[51] Senate Report No. 619, "Mexican Farm Labor Program," 87th Cong., 1st
sess., July 25, 1961.

[52] *Congressional Record*, 107:18770.

[53] Ibid., pp. 18770–18792, 18803–18806, 18808, and 18898–18902.

42–41, with 17 senators not voting.[54] Another administration-backed amendment did not fare so well.

Senator Kenneth Keating of New York proposed that P.L. 78 be amended so that it required employers seeking Mexican nationals to provide domestics with working conditions similar to those offered braceros. Aware of the opposition of many uncommitted senators to such a blanket guarantee, Senator Keating proposed that the housing and health insurance benefits afforded Mexicans not be included within the meaning of "working conditions."[55] Yet despite these deletions, the amendment was attacked as being unrealistic and all but inoperable, and was defeated 49–35, with 16 senators not voting.[56] When the Senate subsequently approved extension of P.L. 78, including the changes recommended by its committee on agriculture as well as Senator McCarthy's "90 percent" formula, it placed itself fundamentally at odds with the House version. A conference was in order. Upon its decision rested the fate of imported Mexican labor.

As is the case with most conference committee decisions, the conference report on H.R. 2010 reflected a compromise on the part of both houses. The conferees recommended that P.L. 78 be extended, with amendments, for two years. Of the suggested changes, the following were particularly noteworthy: (1) Braceros were not to be made available unless "reasonable efforts" had been made to attract domestics, "at wages, standard hours of work, and working conditions comparable to those offered to foreign workers." (2) They were to be employed only in seasonal or temporary occupations, except in specific hardship cases to be determined by the secretary of labor. (3) Mexicans were to be barred from operating or maintaining "power-driven, self-propelled harvesting, planting, or cultivating machinery . . .," except in hardship cases.[57]

Both houses were asked to compromise their original positions.

---

[54] Ibid., p. 18902.   [55] Ibid., p. 18790.

[56] Ibid., pp. 18905–18906.

[57] House Report No. 1198, "Mexican Farm Labor," 87th Cong., 1st sess., September 15, 1961.

The question thus became one of degree: Which side had been asked to sacrifice the most? The House had sought unamended extension. The Senate had requested all the amendments contained in the conference report, plus the McCarthy amendment. On the surface it appeared that the House was asked to compromise more of its position than was the Senate. Yet in the eyes of anti-bracero-ists, the absence of the McCarthy amendment constituted a far greater sacrifice, one that for a time threatened to terminate nineteen years of bracero contracting.

Compared to the subsequent heated Senate debate, House consideration of the conference bill was somewhat perfunctory. For the die-hards on either side of the question, the conference report was unacceptable. Representative George Mahon of Texas contended that his constituents could not operate under such a restrictive law; they would rather have no program at all. On the other hand, Representative Merwin Coad of Iowa deemed the conference bill a true defeat for those forces seeking to improve the lot of domestic farmworkers. In his opinion, they were right back where they had started.[58] Despite such consternation on both sides of the issue, the House accepted the conference version of H.R. 2010 on a voice vote. The bill was then sent to the Senate, where it faced an uncertain future.

In his opening remarks, Senator Everett Jordan of North Carolina attempted to justify the conference bill by terming it the best possible solution under the circumstances. Aware of the strong support among anti-bracero senators for the defunct McCarthy amendment, Senator Jordan rationalized its sacrifice on the grounds that the House absolutely refused to accept the Minnesota senator's "90 percent" formula. Had the Senate conferees demanded that it be included there would have been no bracero program after December 31, 1961.[59] This solution would have been preferable to many of the senators.

The conference bill was unacceptable to both extremes within the Senate, producing a somewhat unique anomaly. Strong sup-

[58] *Congressional Record*, 107:19796–19802.
[59] Ibid., p. 20642.

porters of imported Mexican labor, such as Senators Ralph Yarborough and John Tower of Texas, declared their intention to vote against the bill. Committed anti-braceroists, such as Senators Eugene McCarthy of Minnesota, Kenneth Keating of New York, and William Proxmire of Wisconsin, also vowed to cast negative votes.[60] September, 1961, thus found friend and foe joining forces against an amended extension of P.L. 78 for diametrically opposing reasons. From the outset of Senate consideration of the conference measure it appeared that the bracero program might not be extended in any form.

On the opening day of Senate consideration, Senator McCarthy moved to table H.R. 2010. Die-hards on both sides of the issue spoke in favor of the motion. More moderate voices urged defeat of the McCarthy motion, saying that the conferees had done their best, and their best should be acceptable. Defeat of P.L. 78 would work undue hardship on employers and braceros alike. It might signal a return of the long-dormant wetback tide. The voices of moderation prevailed, but by the slim margin of six votes. The vote, like the debate, produced an anomaly. Both senators from Texas, the largest bracero-using state, voted to table. Both senators from California and Arkansas voted against tabling. One senator each from Arizona and New Mexico voted against the motion, while the other two were paired for it.[61] The vote on Senator McCarthy's motion to table H.R. 2010 produced the first significant split within the congressional ranks of bracero supporters.

Defeated in their effort to table H.R. 2010, anti-bracero senators next turned their efforts toward deferring action on the measure until the next session of Congress. They employed as their principal rationale for such action a letter from Secretary Goldberg to Senator McCarthy. In his correspondence, the secretary of labor expressed displeasure over the conference bill and suggested that inaction on the measure during the first session of the Eighty-seventh Congress would not work any undue hardship on bracero users. P.L. 78 would then expire in December, 1961, but few bra-

60 Ibid., pp. 20642–20645.
61 Ibid.

ceros were contracted during that time of year. Therefore, Congress would have time to act on the matter in the spring of 1962 and thereby make braceros available during the fall.[62]

Pro-bracero senators disagreed with the secretary's reasoning. They contended that a failure to extend P.L. 78 in 1961 would bankrupt many bracero users, promote chaos among those charged with its administration, and create hardships for Mexico and the braceros. Consideration of the question should not be postponed until the next session of Congress. The program should be either extended or terminated during 1961. Their reasoning held forth. Two motions by Senator Keating designed to put off consideration until early in 1961 were defeated.[63]

As Senate debate wore on, it became apparent that the forces opposed to H.R. 2010 were engaged in a mild filibuster against the measure. Yet, despite such delaying tactics, as well as the veiled threat of a presidential veto, the Senate finally voted to accept the conference bill and extend the bracero program to December 31, 1963. The final tally showed forty-one senators supporting extension, thirty-one opposed, and twenty-eight not voting. Texas again split with the other top four bracero-using states when its only senator present for the final vote chose to oppose the conference measure.[64] After a bitter Senate struggle, H.R. 2010 was sent to the White House. There the diplomatic ramifications of the bracero program again proved crucial.

A reluctant President Kennedy signed H.R. 2010 on October 4, 1961. The president's statement made it abundantly clear that he was sorely disappointed at the failure of Congress to further amend the act so that it bettered the lot of domestic farmworkers.

I have signed H.R. 2010 . . . I have done so despite the failure to include in the legislation provisions which I believe necessary to protect domestic farmworkers.

Studies of the operation of the Mexican labor program have clearly established that it is adversely affecting the wages, working conditions,

62 Ibid., pp. 20709–20710.
63 Ibid., pp. 20735–20757.
64 Ibid., p. 20972.

and employment opportunities of our own agricultural workers . . .
The workers most seriously affected are those from underprivileged
groups which are already at the bottom of our economic scale; the conditions under which these people work and live are a matter of grave
concern to me.[65]

In spite of its admitted adverse effect and the failure of Congress
to take steps designed to alleviate the problem, President Kennedy
acquiesced to a two-year extension of the bracero program. He
stated his reasons as follows:

I am aware, however, that some Mexican workers will still be needed next year, in some areas, to supplement our agricultural labor force.
*I am also aware of the serious impact in Mexico if many thousands of
workers employed in this country were summarily deprived of this
much-needed employment.* These considerations impel me to sign H.R.
2010 despite its shortcomings.[66]

Thus, although Mexico never stated officially in 1961 that she
opposed an abrupt termination of the bracero program, reading between the lines of the president's message reveals this opposition,
which President Kennedy was obviously aware of. Without P.L. 78
Mexico would never have permitted large numbers of her citizens
to be contracted for work on United States farms. Without it, in
short, there would have been no Mexican labor program.

While the diplomatic liability inherent in any veto of P.L. 78
weighed heavily in the president's decision to sign H.R. 2010, he
made it clear that the secretary of labor would soon move boldly
where Congress had refused to tread.

The adverse effect of the Mexican farm labor program as it has operated in recent years on the wage and employment conditions of domestic workers is clear and is cumulative in its impact. We cannot afford
to disregard it. We do not condone it. Therefore, I sign this bill with
the assurance that the Secretary of Labor will, by every means at his
disposal, use the authority vested in him under the law to prescribe the

[65] The full text of President Kennedy's remarks is contained in Lee G. Williams, "Recent Legislation Affecting the Mexican Labor Program," *Employment Security Review* 29 (February 1962):31.

[66] Ibid (italics added).

standards and to make the determinations essential for the protection of wages and working conditions of domestic agricultural workers.[67]

Summary

Late in 1961, despite strong opposition within the Senate, congressional supporters of imported Mexican labor managed to extend P.L. 78 for two years. In its amended form, the act excluded braceros from other than temporary or seasonal employment; prohibited them from operating or maintaining power-driven, self-propelled cultivating, planting, or harvesting machinery; and barred them from particular processing, packing, and canning activities. In addition, bracero employers were henceforth required to guarantee domestic farmworkers sanitary and safe working conditions equal to those afforded Mexican nationals.

On balance, the two-year extension of 1961 constituted a marginal triumph for those groups supporting imported Mexican labor. They achieved, first, an extension, which was no mean accomplishment, considering the stance of the Kennedy administration and level of Senate opposition. A close examination of the 1961 version of P.L. 78 indicates that most bracero users were not severely handicapped by the new amendments.

The provision barring braceros from year-round employment affected no more than twenty thousand Mexicans used primarily in ranching activities in Texas and New Mexico. Forbidding the Mexican national to operate particular types of self-propelled machinery was no great concession on the part of employers. Braceros would still be permitted to drive trucks and tractors under this provision. In any case, it is doubtful whether many growers entrusted the use of a $20,000 combine to the hands of a bracero. Exclusion of braceros from certain processing, canning, and packing jobs was aimed primarily at a few thousand Mexicans employed in the production phases of cotton and vegetables. The guarantee of sanitary and safe working conditions was important.

---

[67] Ibid.

It would force bracero employers to further improve the working conditions offered domestics. Still, the guarantee was a far cry from requiring bracero employers to offer native farmworkers the same package of working conditions and fringe benefits provided braceros.

The 1961 struggle over extension of P.L. 78 was another example of how the diplomatic implications of a given program may intervene to determine the fate of what was generally considered a domestic question. Had President Kennedy not been conscious of the bracero program's impact on Mexico, its rural inhabitants, and United States–Mexican relations, he might have vetoed H.R. 2010.

From a purely domestic perspective, the mounting pressure against bracero importation was clearly evidenced at three levels. First, there was the position taken by the new administration against any extension of P.L. 78 unless amended to better protect native farm labor from the adverse effects of imported labor. A second indicator was the narrow passage of H.R. 2010 over the strong objections of an ever-increasing number of anti-bracero senators. Third, and perhaps most important, was the continued proliferation of anti-bracero interest groups.

To the previously mentioned list of groups seeking either an end to or fundamental alteration of the bracero program were added, in 1961, the following names:[68]

United Papermakers and Paperworkers, AFL-CIO
American Veterans Committee
Board of National Missions of the Evangelical and Reformed Church
National Board of the Young Women's Christian Association
United Church Women of Michigan
Bishops' Committee for Migrant Workers
Commission on Christian Social Action of the Evangelical United Brethren Church

[68] House Agriculture Committee Hearings, 1961; and *Congressional Record*, 107:18779, 20735, and 20736.

Bishops' Committee for the Spanish Speaking
Workers Defense League
Christian Family Movement
New York State Citizens Committee on Farm Labor
Colorado Federation of Latin American Groups
Association of California Consumers
Illinois Federation of Mexican-American Organizations
Texas Committee on Migrant Farm Workers
Council for Christian Social Action
National Association of Social Workers

Equally important to the eventual fate of P.L. 78 was the 1961 desertion of the National Grange from the pro-bracero ranks. The Grange sensed that the program was being used as a means to establish wage rates in domestic agriculture. Fred Bailey, legislative consultant to the nation's second most powerful group, observed: "The Grange does not believe that continued extensions of Public Law 78 are in the best interests of a majority of American farmers. We doubt that it is in the long-run best interest of even a minority.

Too many of us in agriculure have leaned too long on Public Law 78 as a crutch—as an excuse for failure to take positive steps which would make the program unnecessary."[69]

Withdrawal by the Grange left the Farm Bureau as the only national farm organization wholeheartedly supporting the bracero program in 1961. Such action was clearly not based on altruistic grounds. With the federal government becoming increasingly involved in the area of domestic farm labor by way of a foreign labor program, the Grange chose to disassociate itself from the program rather than risk deeper governmental involvement. Perhaps the Grange sensed correctly that the degree of involvement had really only begun. Subsequent actions by the Labor Department proved that President Kennedy was not just speaking for public consumption when, in reluctantly signing H.R. 2010, he promised a more vigorous role by the federal government in the field of agricultural labor.

[69] House Agriculture Committee Hearings, 1961, p. 28.

THE 1963 EXTENSION OF PUBLIC LAW 78

With the president's signature in October, 1961, the Mexican labor act was extended two years and scheduled to expire December 31, 1963. Congressional efforts aimed at what was to be the final extension of P.L. 78 did not begin until early in 1963. In the interim, the Kennedy administration moved to counteract the adverse effect of bracero contracting on the wages and working conditions of domestic farmworkers.

The Bracero Agreement of 1961

Oddly enough, one of the first steps taken to counteract the ills associated with the importation of Mexican nationals came at the international level. The bracero agreement of August 31, 1959,[70] originally scheduled to expire June 30, 1961, had been extended to December 31, 1961,[71] and then to January 31, 1962.[72] Late in December, 1961, the United States and Mexico agreed to extend the pact to December 31, 1963, a date coincident with the expiration of P.L. 78. The agreement became effective on February 1, 1962. In its revised form the 1962 extension contained numerous additions and clarifications, four of which reflected the recent amendments to P.L. 78 aimed at adverse effect.[73]

First, braceros were prohibited, except under certain conditions, from remaining in the United States for more than six months. In no case could they remain for more than nine months. Second, occupational insurance benefits for braceros were increased. Third, and perhaps most important, bracero wages were to be no less than the amount set by the secretary of labor in an effort to avoid adverse effect. Fourth, detailed criteria were included to govern the removal of braceros involved in strikes or lockouts.

The latter provision was the result of a series of strikes by California farmworkers in which braceros were involved. The Depart-

---

[70] U.S., Department of State, TIAS 4310; hereafter cited as TIAS.
[71] TIAS 4815.
[72] TIAS 4913.
[73] TIAS, 5160.

ment of Labor became entangled in the disputes because of its administrative responsibilities under the Mexican labor agreement. Contained in the 1951 accord was the stipulation prohibiting employment of braceros during strikes or lockouts. The secretary of labor was empowered to remove braceros already on the job when a strike or lockout occurred if he felt the action seriously affected the operations in which they were engaged.[74] On several occasions during the period 1961–1962 the question of the relationship between braceros and lockouts arose.[75] From the viewpoint of organized labor, Mexican nationals were being used as strikebreakers. Growers contended that the union activities did not constitute bona fide strikes and, therefore, did not affect bracero employment. They claimed the unions arranged phony strikes in which domestics would hire on only to walk off the job immediately, insisting that braceros be removed.[76] The 1962 amendments to Article 22 of the Mexican labor agreement were designed to clarify the position of the Labor Department in such borderline cases. According to the revised provisions, a strike or lockout was legitimate if the secretary of labor determined that 50 percent of the domestic workers on a given farm were on strike or locked out.[77]

Statewide Adverse Effect Rates

Under terms of the revised agreement of 1962, the secretary of labor was empowered to set bracero wages at levels designed to prevent adverse effect.[78] In March, 1962, following hearings held in Washington, Secretary of Labor Goldberg instituted statewide adverse-effect rates for the twenty-four states utilizing braceros.[79] These rates ranged from sixty cents to one dollar an hour and con-

[74] TIAS 2331, p. 1979.

[75] "California's Farm Labor Problems," *Farm Labor Developments*, August, 1963, pp. 12–15; *Hispanic American Report* 14(May 1961):200; *New York Times*, May 28 and 30, 1961.

[76] "California's Farm Labor Problems," p. 14.

[77] TIAS 5160, pp. 2032–2034.

[78] Ibid., pp. 2028–2029.

[79] "Adverse Effect Actions, 1962," *Farm Labor Developments*, May, 1963, pp. 11–13; and *New York Times*, March 30, 1962.

stituted the minimum that growers in particular states could offer in their effort to secure braceros. Prior to the 1962 policy, employers seeking braceros had been required to offer only the prevailing area wage. As of March, 1962, these same individuals were forced to offer at least the statewide average wage. In particular bracero-using regions, the statewide average wage was considerably higher than the area wage. In effect, the new formula was clearly designed to force employers to bid higher for the services of domestic farmworkers. While it constituted somewhat of a departure from prior departmental policy, the 1962 decision was not without precedent.

Actions taken by the secretary of labor to implement his adverse-effect authority under P.L. 78 and the bracero agreement dated back as far as 1953. In that year, Arizona cotton farmers seeking Mexicans were required to pay not less than three dollars for each hundred pounds of cotton picked.[80] In 1956 and 1958 employers were informed by the Labor Department that payment to braceros of wages appreciably lower than those paid by non-bracero users would be deemed an indication of adverse effect.[81] Also in 1958, the Department of Labor promulgated the "40 percent" formula for braceros employed on an hourly basis, and the "90-10" formula for those engaged in piece-rate tasks.[82]

Particularly relevant to the statewide adverse-effect rulings of 1962 was the decision of a federal district court involving bracero employers in New Mexico. In the spring of 1961, the Labor Department determined that growers in Dona Ana County, New Mexico, who employed Mexicans as tractor drivers, irrigators, and general farmworkers would have to pay them not less than the wages found to be prevailing by a government-sponsored survey. The growers considered the action an illegal effort by the secretary of labor to fix farm wages and filed suit against Secretary Goldberg. In its decision, the court upheld the secretary's authority—under

[80] Harold H. Dellon, "The Adverse-Effect Policy for Agricultural Labor," *Farm Labor Developments*, August, 1966, p. 16.

[81] Ibid., pp. 16–17.

[82] See pp. 152–153.

the adverse-effect provisions of the Mexican labor agreement—to determine what wages bracero employers would have to offer.[83]

As a result of the statewide adverse-effect order in March, 1962, the prevailing-wage concept, long the basis of conflict among friend and foe of bracero importation, was clarified. Employers seeking braceros would henceforth be required to offer them, and thus in effect offer domestics, not less than the adverse-effect wage rates for their particular states. The action of Secretary Goldberg early in 1962 constituted a crucial step in the new administration's drive to eliminate the adverse effects associated with bracero importation. Employment of Mexican nationals became far less attractive after March, 1962.

The Changing Bracero Scene, 1959–1962

The statewide adverse-effect policy of 1962 clearly reflected the desire of the Kennedy administration to fully implement the 1961 amendments to P.L. 78 and the Mexican labor agreements. Coincident with the rapid development of cotton mechanization, the adverse-effect policies of the late 1950's and early 1960's radically altered the character of imported Mexican farm labor.

Cotton harvesting had long employed the great majority of imported Mexican nationals. With the advent of adverse-effect regulations, more and more cotton growers turned to mechanized harvesting. In 1956, only 27 percent of all United States cotton was mechanically harvested. By 1959, the figure had risen to 43 percent. In 1961, it was 59 percent. During 1962, 70 percent of all United States cotton was machine harvested.[84]

Even more pertinent to the bracero program, as the figures in Table I reveal, was the increased mechanization of cotton harvesting in the five principal bracero-using states.[85] As a result of ac-

---

[83] *Dona Ana County Farm and Livestock Bureau et al. v. Goldberg et al.*, 200 F. Supp. 210 (D.D.C. 1961). An excellent review of the case is contained in William J. Haltigan, "A Federal Court Looks at the Mexican Program," *Employment Security Review* 29 (May 1962):19–21.

[84] *The Cotton Situation*, May, 1961, p. 42; and May, 1965, p. 21.

[85] Ibid.

TABLE I
Percentage of Cotton Harvested Mechanically in Selected States, 1956–1962

State	1956	1957	1958	1959	1960	1961	1962
California	66	70	71	83	87	93	94
Texas	25	37	35	44	58	64	78
Arizona	45	54	51	62	73	84	92
New Mexico	21	19	38	50	64	73	91
Arkansas	27	15	22	36	42	51	68

celerated cotton mechanization, in combination with the government's adverse-effect policy, the annual number of braceros fell sharply in the late 1950's and early 1960's. In 1956, a record number of 445,197 braceros were imported. In 1959, the figure showed little change and stood at 437,543. Yet by 1960, the number had fallen to 315,846. In 1961, 291,420 braceros were contracted. In 1962, the first year of statewide adverse-effect rulings, only 194,978 Mexicans were contracted for work on United States farms. The 1962 figure was a reduction of approximately 67 percent from the previous year.[86]

Equally revealing was the regional shift in bracero concentration during these years. As a result of accelerated mechanization and increased governmental vigilance, California replaced Texas as the leading contractor of bracero labor, as shown in Table II. In 1962 alone, the number of braceros contracted by Texas growers fell more than 77,000 from the preceding year.[87] Thus, as the congressional supporters of imported Mexican labor renewed their efforts to extend P.L. 78 early in 1963, the entire bracero scene had changed markedly since the last renewal in 1961. The total number of bracero importees had been reduced by around 100,000. California had replaced Texas as the leading bracero contractor. Of even greater importance to the group conflict surrounding imported Mexican farm labor was the accelerated mechanization of the cot-

[86] "Long-Term Trends in Foreign-Worker Employment: Table 3, Foreign Workers Admitted for Temporary Employment in U.S. Agriculture," *Farm Labor Developments*, February, 1968, p. 10; hereafter cited as "Foreign Workers Admitted for Temporary Employment."

[87] "Employment of Foreign Workers in 1963," *Farm Labor Developments*, March, 1964, p. 10.

TABLE II
Number of Braceros Contracted in California and Texas, 1960–1962

State	1960	1961	1962
California	112,995	98,733	116,455
Texas	122,755	117,368	30,152

ton harvest. As machines replaced the bracero in the cotton fields, the supporters of Mexican labor were deprived of one of their principal arguments in behalf of bracero importation.

The Final Extension of Public Law 78

Hearings on extension of the Mexican labor act began in March, 1963. As testimony was presented by friend and foe of imported farm labor, three discernible patterns emerged. There was, on the one hand, the staunchly anti-bracero position that called for an end to the program. In the eyes of such groups as the AFL-CIO, the National Advisory Committee on Farm Labor, and the National Council of Churches, the time for termination had come. No type of amendment to P.L. 78 could render acceptable any further extension.[88] It had long since outlived its usefulness, if indeed it had ever possessed such a virtue.

A second position, and one diametrically opposed to that of the anti-bracero group, was assumed by the longtime supporters of imported Mexican labor. In the eyes of such groups as the Farm Bureau, the Vegetable Growers Association of America, and the National Farm Labor Users Committee, a two-year extension, with amendments, was called for.[89] As might have been expected, the suggested amendments were directed toward the archenemy of agribusiness, the secretary of labor.

As introduced by Congressman E. C. Gathings of Arkansas. H.R. 2009 called for a two-year extension of P.L. 78. It included. in addition, three provisions aimed at curbing the power of the secretary

[88] U.S., Congress, House, Committee on Agriculture, *Mexican Farm Labor Program: Hearings before Subcommittee on H.R. 1836 and H.R. 2009*, 88th Cong., 1st sess., March 27, 28, and 29, 1963, pp. 192–202, 143–158, and 262–268 (hereafter cited as House Agriculture Committee Hearings, 1963).

[89] Ibid., pp. 29–38, 92–96, and 102–105.

of labor. First, the meaning of "temporary or seasonal occupations" was to be defined in such a way as to curtail the secretary's authority over year-round contracting, which he had been granted under the 1961 amendments to P.L. 78 and the revised international agreement of February, 1962. Second, the provision on the use of braceros for the operation or maintenance of power-driven machinery was to be redefined so that it halted the actions taken by the secretary of labor under terms of the 1961 amendments to P.L. 78. Third, the phrase "adverse effect" was to be defined so that it negated the statewide adverse-effect policy inaugurated in March, 1962.[90] In short, the secretary of labor had, in the two years since P.L. 78 had last been extended, proceeded to exercise his authority to the fullest extent. The forces of agribusiness were bent on reducing that authority.

A third approach to P.L. 78, and one favored by the administration, was a compromise between the two polar positions. In testimony before the House Agriculture Committee, Secretary of Labor Willard Wirtz suggested a one-year extension, provided that one crucial amendment was added. The administration felt that there did exist a genuine lack of stoop labor in particular areas of the country, thereby necessitating some bracero contracting. Still, the bracero program, by its very nature, produced adverse effects. Therefore, it was recommended that the act be extended only if it were amended to require employers seeking Mexicans to offer domestics working conditions comparable to those afforded braceros. The phrase "working conditions" was to include workmen's compensation or occupational insurance, housing, and transportation guarantees comparable to those provided braceros.[91] As its asking price for extension, the administration thus requested that native farmworkers be afforded the same benefits provided foreigners. Such an amendment had failed to clear the House on previous occasions. 1963 was to prove no exception.

In its report, the House Committee on Agriculture also assumed a compromise stance. It was, however, a decidedly grower-oriented

[90] Ibid., pp. 1–2.
[91] Ibid., pp. 2–29.

compromise. By a 28–4 vote, the committee recommended a two-year, unamended extension.[92] The Gathings bill, with its three anti–secretary of labor amendments, was thereby rejected, as was the administration proposal. The committee espoused the traditional arguments in favor of bracero importation and thus rejected the call by Secretary Wirtz to equalize working conditions for domestics and braceros. In so doing, the committee went out of its way to criticize the secretary of labor for his past actions in the area of adverse effect.

The Secretary of Labor had recently been setting wage rates for Mexican nationals (which also must be paid to domestic workers by employers of nationals) which he euphemistically calls "the wage to prevent adverse effect." The committee has viewed this action with great concern because, under the guise of making a determination relating to the wages of Mexican workers, the Secretary of Labor actually is establishing a minimum wage for domestic agricultural labor. Clearly it was never the intention of Congress to give the Secretary such authority.[93]

Thus, despite a vigorous minority dissent by three members,[94] the House Agriculture Committee overwhelmingly endorsed an unamended two-year extension of P.L. 78. Yet, to the surprise of all concerned, the full House completely reversed its previous form and, on March 29, 1963, voted not to grant the Mexican labor act a two-year lease on life. With the vote crossing party lines, and 100 members not voting, H.R. 5497 was defeated 174–158.[95] While Texas representatives voted rather solidly in favor of the bill,[96] the California delegation was split badly on the measure. With some of

[92] House Report No. 274, "Continuation of Mexican Farm Labor Program," 88th Cong., 1st sess., May 6, 1963.

[93] Ibid., p. 7.

[94] The three congressmen signing the minority report were Benjamin Rosenthal of New York, Alec Olson of Minnesota, and Spark Matsunaga of Hawaii (Ibid., pp. 10–18).

[95] Of the 158 congressmen voting for extension, 80 were Democrats and 78 were Republicans. Contrariwise, 121 Democrats and 53 Republicans voted against H.R. 5497 (*Congressional Record*, 109:9833–9834).

[96] The most notable exception was Representative Henry Gonzalez of San Antonio who led the floor fight against extension (Ibid., 109:9809).

the most vociferous defenders and critics of the bracero program representing California, eighteen of its congressmen voted for the two-year extension, while twelve voted against.[97]

Grower reaction to the House vote was outspoken and negative. Many predicted calamity. They forecast disaster for vegetable and fruit growers in the Southwest, reduced plantings, and a sharp rise in consumer food prices.[98] "At stake in California are a $180 million tomato crop, a good part of the $348 million annual cotton crop, the multimillion dollar beet crop, the $36 million strawberry crop, the $38 million melon crop, the $28 million asparagus crop."[99]

Whereas the reaction of bracero employers to the defeat of H.R. 5497 was predictable, the Mexican response was somewhat surprising and far more important to the bracero program's survival. Initial Mexican reaction was ambivalent and thus in keeping with the long-held official governmental position toward the bracero program. While he admitted that an end to bracero importation would constitute "a problem of some importance" for both countries, Secretary of the Interior Gustavo Díaz Ordaz contended that Mexico, since it had never viewed the program as permanent, would go along with whatever decision the United States government reached on the matter. The secretary seemed primarily concerned that the host country provide a more adequate program for Mexican citizens if she decided to continue recruitment.[100]

Federal Deputy Everardo Varela responded to the decision by the House in a similar fashion. He noted that termination of the program would cause "immediate social problems for particular sectors of the rural population," but he assured the press that Mexico possessed the resources and ability to handle any such problems

[97] Ibid., 9833–9834. The bracero question had, in fact, split California's Democratic party leadership, with Governor Edmund Brown supporting extension and Jess Unruh, powerful leader of the Democrat-controlled state assembly, opposing further importation (*Hispanic American Report* 16[July 1963]:432).

[98] *New York Times*, May 31 and August 18, 1963; *Hispanic American Report* 16(August 1963):549; and *Congressional Record*, 109:15208–15209.

[99] Editorial in the *Fresno Bee*, June 5, 1963, as quoted in the *Congressional Record*, 109:15208.

[100] *Hispano Americano*, June 10, 1963, p. 10.

in the long run.[101] *El Universal* editorialized that, with the projected opening of some 120,000 hectares of land in the tropical zone, Mexico could employ those who might be displaced by termination of the program.[102] Perhaps the initial Mexican reaction was best summed up by columnist Carlos Ortiz. He surmised that, while Mexico would feel some initial pangs of readjustment, she would muddle through because of her expertise at the art of *echarle un hueso más al caldo*, that is, "throwing another bone in the pot."[103]

Although she initially assumed an ambivalent, if not lighthearted, attitude toward the demise of H.R. 5497, Mexico soon made known officially that she did not want the bracero program to be abruptly terminated. In a diplomatic dispatch of June 21, 1963, which was not made public until August 15, when Senator William Fulbright of Arkansas had it placed in the *Congressional Record*, Ambassador Antonio Carillo Flores revealed the true Mexican reaction.[104] The Mexican government opposed any sudden termination of the program for five reasons.

First, an abrupt end to legalized contracting would not mean an end to the northward migration of Mexican workers. Instead, it would signal a return of the wetback problem.

It is not to be expected that the termination of an international agreement governing and regulating the rendering of service of Mexican workers in the United States will put an end to that type of seasonal migration. The aforesaid agreement is not the cause of that migration; it is the effect or result of the migratory phenomenon. Therefore, the absence of an agreement would not end the problem but rather would give rise to a de facto situation: the illegal introduction of Mexican workers into the United States.[105]

A second basis of Mexican opposition lay in her concern over the growing number of permanent emigrees to the United States. As the number of contracted braceros had dropped from 1959 to 1962, there had been a corresponding increase in the number of

101 *El Universal*, June 2, 1963.
102 Ibid., May 31, 1963.
103 "La cuestion de los braceros" (Ibid., June 4, 1963).
104 *Congressional Record*, 109:15203–15204.
105 Ibid., 15204.

Mexican farmworkers applying for and obtaining resident visas to come to the United States. Ambassador Carillo Flores indicated that thirty thousand such Mexicans migrated to the United States in 1961, and some forty thousand in 1962. Mexico was thus concerned lest an abrupt end to P.L. 78 cause a damaging flood tide of permanent visa applications within Mexico's agricultural sector.[106]

Another reason for continuing the program was said to be its salutary effects on the United States farmworkers. "It is not considered that the contracting of Mexican workers under the international agreement has produced unfavorable effects on American workers. Quite the contrary. The benefits granted the contracted braceros . . . have provided a pattern that can be followed for domestic workers who lack such protection."[107]

The fourth, and in all likelihood the paramount, reason for Mexican concern over termination of bracero recruitment revolved around the program's economic impact.

It should be considered that on various occasions when at international meetings on migrant worker problems representatives of the Government of the United States have indicated their purpose of decreasing the contracting until the elimination point is reached, the Mexican representatives have requested that an attempt be made to make the decrease gradually, in order to give Mexico an opportunity to reabsorb the workers who have habitually been working in the United States and thus stave off the sudden crisis that would come from an increase in national unemployment. The stoppage of the contracts at the start of 1964 would leave approximately 200,000 persons out of work.[108]

What the ambassador did not say, but what was understood by all students of the bracero program, was that each bracero supported an average of four persons. An end to recruitment would mean that 800,000 Mexicans would be faced with the prospect of going hungry.[109] President López Mateos and the members of

---

[106] Ibid.
[107] Ibid.
[108] Ibid.
[109] *Hispanic American Report* 16(July 1963):433; and 16(August 1963):548.

Mexico's governing elite were obviously well aware of pressures emanating from the marginal, ever-restless peasant sector in support of continued bracero contracting. As had been the case throughout its history, the potentially explosive demands of the Mexican peasant weighed heavily in the decision of the Mexican government to overtly support a continuation of the bracero program.

▬ Fifth, and closely associated with Mexico's opposition to termination on economic grounds, was the bracero program's diplomatic impact. It had proved beneficial to both nations. More specifically from the Mexican perspective, the program had led to a "virtual extinction of discrimination against and segregation of persons of Mexican nationality in areas of the United States where such practices once existed" "There is no doubt," the note concluded, "that this has been a firm foundation for the good relations between the peoples of the two countries."[110]

▬ In giving these five reasons against termination of the bracero program, the Mexican government, perhaps unknowingly, placed itself in league with grower interests in the United States. Thus, Mexico was largely responsible for the final extension of P.L. 78.

Defeated in the House, supporters of Mexican labor turned elsewhere in their efforts to salvage an extension of P.L. 78. California Governor Edmund Brown, who had previously given strong endorsement to pro-bracero testimony by a California delegation before the House Agriculture Committee,[111] reportedly urged President Kennedy not to let the program die in 1963.[112] While numerous extension bills were being introduced in both houses, Senator Fulbright, advised of the Mexican note of June 21, came out in favor of extension.[113]

As a result of both domestic and foreign pressure, the Senate Committee on Agriculture reported on July 22 in favor of an unamended one-year extension of the bracero act. Rationalizing in

---

[110] *Congressional Record*, 109:15204.
[111] House Agriculture Committee Hearings, 1963, pp. 55–65.
[112] *Hispanic American Report* 16(August 1963):549.
[113] Ibid.

much the same way as its counterpart in the House had, the Senate committee leaned heavily on the testimony of Labor Secretary Wirtz in calling for a one-year prolongation. The committee, for essentially the same reasons put forth by the House Agriculture Committee in its report of May 6, 1963, refused, however, to accept the administration-sponsored amendments designed to equalize the working conditions of domestics and foreigners.[114]

Senate consideration of S. 1703 was delayed, however, as a result of some adroit parliamentary maneuvering by a longtime opponent of imported labor. When the measure originally came up for consideration on July 31, Senator William Proxmire of Wisconsin raised a point of order concerning the absence of a quorum during actual voting on the bill by the Senate Agriculture Committee. This rare and technical challenge to the authority of a committee chairman was upheld, despite the heated protests of Chairman Ellender.[115] S. 1703 was thus again referred to committee, reported for a second time on August 6,[116] and finally brought before the Senate on August 15.

As had been the case with previous considerations of P.L. 78, Senate debate centered around the merits and demerits of the bracero program. Senator Eugene McCarthy of Minnesota lived up to his past performances as a leader of the Senate's anti-bracero wing by again introducing the administration-sponsored amendment.[117] In his call for equal working conditions for domestics and braceros, Senator McCarthy relied heavily on testimony by Under Secretary of Labor John Hennings before a subcommittee of the Senate Labor Committee. Secretary Hennings, despite terming P.L. 78 a "wretched law" and a "betrayal" of domestic farmworkers, supported a one-year extension, *provided* that the administration amendment was included. Such an amendment was deemed neces-

---

[114] Senate Report No. 372, "Extension of Mexican Farm Labor Program," 88th Cong., 1st sess., July 22, 1963.

[115] *Congressional Record*, 109:13791.

[116] Senate Report No. 391, "Extension of Mexican Farm Labor Program," 88th Cong., 1st sess., August 6, 1963.

[117] *Congressional Record*, 109:15190.

sary, because without it the secretary of labor could not possibly provide equal working conditions by administrative fiat. Only Congress could equalize these conditions by amending P.L. 78.[118]

History repeated itself when a slightly modified version of the original McCarthy amendment carried by a narrow margin of 44–43, with 12 senators not voting.[119] At this juncture, Senator Fulbright, who had himself sponsored a bill calling for a three-year phase out of bracero contracting, introduced for Senate consideration the June 21 dispatch of Ambassador Carillo Flores.[120] The Arkansas senator then suggested that, had they realized how important the bracero program was to Mexico, perhaps many of the senators who had supported the McCarthy amendment would not have done so.[121] It had become clear during House debates of 1961 and 1963 that the lower chamber would not accept the so-called equal-conditions amendment. If this were to be the Senate's asking price for extension, the bracero program was doomed.

Senator Thomas Kuchel of California joined Senator Fulbright in stressing the diplomatic ramifications of imported labor. Recalling his experiences during the third Mexico–United States Interparliamentary Conference, the Californian observed that "every Mexican representing a district or a state in Mexico and every American there—both Democrats and Republicans—voted unanimously that it was in the interests of both countries that this program be continued."[122]

Other pro-bracero senators joined in expressing support for extension of P.L. 78 on diplomatic grounds. Senator John Tower of Texas observed: "We are denying a number of underprivileged Mexican people work that they need and desire . . . If we should kill the program we would deny the satisfaction of a great need to

[118] Ibid., p. 15194.
[119] Ibid., p. 15202.
[120] Ibid., pp. 15203–15204.
[121] Ibid., p. 15207.
[122] Ibid. Evidence to substantiate Senator Kuchel's remarks is contained in Report of the Senate Delegation, "Mexican–United States Interparliamentary Group," 88th Cong., 1st sess., December 2, 1963, pp. 10–11.

people who would be our best friends—the people of the great Republic of Mexico."[123]

Senator Barry Goldwater of Arizona, soon to be the Republican presidential nominee, emphasized the program's diplomatic importance. "I have yet to meet a Mexican official who has not told me that this is the most constructive thing that the United States has ever done to better the relationship between our countries."[124]

Yet despite these and other pro-bracero arguments which, in effect, equated the bracero program with one of foreign aid, a motion by Senator Ellender to reconsider the vote on the McCarthy amendment was defeated on a tie vote when Senator McCarthy moved to table.[125] At this stage in the Senate's consideration of S. 1703, the words of Father James Vizzard, S.J., director of the National Catholic Rural Life Conference, appeared to hold the most appeal for a majority of senators. "Why should the poorest people in the United States, our domestic farmworkers, be required to carry a burden of a purported foreign aid program, which if conducted, and it should be conducted, should be paid out of the tax funds of the general citizenry. We are for assistance to Mexico, but not at the cost of the poorest people in the United States."[126]

After one day's consideration the Senate voted 65–25 to pass S. 1703, which included the hotly debated McCarthy amendment.[127] The many Senate votes on the issue defied party labels and divided instead along liberal-conservative lines. Those voting against the McCarthy amendment were either conservative Republicans or southern Democrats, while those in favor were either liberal Republicans or northern Democrats. A hard-core group of eighteen senators was opposed to any extension, while twenty or more favored only a one-year, fundamentally amended extension.[128] Any prolongation of P.L. 78, minus the administration

[123] *Congressional Record*, 109:15210.
[124] Ibid., p. 15212.
[125] Ibid., p. 15213.
[126] Ibid., p. 15215.
[127] Ibid., p. 15219.
[128] *Hispanic American Report* 16(October 1963):753–754.

amendment, would have to overcome a growing number of anti-bracero senators.

After the Senate action of August 15, the next move was left up to the House. Following a one-day hearing on August 21, the Subcommittee on Equipment, Supplies, and Manpower of the House Committee on Agriculture refused to accept the McCarthy amendment and recommended, instead, a simple, unamended one-year extension.[129] Despite its abbreviated length, the August 21 hearing was important for two reasons: (1) Domestically, it illustrated once again with great clarity the contradictory, dual nature of the bracero program during its latter years.[130] (2) Internationally, the hearing revealed the State Department's growing concern that the program might end in 1963.[131]

In its report of September 6, the full House Committee on Agriculture followed the advice of its subcommittee by recommending a one-year unamended extension of P.L. 78. The committee rejected outright, for essentially the same reasons it had put forth in its previous report of May 6,[132] the administration-sponsored McCarthy amendment.

In a response to the majority's decision in favor of unamended extension, the four dissenting committee members issued an elaborate, stinging minority report.[133] Terming the one-year extension a "farce," the minority report charged P.L. 78 with a multitude of sins. It contended that the Mexican labor program (1) disadvantaged United States workers, (2) caused poverty, (3) ran counter to the free enterprise system, (4) abetted rural unemploy-

---

[129] *New York Times*, August 22, 1963.

[130] For an excellent illustration of the seemingly irreconcilable arguments surrounding P.L. 78 in 1963, note the testimony of Millard Cass, deputy under secretary of labor (U.S., Congress, House, Committee on Agriculture, *Extend the Mexican Farm Labor Program: Hearing before Subcommittee on H.R. 7185, H.R. 7191, and S. 1703*, 88th Cong., 1st sess., August 21, 1963, pp. 5–38).

[131] Statement of Robert M. Sayre, acting director, Office of Caribbean and Mexican Affairs, Department of State (Ibid., pp. 38–41).

[132] House Report No. 722, "One-Year Extension of Mexican Farm Labor Program," 88th Cong., 1st sess., September 6, 1963, pp. 1–19.

[133] Ibid., pp. 20–34.

ment, (5) aided large farms and hurt family farms, and (6) subsidized bracero users. The report maintained further that (1) domestics were available for stoop labor if greater benefits were offered, (2) growers opposed recruitment of natives, and recruitment was thus inadequate, (3) termination of P.L. 78 would not harm consumers, (4) Mexico opposed the program, (5) ex-braceros were easy communist prey, and (6) P.L. 78 did not end the wetback problem. The minority report concluded with a strong moral condemnation of imported Mexican farm labor. "Public Law 78 is a bad law. It is an immoral law. It is a Government program which uses one poverty-stricken group of men to compete against another poverty-stricken group to create still more poverty. It violates the basic beliefs of our Nation."[134]

Consideration on the floor of the House of an unamended, one-year extension began October 31, 1963. Debate for and against the measure tended to conform to the majority and minority opinions expressed in the September 6 report of the House Agriculture Committee. Anti-bracero representatives offered three separate amendments designed (1) to assure a phase out of P.L. 78 by the end of 1964, (2) to prohibit the use of braceros in surplus crops, and (3) to afford domestics working conditions equal to those granted braceros. Each was defeated by a majority of at least twenty votes. After one day's debate, a simple one-year extension was approved by a vote of 173-160, with 94 representatives not voting.[135]

From the welter of pro and con arguments, four facts emerged from what proved to be the final House debate over the Mexican labor act. First, in their effort to secure extension, pro-bracero congressmen relied heavily on diplomatic and consumer-price arguments. They contended that defeat of P.L. 78 would be bad for United States–Mexican relations and bad for the price-conscious housewife.[136]

Second, opposition to P.L. 78 was based primarily on moral

[134] Ibid., p. 34.
[135] *Congressional Record*, 109:20698–20731.
[136] Ibid.

grounds. Not only was the act deemed disadvantageous to the domestic farmworker, but the entire bracero program was also condemned as immoral. According to one representative, the over-riding characteristic of bracero labor was that it constituted a "question of morals."[137] In the eyes of another, bracero labor was slave labor: "This is a slave bill . . . It is a slave labor bill . . . Many of us thought that Lincoln freed the slaves about 100 years ago, but if we want to continue this kind of operation and continue this kind of slave labor in this country, as we have since 1951, we will be looking for another Abraham Lincoln after 1968."[138]

Third, lobbying in behalf of prolongation reached a high point during House consideration. Representative John Fogarty of Rhode Island observed: "In the 23 years I have been a member of this Congress I have never been lobbied by so many high-handed, brazen lobbyists as I have in the past 3 or 4 weeks in behalf of extension of Public Law 78."[139]

Fourth, and most important, it became evident from the statements of congressmen on both sides of the question that this was to be the final extension of issue. "I plan," observed Representative Albert Quie of Minnesota, "to vote for this 1-year extension and that is the end of my support for this program."[140] Representative Melvin Laird of Wisconsin stated, "I am going to support this 1-year extension with the understanding that the program will be terminated."[141] Such opinions were substantiated during Senate consideration.

In his lead-off statement before the upper chamber, Senator Allen Ellender of Louisiana, the man generally credited with being the architect of P.L. 78, made it clear that, if granted, this would indeed be the final prolongation of the Mexican labor act.

---

137 Remarks of Representative Spark Matsunaga of Hawaii (Ibid., 109:20700).
138 Remarks of Representative John Fogarty of Rhode Island (Ibid., 109: 20707).
139 Ibid.
140 Ibid., 109:20704.
141 Ibid., 20708.

"If that is done, all persons will be on notice that, beginning in 1965, other methods will have to be used to provide for stoop labor. What they will be, I am unable to say at this time. However, the farmers will at least be warned in advance."[142]

As their counterparts in the House had done previously, anti-bracero senators expressed doubts about the final nature of any extension. "It has been said," observed Senator Harrison Williams of New Jersey, "that the poor are always with us; I am beginning to think that the braceros will always be with us."[143] Yet, despite such skepticism and despite repeated contentions that the Mexican labor act had fostered a system of "involuntary servitude"[144] and "rented 'slaves,' "[145] the Senate, on December 4, 1964, agreed to a one-year, unamended extension of P.L. 78.[146] On December 20, the international agreement with Mexico was extended to December 31, 1964.[147] The bracero program was thus granted its final lease on life.

Summary

On May 29, 1963, when the House of Representatives voted not to extend P.L. 78, it appeared that the bracero program would end as of December 31, 1963. At this stage, however, a fundamental change occurred in the long-held Mexican attitude of official ambivalence toward bracero contracting. Analysis of President Kennedy's remarks in signing the 1961 extension of P.L. 78 revealed the presence of subtle, behind-the-scenes Mexican pressure in favor of prolongation.[148] There was nothing subtle in the Mexican

---

[142] Ibid., 23155.

[143] Ibid., 23163. In a similar vein, note the observation of Representative John Kyl of Iowa: "We have made more progress in phasing out prayer in the last 3 or 4 years than we have in phasing out the bracero program" (Ibid., 109: 20706).

[144] Remarks of Senator Paul Douglas of Illinois (Ibid., 109:23156).

[145] Remarks of Senator Eugene McCarthy of Minnesota (Ibid., 109:23156).

[146] Ibid., 109:23223.

[147] TIAS 5492.

[148] See p. 173.

action of June, 1963. Combined with pressure from domestic growers, the Mexican stance of 1963 ensured the bracero program an additional year's longevity. Had it not been for its diplomatic ramifications, the bracero program would not have been extended beyond 1963, and perhaps not beyond 1961. Theoretically, this development provides an important insight for the student of interest groups and the foreign policy process. In the event of stalemate or relative balance among competing domestic forces, pressure from the international environment may prove decisive.

A majority of southwestern employers appeared to grudgingly accept the fact that after 1964 large-scale bracero contracting would be a thing of the past.[149] Though obviously concerned, Mexico too, as she had always said she would, recognized the United States decision as final.[150] Some growers, however, refused to accept the inevitable and continued to pressure for a "final" extension of P.L. 78.[151] Their efforts were in vain.

Congressional supporters of bracero labor were earnest when, in 1963, they promised no further efforts to extend P.L. 78. They realized that political reality dictated an end to the program. The extensions of 1961 and 1963 had been achieved by the narrowest of margins and then only with an invaluable assist from the international environment. Adverse-effect policies promulgated by the Department of Labor during the late 1950's and early 1960's, in combination with accelerated mechanization of the cotton harvest, had drastically reduced bracero contracting. As a result, during 1963 and 1964 less than 190,000 Mexicans were employed on less than 1 percent of all United States farms.[152]

Perhaps more important was that domestic opposition to bracero contracting continued to mount during the 1960's. In the process, anti-braceroists assumed an increasingly moral stance against im-

[149] *New York Times*, February 23, and April 20, 1964.

[150] Ibid., February 23, March 8, November 14, and December 6, 1964.

[151] Ibid., January 1, 9, 16, February 6, March 14, and 29, April 3, and 16, 1965.

[152] *Congressional Record*, 109:20700; and "Foreign Workers Admitted for Temporary Employment."

ported farm labor. To the steadily growing list of anti-bracero interest groups were added, in 1963, the following names:[153]

Emergency Committee to Aid Farmworkers
Commission on Social Action of Reform Judaism
Americans for Democratic Action
Imperial Valley Farm Labor Contractors Association
American Veterans Committee
Socialist Party–Social Democratic Federation
International Longshoremen's and Warehousemen's Union
Mexican-American Educational Conference Committee
Congregational and Christian Conference of Illinois

As a result, a system of imported Mexican labor, with all the economic and moral ills it was said to engender, appeared increasingly out of place during the New Frontier administration of President John F. Kennedy. With the election of Lyndon B. Johnson, a man pledged to achieve the Great Society for all United States citizens—which presumably included the lowly migrant farmworker—the bracero program became an even greater anachronism. Therefore, the 1963 extension of P.L. 78 proved to be a finale to twenty-two years of large-scale bracero contracting.

[153] House Agriculture Committee Hearings, 1963; and *Congressional Record*, 109:20716.

CHAPTER 6

Closing Observations

MEXICAN NATIONALS have worked in the fields of the Southwest since the turn of the century. Substantial numbers of braceros were recruited directly by United States employers during World War I. With the economic depression of the 1930's the flow of braceros was virtually terminated. With United States involvement in World War II, a chronic shortage of manpower necessitated the launching of a program of large-scale, government-sponsored bracero contracting.

In 1942, the United States and Mexico concluded the initial bracero agreement. The 1942 accord and its 1943 successor served as the international basis of bracero contracting until 1948. During this wartime era various public laws provided a statutory foundation for the bracero program, while recruitment and contracting were conducted by the Department of Agriculture.

From 1948 to 1951, Mexican farmworkers were recruited under a series of revised international agreements. Under these accords the legal contractor was no longer the United States government, but the individual grower. Neither Mexico nor the United States was pleased with this system of direct employer recruitment. With the outbreak of war in Korea, bracero contracting was again established on a government-to-government basis.

Faced with a growing manpower shortage, as well as indigenous and Mexican demands, Congress granted for the first time in 1951 specific statutory authority for contracting Mexican farmworkers. Shortly after the enactment of P.L. 78, Mexico and the United States concluded the bracero agreement of 1951. The 1951 accord contained elaborate guarantees and benefits for the bracero and served as the international framework for bracero contracting until 1965.

From its inception, Public Law 78 charged the secretary of labor with the incompatible functions of recruiting Mexican labor while simultaneously protecting domestic farmworkers from any ill effects stemming from bracero contracting. The act was extended on six different occasions during its fourteen-year existence. As the bracero program grew more massive and its adverse effect increased, the secretary of labor moved to counter its negative impact and, thereby, to improve the working conditions of domestic farm labor. As a result, opposition to extension of the ever-more-exclusive program mounted among the general public and within Congress. From 1960 on, the congressional struggle over prolongation became more intense. Only the built-in access enjoyed by congressional proponents in league with Mexican pressure enabled the program to survive in 1961 and 1963. In the final analysis the bracero program became a victim of the changing political, social, and group milieu that characterized the early 1960's.

CONCLUSIONS

During its twenty-two–year history, the bracero program afforded a rare example of the interplay of group pressures at the national and international level. Viewed from a broad perspective, the group processes involved in large-scale bracero contracting provide six summary points of interest, four of which relate specifically to the foreign policy process.

Within an international context the bracero program is important first because it shows the impact that a restricted international environment (United States–Mexican relations) can have on the domestic political process in both nations. In the case of Mexico, the bracero program was a crucial source of foreign exchange and a political safety valve. In addition, it was indirectly responsible for a rejuvenated, long-overdue concern on the part of Mexican officials about the plight of the nation's rural sector. The mad rush to become a bracero or a wetback, the abandonment of private landholdings, and the resultant exploitation and bloody confrontations awakened a somewhat lethargic officialdom to the conditions of abject poverty that characterized much of rural Mexico.

In the case of the United States, the bracero program's impact produced both short- and long-range results. In its short-term effects, Mexican labor was undoubtedly important for the cultivation and harvesting of crops in the Southwest. At the national level, Mexican pressure for prolongation constituted a decisive factor in the program's longevity during the 1960's. Pressure from the international environment was largely responsible for the continuation of an otherwise unpopular program.

As to its long-range effect, the Mexican labor program was indirectly responsible for a marked improvement in the wages and working conditions of domestic farm labor. Perhaps the greatest irony of large-scale bracero contracting was the benefits granted foreigners but denied United States citizens. Such an anomaly could not long endure in a democratic political system. Utilizing the bracero system as a wedge, supporters of a better life for native farmworkers achieved in a comparatively short time span state and national legislation that otherwise would have entailed a far longer period. As was the case with Mexico and its rural sector, an international program proved indirectly responsible for producing national concern over a previously neglected segment of United States society.

Second, the international environment can effect a particular foreign policy. The impact of the international events external to United States–Mexican relations proved crucial to the content and functioning of the Mexican labor system. This impact was particularly evident during World War II and the Korean War. In both instances the exigencies arising from international confrontation proved vital to the very existence and character of the bracero program. Had it not been for the Second World War it is doubtful whether a formal bracero agreement would have been concluded. Had the need for manpower not been so great, Mexico would not have achieved a formal, government-sponsored system of labor contracting. The same may be said for the even more formalized and detailed agreement of 1951. Events emanating from the greater international environment rendered Mexican labor so necessary that the United States was willing to conclude an international accord despite domestic pressures to the contrary.

Third, the element of timing is closely associated with the impact of the entire international milieu on the bracero program. Domestically it has long been recognized that timing is crucial to achieving group ends. Labor unions generally time their strikes to coincide with a vulnerable period for their management counterparts.

Mexico proved most adroit at this particular art by timing her demands to coincide with crisis periods. The concessions that Mexico was able to wring from United States negotiators were due in large part to the time factor, which accounted for the elaborate government-sponsored guarantees contained in the agreements of 1942 and 1951. Mexico, realizing that the United States was in dire need of manpower because of international confrontations, demanded and got agreements that might have proved unobtainable in periods in international calm. The same may be said of the periodic revisions of the 1951 accord. In requesting changes beneficial to her nationals, Mexican negotiators timed their demands to coincide with the period of greatest need among United States growers. The results were invariably the same: Mexico got the revisions she demanded because employers had to have braceros, even at the Mexican asking price.

Yet the element of timing, which Mexico utilized so adroitly, proved a two-edged sword. During the 1954 episode over unilateral recruitment, the United States correctly sensed Mexico's true need for the bracero program, as well as her intentions merely to extend the agreement in order to acquire a stronger bargaining position. Washington thus enacted an amendment to P.L. 78 authorizing unilateral recruitment, presented the Mexican negotiators with a list of negotiable demands, and then threatened to abrogate the 1951 accord and recruit unilaterally if the Mexicans refused to compromise. Mexico realized that they had been outmaneuvered in the use of the time element as a pressure tactic, and compromised.

Fourth, the bracero program is important because it demonstrates how domestic group pressures can influence the conduct of foreign policy. In what is perhaps a variant from the norm, the disproportionate access enjoyed by employer interests did not generally prove detrimental to United States foreign policy. On the contrary, the reverse was true. With the possible exceptions of the period of direct grower recruitment from 1948–1951 and the brief interval of unilateral contracting, grower access proved a catalyst to improved United States–Mexican relations. Relations were especially good in 1961 and 1963 when the demands of grower interests and those of the Mexican government coalesced to bring about the final two extensions of P.L. 78. Whereas disproportionate access on the part of particular interest groups may well be harmful to the national interest, as expressed in foreign policy, such was not the case with the bracero program.

Domestically, the bracero program is important for what it reveals about the doctrine of countervailing powers and for the insights it offers in the area of group conflict and the administrative process.

That a small minority of southwestern growers was able to prolong for several years a program that many observers deemed temporary as well as detrimental to the country, particularly to domestic farmworkers, may well be cause for concern among students of democratic government. Yet, for two reasons, it should not be cause for undue alarm: (1) The program's longevity can be explained by examining the group processes surrounding imported Mexican labor. (2) In time the disproportionate power of grower interests was counteracted by superior forces representing the general interest.

Although a multitude of reasons may be offered to explain the success of grower interests in securing extension of P.L. 78, five appear to be fundamental: (1) location of the congressional struggle, (2) political access, (3) organization and tactics, (4) ineffectiveness of the opposition, and (5) congruence between the interests of employers and those of the Mexican government. Of these, the first and last reasons are particularly salient.

The bracero program does not provide the first nor will it provide the final illustration of the effectiveness of small minorities within the congressional process. In their positions as chairmen of agricultural committees and subcommittees in both houses, pro-bracero congressmen were most strategically located. In league with conservative elements in both parties they were able to counteract the apparent numerical superiority of anti-bracero forces in Congress. It must also be recalled by those who criticize minority rule in the case of bracero labor that such rule was exercised wholly within the democratic framework of congressional procedures, and that an exercise of minority power need not necessarily prove detrimental to the national interest. Evaluation of the public interest differs, of course, according to one's own particular viewpoint.

The final reason—that of congruence between domestic and foreign pressures—is equally significant in explaining the bracero program's longevity. It is particularly noteworthy that students of the program have tended to overlook this point.[1] This crucial factor

[1] As an example, note the excellent summary statement by Ellis W. Hawley in "The Politics of the Mexican Labor Issue, *Agricultural History* 40(July

enabled the program to survive in the 1960's, despite what appeared to be overwhelming opposition.

Nevertheless, no degree of congruence between domestic and international pressures can forever prolong largely unpopular legislation. Although some may argue that twenty-two years of imported Mexican farm labor constituted a refutation of the theory of countervailing powers, the inescapable fact remains that with the bracero program's ultimate demise the theory was again vindicated. One of the primary reasons for its vindication lies within the theory itself.

John Kenneth Galbraith and other proponents of the pluralist model[2] contend that, should the group milieu surrounding a particular program become so unbalanced that it poses a threat to the national interest, government, because of its unique role as representative of the entire national interest, should intervene to rectify the situation. In the case of the bracero program, the government as a whole did not move to counteract the disproportionate power and access enjoyed by agribusiness. Instead, a particular arm of government, the Department of Labor, served as the equalizing agent.

Effective political access may be administrative as well as legislative or executive. In the case of P.L. 78, it was the access of anti-bracero forces to the secretary of labor that proved decisive. While he was himself unable to bring about an end to large-scale bracero recruitment, the secretary of labor was able to render the procurement of braceros so inconvenient that their employment became all but prohibitive. Foiled in their effort to terminate P.L. 78 congressionally, anti-braceroists utilized their access to an administrative department in a successful effort to render bracero contracting incompatible to the majority of southwestern growers. Employer access to important centers of congressional power was thus counterbalanced during the 1960's by the administrative access enjoyed by anti-bracero interests.

1966):157–176. As a lone possible exception, see James F. Creagan, "Public Law 78: A Tangle of Domestic and International Relations," *Journal of Inter-American Studies* 7 (October 1965):541–556.

   2 John Kenneth Galbraith, *American Capitalism: The Concept of Countervailing Power*, chap. 10.

FURTHER RESEARCH

This case study of the Mexican labor program provides but one example of the wide range of research possibilities at the national and the international level. From a broad international perspective, additional studies are needed to assess the relationship between particular foreign policy environments and the entire international milieu. On the subject of the foreign policy dimension of the bracero program, research will be hampered in the near future because of the program's diplomatically sensitive nature. When diplomatic files on the program are opened to scholars, two areas will deserve special attention: (1) the extent of Mexican pressure in behalf of prolongation, and (2) the import of contacts between United States grower interests and Mexican officials. The former should provide further insights into the area of international pressure politics, while the latter should afford information on the relationship between foreign policy and interaction with particular nongovernmental interest groups in foreign countries.

At the domestic level, research possibilities are abundant in both Mexico and the United States. Subnationally, studies similar to Hancock's work on Chihuahua[3] could be repeated at the state and municipal level in both nations, which should provide important data concerning the impact of international programs on local political cultures. Another topic with wide-ranging comparative implications is the group struggle that surrounded the bracero program in Mexico. A thorough analysis of this conflict would prove a welcome addition to the growing list of case studies focusing on group conflict in developing nations.

A final and very important area in need of further research is the entire question of domestic group pressures and foreign policy. The interest group–foreign policy relationship has only recently been explored by United States and foreign scholars.[4] Further re-

[3] Richard H. Hancock, *The Role of the Bracero in the Economic and Cultural Dynamics of Mexico: A Case Study of Chihuahua.*

[4] Under the leadership of Bernard Cohen and James Rosenau this long-neglected relationship is finally receiving the attention it deserves. As examples

search is needed at two levels: (1) group pressures and the overall conduct of foreign policy in the United States and in other countries, and (2) case studies of group conflict surrounding particular foreign policy questions. Problems of foreign policy are by their very nature more removed from popular control and participation than are questions of domestic policy. But removal need not mean isolation, which is especially true in the case of interest groups and the foreign policy process.

---

of recent scholarship in this area, note the following: Bernard C. Cohen, *The Influence of Non-Governmental Groups on Foreign Policy Making*; idem, *The Political Process and Foreign Policy: The Making of the Japanese Peace Settlement*; Fred W. Riggs, *Pressures on Congress: A Study of the Repeal of Chinese Exclusion*; Franklin L. Burdette, "The Influence of Non-Congressional Pressures on Foreign Policy," *Annals of the American Academy of Political and Social Science* 289(September 1953):92–99; Kenneth B. Adler and Davis Bobrow, "Interest and Influence in Foreign Affairs," *Public Opinion Quarterly* 20(1956): 89–101; James N. Rosenau, *Public Opinion and Foreign Policy: An Operational Formulation*; James N. Rosenau, ed., *Domestic Sources of Foreign Policy*; R. Barry Farrell, ed., *Approaches to Comparative and International Politics*; and Wolfram F. Hanreider, "Compatibility and Consensus: A Proposal for the Conceptual Linkage of External and Internal Dimensions of Foreign Policy," *American Political Science Review* 61(December 1967):971–982.

BIBLIOGRAPHY

GOVERNMENT DOCUMENTS

Barlow, Frank D., Jr., and Grady B. Crowe. *Mexican Cotton: Production, Problems, Potentials.* Foreign Agricultural Service, United States Department of Agriculture, Foreign Agriculture Report no. 98. Washington, D.C.: Government Printing Office, 1957.

Dirección General de Estadística. *Compendido Estadístico, 1951.* Mexico City: Secretaría de Economia, 1952.

———. *Compendido Estadístico, 1952.* Mexico City: Secretaría de Economia, 1953.

Jones, Robert C. *Los braceros mexicanos en los estados unidos durante el periodo belico.* Washington, D.C.: Union Panamericana, 1946.

Kinkead, Alice C. *Labor Unionism in Agriculture: A Brief History and Summary of Pro and Con Arguments.* Washington, D.C.: Library of Congress Legislative Reference Service, 1967.

McElroy, Robert C., and Earl E. Gavett. *Termination of the Bracero Program: Some Effects on Farm Labor and Migrant Housing Needs.* Economic Research Service, United States Department of Agriculture, Agriculture Economic Report no. 77. Washington, D.C.: Government Printing Office, 1965.

Rasmussen, Wayne D. *A History of the Emergency Farm Labor Supply Program 1943–47.* Agriculture Monograph no. 13. Washington, D.C.: U.S. Department of Agriculture, 1951.

Report of the Combined Mexican Working Party. *The Economic De-*

velopment of Mexico. Baltimore: Johns Hopkins University Press, 1953.

Report of the President's Commission on Migratory Labor. *Migratory Labor in American Agriculture.* Washington, D.C.: Government Printing Office, 1951.

Report of the Senate Committee on Labor and Welfare. *California Farm Labor Problems, Part I.* Sacramento: Senate of the State of California, 1961.

Report of the Senate Delegation. "Mexican–United States Interparliamentary Group," 88th Cong., 1st sess., December 2, 1963. Washington, D.C.: Government Printing Office, 1963.

Rich, Spencer A. *United States Agricultural Policy in the Postwar Years, 1945–1963.* Washington, D.C.: Congressional Quarterly Service, 1963.

U.S. Bureau of the Census. *Historical Statistics of the United States, Colonial Times to 1957.* Washington, D.C.: Government Printing Office, 1960.

U.S., Congress, House, Committee on Agriculture. *Extend the Mexican Farm Labor Program: Hearing before Subcommittee on H.R. 7185, H.R. 7191, S. 1703,* 88th Cong., 1st sess., August 21, 1963. Washington, D.C.: Government Printing Office, 1963.

———. *Extension of Mexican Farm Labor Program: Hearings on H.R. 3480,* 83d Cong., 1st sess., March 24, 25, and 26, 1953. Washington, D.C.: Government Printing Office, 1953.

———. *Extension of Mexican Farm Labor Program: Hearings before Subcommittee on H.R. 9869 and others,* 86th Cong., 2d sess., March 22, 23, 24, 25, and 31, 1960. Washington, D.C.: Government Printing Office, 1960.

———. *Extension of Mexican Farm Labor Program: Hearings before Subcommittee on H.R. 2010,* 87th Cong., 1st sess., March 6–9 and 17, 1961. Washington, D.C.: Government Printing Office, 1961.

———. *Farm Labor: Hearings on H.R. 2955, H.R. 3048,* 82d Cong., 1st sess., March 8–14, 1951. Washington, D.C.: Government Printing Office, 1951.

———. *Farm Labor and Mexican Labor: Hearings before Subcommittee on H.R. 7028 and others,* 85th Cong., 2d sess., February 28, March 1 and 3, June 9–12, and July 2, 1958. Washington, D.C.: Government Printing Office, 1958.

———. *Mexican Farm Labor: Hearings on H.J. Res. 355,* 83d Cong., 2d sess., February 3, 5, 8, 9, 10, and 11, 1954. Washington, D.C.: Government Printing Office, 1954.

———. *Mexican Farm Labor Program: Hearings before Subcommittee* on H.R. *3822*, 84th Cong., 1st sess., March 16–22, 1955. Washington, D.C.: Government Printing Office, 1955.

———. *Mexican Farm Labor Program: Hearings before Subcommittee on H.R. 1836 and H.R. 2009*, 88th Cong., 1st sess., March 27, 28, and 29, 1963. Washington, D.C.: Government Printing Office, 1963.

———. Report No. 274, "Continuation of the Mexican Farm Labor Program," 87th Cong., 1st sess., April 24, 1961. Washington, D.C.: Government Printing Office, 1961.

———. Report No. 274, "Continuation of Mexican Farm Labor Program," 88th Cong., 1st sess., May 6, 1963. Washington, D.C.: Government Printing Office, 1963.

———. Report No. 722, "One-Year Extension of the Mexican Farm Labor Program," 88th Cong., 1st sess., September 6, 1963. Washington, D.C.: Government Printing Office, 1963.

———. Report No. 1198, "Mexican Farm Labor," 87th Cong., 1st sess., September 15, 1961. Washington, D.C.: Government Printing Office, 1961.

———. Report No. 1199, "Mexican Agricultural Workers," 83d Cong., 2d sess., February 12, 1954. Washington, D.C.: Government Printing Office, 1954.

———. Report No. 1954, "Farm Labor Program," 86th Cong., 2d sess., June 12, 1960. Washington, D.C.: Government Printing Office, 1960.

U.S., Congress, House, Committee on the Judiciary. *Study of Population and Immigration Problems, Administrative Presentations (III), Admission of Aliens into the United States for Temporary Employment, and "Commuter Workers": Hearing before Subcommittee*, 88th Cong., 1st sess., June 24, 1963. Washington, D.C.: Government Printing Office, 1963.

U.S., Congress, Senate, Committee on Agriculture and Forestry. *Extension of the Mexican Farm Labor Program: Hearings on S. 1207*, 83d Cong., 1st sess., March 23 and 24, 1953. Washington, D.C.: Government Printing Office, 1953.

———. *Extension of Mexican Farm Labor Program: Hearings before Subcommittee on S. 1466, S. 1945, and H.R. 2010*, 87th Cong., 1st sess., June 12 and 13, 1961. Washington, D.C.: Government Printing Office, 1961.

———. *Farm Labor: Hearings on S. 949, S. 984, and S. 1106*, 82d Cong., 1st sess., March 13–16, 1951. Washington, D.C.: Government Printing Office, 1951.

———. Report No. 214, "Importation of Foreign Agricultural Workers," 82d Cong., 1st sess., April 11, 1951. Washington, D.C.: Government Printing Office, 1951.

————. Report No. 372, "Extension of Mexican Farm Labor Program," 88th Cong., 1st sess., July 22, 1963. Washington, D.C.: Government Printing Office, 1963.

————. Report No. 391, "Extension of Mexican Farm Labor Program," 88th Cong., 1st sess., August 6, 1963. Washington, D.C.: Government Printing Office, 1963.

————. Report No. 619, "Mexican Farm Labor Program," 87th Cong., 1st sess., July 25, 1961. Washington, D.C.: Government Printing Office, 1961.

————. Report No. 1145, "Assisting in Preventing Aliens from Entering or Remaining in the United States Illegally," 82d Cong., 2d sess., February 4, 1952. Washington, D.C.: Government Printing Office, 1952.

————. Report No. 1901, "Mexican Farm Labor," 86th Cong., 2d sess., August 23, 1960. Washington, D.C.: Government Printing Office, 1960.

U.S., Congress, Senate, Committee on Appropriations. *Department of Agriculture and Related Agencies Appropriations: Hearing before Subcommittee on H.R. 10509*, 90th Cong., 1st sess., Fiscal Year 1968. Washington, D.C.: Government Printing Office, 1968.

U.S., Congress, Senate, Committee on Labor and Labor-Management Relations. *Migratory Labor, Part I: Hearing before Subcommittee*, 82d Cong., 2d sess., February 5, 6, 7, 11, 14, 15, 27, 28, 29, and March 27, 28, 1952. Washington, D.C.: Government Printing Office, 1952.

U.S., *Congressional Record*, 1951–1963.

U.S., Department of Agriculture, *Agricultural Statistics, 1966*. Washington, D.C.: Government Printing Office, 1966.

U.S., Department of Justice. *Annual Report of the Immigration and Naturalization Service, 1949*. Washington, D.C.: Government Printing Office, 1949.

————. *Annual Report of the Immigration and Naturalization Service, 1955*. Washington, D.C.: Government Printing Office, 1955.

U.S., Department of Justice, Immigration, and Naturalization Service. "Mexican Agricultural Laborers Admitted and Mexican Aliens Located in Illegal Status, Years Ended June 30, 1949–1967." Washington, D.C.: Government Printing Office, 1968.

U.S., Department of Labor. *Farm Labor Fact Book*. Washington, D.C.: Government Printing Office, 1959.

————. "Report of Operations of Mexican Farm Labor Program Made Pursuant to Conference Report No. 1449," House of Representatives, 84th Cong., 1st sess., January 1–June 30, 1959. Washington, D.C.: Government Printing Office, 1959.

————. *Information Concerning Entry of Mexican Agricultural Workers into the United States: Public Law 78, 82d Congress, as Amended; Migrant Labor Agreement of 1951, as Amended and Pertinent Interpretations; Standard Work Contract, as Amended and Pertinent Interpretations; Joint Operating Instructions.* Washington, D.C.: Government Printing Office, 1962.

————. Bureau of Employment Security. "Mexican Farm Labor Program, Consultants Report." Washington, D.C.: Government Printing Office, 1959.

————. *Hired Farm Workers in the United States.* Washington, D.C.: Government Printing Office, 1961.

U.S., Department of State. "Mexico, Mexican Agricultural Workers, Agreement Effected by Exchange of Notes Signed at Mexico August 1, 1949; Entered into Force August 1, 1949. And Amendments and Interpretations Effected by Exchange of Notes," TIAS 2260, *United States Treaties and Other International Agreements*, vol. 2, pt. 1, 1951, pp. 1048–1155. Washington, D.C.: Government Printing Office, 1952.

————. "Mexico, Mexican Agricultural Workers, Agreement Amending the Agreement of August 11, 1951. Effected by Exchange of Notes Signed at Mexico January 10 and 31, 1952; Entered into Force January 31, 1952. And Extending the Agreement of August 11, 1951. Effected by Exchange of Notes Signed at Mexico February 8, 1952; Entered into Force February 8, 1952. And Exchanges of Notes Signed at Mexico March 31 and April 9, 1952; Entered into Force April 9, 1952," TIAS 2531, *United States Treaties and Other International Agreements*, vol. 3, pt. 3, 1952, pp. 3958–3962. Washington, D.C.: Government Printing Office, 1955.

————. "Mexico, Mexican Agricultural Workers, Agreement Extending the Agreement of August 11, 1951. Effected by Exchange of Notes Signed in Mexico May 19, 1952; Entered into Force May 19, 1952," TIAS 2586, *United States Treaties and Other International Agreements*, vol. 3, pt. 3, 1952, pp. 4341–4393. Washington, D.C.: Government Printing Office, 1955.

————. "Mexican Agricultural Workers, Agreement between the United States of America and Mexico, Provisionally Extending Agreement of August 11, 1951, as Amended, Effected by Exchange of Notes Signed at Washington December 30 and 31, 1953; Entered into Force December 31, 1953," TIAS 2928, *United States Treaties and Other International Agreements*, vol. 5, pt. 1, 1954, pp. 353–358. Washington, D.C.: Government Printing Office, 1955.

————. "Mexican Agricultural Workers, Agreements between the

United States of America and Mexico, Renewing and Amending the Agreement of August 11, 1951, as Amended, and Establishing a Joint Migratory Labor Commission, Effected by Exchanges of Notes Signed at Mexico March 10, 1954; Entered into Force March 10, 1954," TIAS 2932, *United States Treaties and Other International Agreements*, vol. 5, pt. 1, 1954, pp. 379–415. Washington, D.C.: Government Printing Office, 1955.

————. "Mexico, Agricultural Workers: Recommendations by Joint Migratory Labor Commission, Agreement Effected by Exchange of Notes Dated at Mexico, D. F., April 14, 1955; Entered into Force April 14, 1955," TIAS 3242, *United States Treaties and Other International Agreements*, vol. 6, pt. 1, 1955, pp. 1017–1030. Washington, D.C.: Government Printing Office, 1956.

————. "Mexico, Agricultural Workers, Agreement Extending the Agreement of August 11, 1951, as Amended and Extended. Effected by Exchange of Notes Dated at Mexico, December 23, 1955; Entered into Force December 23, 1955," TIAS 3454, *United States Treaties and Other International Agreements*, vol. 6, pt. 5, 1955, pp. 6058–6062. Washington, D.C.: Government Printing Office, 1956.

————. "Mexico, Mexican Agricultural Workers, Agreement Extending the Agreement of August 11, 1951, as Amended and Extended. Effected by Exchange of Notes Signed at Mexico December 20, 1956; Entered into Force December 20, 1956," TIAS 3714, *United States Treaties and Other International Agreements*, vol. 7, pt. 3, 1956, pp. 3427–3431. Washington, D.C.: Government Printing Office, 1957.

————. "Mexico, Mexican Agricultural Workers, Agreements Extending the Agreement of August 11, 1951, as Amended and Extended. Effected by Exchange of Notes Signed at Mexico August 31, 1959; Entered into Force August 31, 1959. And Exchange of Notes Signed at Mexico July 28 and 30, 1959; Entered into Force July 30, 1959. And Exchange of Notes Signed at Mexico June 24 and 27, 1959; Entered into Force June 27, 1959," TIAS 4310, *United States Treaties and Other International Agreements*, vol. 10, pt. 2, 1959, pp. 1630–1637. Washington, D.C.: Government Printing Office, 1960.

————. "Mexico, Mexican Agricultural Workers, Agreement Extending and Supplementing the Agreement of August 11, 1951, as Amended and Extended. Effected by Exchange of Notes Signed at Mexico June 27, 1961; Entered into Force June 27, 1961," TIAS 4815, *United States Treaties and Other International Agreements*, vol. 13, pt. 1, 1961, pp. 1081–1084. Washington, D.C.: Government Printing Office, 1962.

————. "Mexico, Mexican Agricultural Workers, Agreement Extending the Agreement of August 11, 1951, as Amended and Extended. Effected by Exchange of Notes Signed at Mexico December 11, 1961; Entered into Force December 11, 1961," TIAS 4913, *United States Treaties and Other International Agreements*, vol. 13, pt. 3, 1961, pp. 3130 3131. Washington, D.C.: Government Printing Office, 1962.

————. "Mexico, Migratory Workers: Mexican Agricultural Workers, Agreement Amending and Extending the Agreement of August 11, 1951 as Amended and Extended, and Including Joint Interpretations of 1961. Effected by Exchanges of Notes Signed at Mexico December 29, 1961; Entered into Force February 1, 1962," TIAS 5160, *United States Treaties and Other International Agreements*, vol. 13, pt. 2, 1962, pp. 2022–2064. Washington, D.C.: Government Printing Office, 1963.

————. "Mexico, Migratory Workers: Mexican Agricultural Workers, Agreement Extending the Agreement of August 11, 1951, as Amended and Extended. Effected by Exchange of Notes Signed at Mexico December 20, 1963; Entered into Force December 20, 1963," TIAS 5492, *United States Treaties and Other International Agreements*, vol. 14, pt. 2, 1963, pp. 1804–1806. Washington: Government Printing Office, 1964.

U.S. President. "Recommendations Supplementing the Provisions of S. 984, an Act Relating to the Recruitment and Employment of Agricultural Workers from Mexico," House Document No. 192, 82d Cong., 1st sess., July 13, 1951. Washington, D.C.: Government Printing Office, 1951.

U.S., Statutes at Large, Volumes 56, 57, 61, 62, 65, 66, 67, 69, and 72.

Wylie, Kathryn H. *Mexico as a Market and Competitor for U.S. Agricultural Products*. Foreign Agricultural Service, United States Department of Agriculture, Foreign Agriculture Report no. 99. Washington, D.C.: Government Printing Office, August, 1957.

THESES AND DISSERTATIONS

Copp, Nelson G. " 'Wetbacks' and Braceros: Mexican Migrant Laborers and American Immigration Policy, 1930–1960." Ph.D. Dissertation, Boston University Graduate School, 1963.

Elac, John C. "The Employment of Mexican Workers in United States Agriculture, 1900–1960: A Binational Economic Analysis." Ph.D. Dissertation, University of California at Los Angeles, 1961.

Graves, Ruth Parker. "A History of the Interrelationships between Imported Mexican Labor, Domestic Migrants, and the Texas Agricultural Economy." Master's Thesis, The University of Texas at Austin, 1960.

Lyon, Richard M. "The Legal Status of American and Mexican Migratory Farm Labor: An Analysis of United States Farm Labor Legislation, Policy, and Administration." Ph.D. Dissertation, Cornell University, 1954.

Meador, Bruce Staffel. " 'Wetback' Labor in the Lower Rio Grande Valley." Master's Thesis, The University of Texas at Austin, 1951.

Moore, Woodrow. "El problema de la emigración de los braceros." Master's Thesis, Universidad Nacional Autónoma de México, 1961.

Pfeiffer, David G. "The Mexican Farm Labor Supply Program—Its Friends and Foes." Master's Thesis, The University of Texas at Austin, 1963.

Tomasek, Robert D. "The Political and Economic Implications of Mexican Labor in the United States under the Non Quota System, Contract Labor Program, and Wetback Movement." Ph.D. Dissertation, University of Michigan, 1957.

Vargas y Campos, Gloria R. "El problema del bracero mexicano." Ph.D. Dissertation, Universidad Nacional Autónoma de México, 1964.

BOOKS

Adams, Richard N., et al. *Social Change in Latin America Today: Its Implications for United States Policy*. New York: Harper and Row, 1960.

Almond, Gabriel A. *The American People and Foreign Policy*. New York: Frederick A. Praeger, 1967.

————, and Sydney Verba. *The Civic Culture: Political Attitudes and Democracy in Five Nations*. Boston: Little, Brown and Co., 1965.

Anderson, Henry P. *The Bracero Program in California with Particular Reference to Health Status, Attitudes, and Practices*. Berkeley: School of Public Health, University of California, 1961.

Bailey, Stephen K. *Congress Makes a Law: The Story behind the Employment Act of 1946*. New York: Columbia University Press, 1950.

Bauer, Raymond, et al. *American Business and Public Policy: The Politics of Foreign Trade*. New York: Atherton Press, 1963.

Bentley, Arthur F. *The Process of Government*. Chicago: University of Chicago Press, 1908.

Berman, Daniel M. *A Bill Becomes a Law: The Civil Rights Act of 1960*. New York: MacMillan Co., 1962.

Blaisdell, Donald C. *American Democracy under Pressure*. New York: Ronald Press Co., 1957.

Brandenburg, Frank. *The Making of Modern Mexico*. Englewood Cliffs, New Jersey: Prentice-Hall, 1964.

Bryce, Lord. *The American Commonwealth*. 4th ed. New York: Mac-Millan Co., 1910.

Burma, John H. *Spanish-Speaking Groups in the United States*. Durham, North Carolina: Duke University Press, 1954.

Chase, Stuart. *Democracy under Pressure: Special Interest vs. the Public Welfare*. New York: Twentieth Century Fund, 1945.

Cline, Howard F. *Mexico: Revolution to Evolution, 1940–1960*. New York: Oxford University Press, 1962.

———. *The United States and Mexico*. Cambridge: Harvard University Press, 1961.

Cohen, Bernard C. *The Influence of Non-Governmental Groups on Foreign Policy Making*. Princeton: Center for International Studies, 1959.

———. *The Political Process and Foreign Policy: The Making of the Japanese Peace Settlement*. Princeton: Princeton University Press, 1957.

Crow, John A. *Mexico Today*. New York: Harper Brothers, 1957.

de Tocqueville, Alexis. *Democracy in America*. New York: Washington Square Press, 1964.

Easton, David. *A Framework for Political Analysis*. Englewood Cliffs, New Jersey: Prentice-Hall, 1965.

———. *A Systems Analysis of Political Life*. New York: John Wiley and Sons, 1965.

Eckstein, Harry. *Pressure Group Politics: The Case of the British Medical Association*. Stanford: Stanford University Press, 1960.

Ehrmann, Henry W. *Organized Business in France*. Princeton: Princeton University Press, 1957.

———, ed. *Interest Groups on Four Continents*. Pittsburgh: University of Pittsburgh Press, 1958.

Engler, Robert. *The Politics of Oil: A Study of Private Power and Democratic Directions*. New York: MacMillan Co., 1961.

Fisher, Lloyd H. *The Harvest Labor Market in California*. Cambridge: Harvard University Press, 1953.

Freithaler, William O. *Mexico's Foreign Trade and Economic Development*. New York: Frederick A. Praeger, 1968.

Galarza, Ernesto. *Merchants of Labor: The Mexican Bracero Story; An Account of the Managed Migration of Mexican Farmworkers in California 1942–1960*. Santa Barbara, California: McNally and Loftin, 1964.

————. *Strangers in Our Fields*. Rev. ed. Washington, D.C.: United States Section, Joint United States–Mexico Trade Union Committee, 1956.

Galbraith, John Kenneth. *American Capitalism: The Concept of Countervailing Power*. Rev. ed. Boston: Houghton Mifflin Co., 1956.

Gonzalez Casanova, Pablo. *La democracia en México*. Mexico City: ERA, 1965.

Gross, Bertram. *The Legislative Struggle: A Study of Social Combat*. New York: McGraw-Hill Book Co., 1953.

Hadwiger, Don F., and Ross B. Talbot. *Pressures and Protests: The Kennedy Farm Program and the Wheat Referendum of 1963*. San Francisco: Chandler Publishing Co., 1965.

Hancock, Richard H. *The Role of the Bracero in the Economic and Cultural Dynamics of Mexico: A Case Study of Chihuahua*. Stanford, California: Hispanic American Society, 1959.

Hathaway, Dale E. *Government and Agriculture: Public Policy in a Democratic Society*. New York: MacMillan Co., 1963.

Herring, E. Pendelton. *Group Representation before Congress*. Baltimore: Johns Hopkins University Press, 1929.

Janowitz, Morris. *The Military in the Political Development of New States: An Essay in Comparative Analysis*. Chicago: University of Chicago Press, 1964.

Kaplan, Morton A. *System and Process in International Politics*. New York: John Wiley and Sons, 1957.

Key, V. O., Jr. *Politics, Parties, and Pressure Groups*. 5th ed. New York: Thomas Y. Crowell Co., 1966.

————. *Public Opinion and American Democracy*. New York: Alfred A. Knopf, 1961.

Kibbe, Pauline R. *Latin Americans in Texas*. Albuquerque: University of New Mexico Press, 1946.

Kile, Orville M. *The Farm Bureau through Three Decades*. Baltimore: Waverly Press, 1948.

Kornhauser, William. *The Politics of Mass Society*. Glencoe, Illinois: Free Press, 1959.

Lane, Robert E. *Political Life: Why People Get Involved in Politics*. Glencoe, Illinois: Free Press, 1959.

La Palombara, Joseph. *Interest Groups in Italian Politics*. Princeton: Princeton University Press, 1964.

Latham, Earl. *The Group Basis of Politics: A Study in Basing-Point Legislation*. Ithaca, New York: Cornell University Press, 1952.

Lewis, Oscar. *Life in a Mexican Village: Tepoztlan Restudied*. Urbana: University of Illinois Press, 1951.

Lindbloom, Charles E. *The Intelligence of Democracy: Decision Making through Mutual Adjustment.* New York: Free Press, 1965.

Lipset, Seymour M. *Political Man: The Social Basis of Politics.* Garden City, New York: Doubleday and Co., 1960.

McClelland, Charles A. *Theory and the International System.* New York: MacMillan Co., 1966.

McClelland, David. *The Achieving Society.* Princeton: D. Van Nostrand Co., 1961.

McConnell, Grant. *The Decline of Agrarian Democracy.* Berkeley: University of California Press, 1953.

McCune, Wesley, *Who's behind Our Farm Policy?* New York: Frederick A. Praeger, 1956.

Macridis, Roy C., ed. *Foreign Policy in World Politics.* 2d ed. Englewood Cliffs, New Jersey: Prentice-Hall, 1964.

———, and Bernard C. Brown, ed. *Comparative Politics: Notes and Readings.* 3d ed. Homewood, Illinois: Dorsey Press, 1968.

Meynaud, Jean. *Les groupes de pressiones en France.* Paris: Librairie Armand Colin, 1958.

Michels, Robert. *Political Parties: A Sociological Study of Oligarchical Tendencies of Modern Democracy.* New York: Free Press, 1962.

Morin, Alexander. *The Organizability of Farm Labor in the United States.* Cambridge: Harvard University Press, 1952.

Mosk, Stanford A. *Industrial Revolution in Mexico.* Berkeley: University of California Press, 1954.

Myrdal, Gunnar. *An American Dilemma: The Negro Problem and Modern Democracy.* New York: Harper and Row, 1962.

Odegard, Peter. *Pressure Politics: The Story of the Anti-Saloon League.* New York: Columbia University Press, 1928.

Olson, Mancur, Jr. *The Logic of Collective Action: Public Goods and the Theory of Groups.* Cambridge: Harvard University Press, 1965.

Padfield, Harland, and William E. Martin. *Farmers, Workers, and Machines: Technological and Social Changes in Farm Industries of Arizona.* Tucson: University of Arizona Press, 1965.

Padgett, L. Vincent. *The Mexican Political System.* Boston: Houghton Mifflin Co., 1966.

Riggs, Fred W. *Pressures on Congress: A Study of the Repeal of Chinese Exclusion.* New York: King's Crown Press, 1950.

Rosecrance, Richard N. *Action and Reaction in World Politics: International Systems in Perspective.* Boston: Little, Brown, and Co., 1963.

Rosenau, James N. *Public Opinion and Foreign Policy: An Operational Formulation.* New York: Random House, 1961.

Salinas, José Lázaro. *La emigración de braceros: Vision objectiva de un problema mexicano.* Mexico City, 1955.

Schattschneider, E. E. *Politics, Pressures, and the Tariff: A Study of Free Enterprise in Pressure Politics as Shown in the 1929–1930 Revision of the Tariff.* Englewood Cliffs, New Jersey: Prentice-Hall, 1935.

————. *The Semi-Sovereign People: A Realist's View of Democracy.* New York: Holt, Rinehart, and Winston, 1960.

Scott, Robert E. *Mexican Government in Transition.* Rev. ed. Urbana: University of Illinois Press, 1964.

Shotwell, Louisa R. *The Harvesters: The Story of the Migrant People.* New York: Doubleday and Co., 1961.

Simpson, Lesley Bird. *Many Mexicos.* 3d ed. Berkeley: University of California Press, 1959.

Topete, Jesus. *Aventuras de un bracero.* Mexico City: AmeXica, 1949.

Truman, David B. *The Governmental Process: Political Interest and Public Opinion.* New York: Alfred E. Knopf, 1951.

Tucker, William P. *The Mexican Government Today.* Minneapolis: University of Minnesota Press, 1957.

Vernon, Raymond. *The Dilemma of Mexico's Development: The Role of the Private and Public Sectors.* Cambridge: Harvard University Press, 1963.

Whetten, Nathan L. *Rural Mexico.* Chicago: University of Chicago Press, 1948.

Wilson, H. H. *Pressure Group: The Campaign for Commercial Television in England.* New Brunswick, New Jersey: Rutgers University Press, 1961.

Zeigler, Harmon. *Interest Groups in American Society.* Englewood Cliffs, New Jersey: Prentice-Hall, 1964.

ARTICLES

Adler, Kenneth B., and Davis Bobrow. "Interest and Influence in Foreign Affairs." *Public Opinion Quarterly* 20(1965):89–101.

"Adverse Effect Actions, 1962." *Farm Labor Developments,* May, 1963, pp. 11–13.

Ainsworth, Robert G. "Causes and and Effects of Declining Cotton Employment." *Farm Labor Developments,* September–October, 1967, p. 32.

Almond, Gabriel. "The Political Attitudes of German Business." *World Politics,* 8(January 1956):157–186.

————. "Research Note: A Comparative Study of Interest Groups and the Political Process." *American Political Science Review* 52(March 1958):270–282.

"An Interview with Secretary Mitchell." *The Reporter*, January 22, 1959, p. 20.

Bailey, Lindwood K., and Samuel Vernoff. "Agricultural Wage Policy Developments During 1958." *Employment Security Review* 26(February 1959):12–14.

Beer, Samuel H. "Group Representation in Britain and the United States." *Annals of the American Academy of Political and Social Science* 319(September 1958):126–140.

Blaisdell, Donald C. "Pressure Groups, Foreign Policies, and International Politics." *Annals of the American Academy of Political and Social Science* 319(September 1958):149–157.

Blanksten, George I. "Political Groups in Latin America." *American Political Science Review* 53(March 1959):106–127.

Brandenburg, Frank. "Organized Business in Mexico." *Inter-American Economic Affairs* 13(1958):26–52.

Burdette, Franklin L. "The Influence of Noncongressional Pressures on Foreign Policy." *Annals of the American Academy of Political and Social Science* 289(Septmeber 1953):92–99.

"California's Farm Labor Problems." *Farm Labor Developments*, August, 1963, pp. 12–15.

Carey, James B. "Organized Labor in Politics." *Annals of the American Academy of Political and Social Science* 319(September 1958): 52–64.

Celler, Emanuel. "Pressure Groups in Congress." *Annals of the American Academy of Political and Social Science* 319(September 1958): 1–9.

Coalson, George O. "Mexican Contract Labor in American Agriculture." *Southwestern Social Science Quarterly* 33(September 1952): 228–238.

Coombs, S. W. "Bracero's Journey." *Americas* 15(December 1963):7–11.

Creagan, James F. "Public Law 78: A Tangle of Domestic and International Relations." *Journal of Inter-American Studies* 7(October 1965):541–556.

de Grazia, Alfred. "Nature and Prospects of Political Interest Groups." *Annals of the American Academy of Political and Social Science* 319 (September 1958):113–122.

Dellon, Harold H. "The Adverse-Effect Policy for Agricultural Labor." *Farm Labor Developments*, August, 1966, pp. 15–26.

Dowling, R. E. "Pressure Group Theory: Its Methodological Range." *American Political Science Review* 54(December 1960):944–954.

Easton, David. "An Approach to the Analysis of Political Systems." *World Politics* 9(April 1957):383–400.

Eckels, R. P. "Hungry Workers, Ripe Crops, and the Non-Existent Mexican Border." *The Reporter*, April 13, 1954, pp. 28–32.

Eckstein, Harry. "Group Theory and the Comparative Study of Pressure Groups." In *Comparative Politics: A Reader*, edited by Harry Eckstein and David E. Apter, pp. 389–397. New York: Free Press, 1966.

"Employment of Foreign Workers in 1963." *Farm Labor Developments*, March, 1964, pp. 1 and 9–13.

Fernbach, F. L. "Organized Labor Views Labor Mobility Needs." In *Labor Mobility and Population in Agriculture*, pp. 176–183. Ames: Iowa State University Press, 1961.

Fisher, O. C. "Big Labor Dooms Bracero Program." *Human Events*, March 3, 1962, p. 153.

Friedrich, Carl J. "International Politics and Foreign Policy in Developed (Western) Systems." In *Approaches to Comparative and International Politics*, edited by R. Barry Farrell, pp. 97–119. Evanston, Illinois: Northwestern University Press, 1966.

Friese, Gordon B. "A Day in the Life of a Foreign Labor Service Representative." *Employment Security Review* 24(March 1957):3–6.

Fuchs, Lawrence H. "Minority Groups and Foreign Policy." *Political Science Quarterly* 74(June 1959):161–175.

Galarza, Ernesto. "They Work for Pennies." *American Federationist* 59(April 1952):10–13 and 29.

Gerson, Louis L. "Immigrant Groups and American Foreign Policy." In *Issues and Conflicts: Studies in Twentieth-Century American Diplomacy*, edited by George L. Anderson, pp. 172–192. Lawrence: University of Kansas Press, 1959.

Gilmore, N. R., and G. W. Gilmore. "Bracero in California," *Pacific Historical Review* 32(August 1963):265–282.

Gilpatrick, Thomas W. "Price Support Policy and the Midwest Farm Vote." *Midwest Journal of Political Science* 3(November 1959):319–335.

Goott, Daniel. "Employment of Foreign Workers in United States Agriculture." *Department of State Bulletin*, July 18, 1949, pp. 43–46.

Hagan, Charles B. "The Group in a Political Science." In *Approaches to the Study of Politics*, edited by Roland Young, pp. 38–51. Evanston, Illinois: Northwestern University Press, 1958.

Hale, Myron Q. "The Cosmology of Arthur F. Bentley." *American Political Science Review* 54(December 1960):955–961.

Haltigan, William J. "A Federal Court Looks at the Mexican Labor Program." *Employment Security Review* 29(May 1962):19–21.

Hanreider, Wolfram F. "Compatibility and Consensus: A Proposal for the Conceptual Linkage of External and Internal Dimensions of Foreign Policy." *American Political Science Review* 61(December 1967):971–982.

Hardin, Charles M. "American Agriculture." *Review of Politics* 20 (April 1958):169–208.

———. "Congressional Farm Politics and Economic Foreign Policy." *Annals of the American Academy of Political and Social Science* 331(September 1960):98–102.

Hasiwar, Hank. "Darkness in the Valley." *American Federationist* 58 (June 1951):23–25 and 31.

Hawley, Ellis W. "The Politics of the Mexican Labor Issue." *Agricultural History* 40(July 1966):157–176.

Hayes, Edward F., et al. " 'Operation Wetback'—Impact on the Border States." *Employment Security Review* 22(March 1955):16–17.

Kelly, Willard F. "The Wetback Issue." *I and N Reporter* 2(January 1954):37–39.

Kissinger, Henry A. "Domestic Structure and Foreign Policy." *Daedalus* 95(1966):503–529.

Krainock, Louis. "Organized Labor Views the Farm Worker Problem." In *Proceedings: Western Interstate Conference on Migratory Labor*, pp. 31–35. San Francisco: Council of State Governments, 1960.

Krichefsky, Gertrude D. "Importation of Alien Laborers." *I and N Reporter* 5(July 1956):4–8.

La Palombara, Joseph. "The Utility and Limitations of Interest Group Theory in Non-American Field Situations." *Journal of Politics* 22 (February 1960):29–49.

Larin, Don. "Annual Work Plans for Agricultural Migrants." *Employment Security Review* 22(March 1955):3–4.

Latham, Earl. "The Group Basis of Politics: Notes for a Theory." *American Political Science Review* 46(June 1952):376–397.

Le Berthon, Ted. "At the Prevailing Rate." *Commonweal*, November 1, 1957, pp. 122–125.

Lee, John Franklin. "Statutory Provisions for Admission of Mexican Agricultural Workers—An Exception to the Immigration and Nationality Act of 1952." *George Washington Law Review* 24(March 1956):464–477.

Leiserson, Avery. "Organized Labor as a Pressure Group." *Annals of the American Academy of Political and Social Science* 274(March 1951):108–117.

"Long-Term Trends in Foreign-Worker Employment." *Farm Labor Developments*, February, 1967, pp. 11–14.

Lowi, Theodore. "How Farmers Get What They Want." *The Reporter*, May 26, 1964, pp. 34–37.

McClosky, Herbert, et al. "Issue Conflict and Consensus among Party Leaders and Followers." *American Political Science Review* 54(June 1960):406–427.

McCune, Wesley. "Farmers in Politics." *Annals of the American Academy of Political and Social Science* 319(September 1958):32–40.

McLellan, Andrew C. "Thirty Cents an Hour!" *American Federationist* 62(May 1955):23–24.

McLellan, David S., and Charles E. Woodhouse. "The Business Elite and Foreign Policy." *Western Political Quarterly* 13(March 1960): 172–190.

Macridis, Roy C. "Interest Groups in Comparative Analysis." *Journal of Politics* 23(February 1961):25–45.

McWilliams, Carey. "They Saved the Crops." *The Inter-American* 2(August 1943):10–14.

Maisel, Albert Q. "The Mexicans among Us." *Reader's Digest* 68 (March 1956):177–186.

Masland, John W. "Pressure Groups and American Foreign Policy preceding Pearl Harbor." *Public Opinion Quarterly* 6(1942):115–122.

Mayer, Arnold. "The Grapes of Wrath, Vintage 1961." *The Reporter*, February 2, 1961, pp. 34–37.

"Migrants and Machines." *New Republic*, July 24, 1961, pp. 7–8.

"Migrant Workers' Plight," *Fortune*, November, 1959, pp. 274, 275.

Milbrath, Lester W. "Interest Groups and Foreign Policy." In *Domestic Sources of Foreign Policy*, edited by James N. Rosenau, pp. 231–251. New York: Free Press, 1967.

Mitchell, H. L. "Unions of Two Countries Act on Wetback Influx." *American Federationist* 61(January 1954):28–29.

Nix, James. "Effects of Cotton Harvest Mechanization on Hired Seasonal Labor." *Employment Security Review*, 30(January 1963):12–15.

Odegard, Peter. "A Group Basis of Politics: A New Name for an Ancient Myth." *Western Political Quarterly* 11(September 1958): 689–702.

Pye, Lucian W. "The Non-Western Political Process." *Journal of Politics* 20(August 1958):468–486.

Raskin, A. H. "For 50,000—Still 'Tobacco Road.' " *New York Times Magazine*, April 24, 1960, pp. 14, 128–130.

Romualdi, Serafino. "Hands across the Border." *American Federationist* 61(June 1954):19–20.

Rooney, James F. "The Effects of Imported Mexican Farm Labor in a California County." *The American Journal of Economics and Sociology* 20(October 1961):513–521.

Rosenau, James N. "Pretheories and Theories of Foreign Policy." In *Approaches to Comparative and International Politics*, edited by R. Barry Farrell, pp. 27–92. Evanston, Illinois: Northwestern University Press, 1966.

Rothman, Stanley. "Systematic Political Theory: Observations on the Group Approach." *American Political Science Review* 54(March 1960):15–33.

Scruggs, Otey M. "Evolution of the Mexican Farm Labor Agreement of 1942." *Agricultural History* 34(July 1960):140–149.

———. "Texas, Good Neighbor?" *Southwestern Social Science Quarterly* 43(September 1962):118–125.

———. "The United States, Mexico, and the Wetback: 1942 1947." *Pacific Historical Review* 4(May 1961):316–329.

Secretaría de Industria y Comercio, Dirección General de Estadística. *Revista de Estadística*. Vols. 19–23, March–April, 1956, to February, 1960.

Skilling, H. Gordon. "Interest Groups and Communist Politics." *World Politics* 18(April 1966):435–451.

Soth, Lauren K. "Farm Policy, Foreign Policy, and Farm Opinion." *Annals of the American Academy of Political and Social Science* 331(September 1960):103–109.

Spradlin, T. Richard. "The Mexican Farm Labor Importation Program —Review and Reform (Parts I and II)." *The George Washington Law Review* 30(October 1961):84–122; and 30(December 1961):311–327.

Sprout, Harold H. "Pressure Groups and Foreign Policies." *Annals of the American Academy of Political and Social Science* 179(May 1935):114–123.

Swing, J. M. "A Workable Labor Program." *I and N Reporter* 4(November 1955): 15–16.

Table 39, Upland Cotton: Percentage Harvested by Hand and Mechanically, by States and the United States, 1956 to Date, in *The Cotton Situation*, May 1961, p. 42.

Table 21, Upland Cotton: Percentage Harvested by Hand and Mechanically, by States and the United States, 1960 to Date, in *The Cotton Situation*, May, 1965, p. 21.

Taylor, Robert W. "Arthur F. Bentley's Political Science." *Western Political Quarterly* 5(June 1952):214–230.

Tomasek, Robert D. "The Migrant Labor Program and Pressure Politics." *Journal of Politics* 23(May 1961):295–319.

"U.S. and Mexico Reach Agreement on Agricultural Workers." *Department of State Bulletin*, February 19, 1951, p. 300.

"U.S., Mexico to Extend Migratory Labor Agreement." *Department of State Bulletin*, March 3, 1952, p. 359.

Watson, Richard A. "The Tariff Revolution: A Study in Shifting Party Attitudes." *Journal of Politics* 18(November 1956):678–701.

"The Wetbacks." *Time*, April 9, 1951, p. 24.

"Wetbacks: Can the States Act to Curb Illegal Entry?" *Stanford Law Review* 6(March 1954):287–322.

"Wetbacks, Cotton, and Korea." *The Nation*, May 5, 1951, p. 408.

"Wetbacks in Middle of Border War," *Business Week*, October 24, 1963, p. 62–66.

"Wetbacks Swarm In." *Life*, May 21, 1951, pp. 33–37.

Wilcox, Walter M. "The Wartime Use of Manpower on Farms." *Journal of Farm Economics* 28(August 1946):723–741.

Williams, Harrison A., Jr. "For a National Task—A National Program." In *Proceedings: Western Interstate Conference on Migratory Labor*, pp. 3–13. San Francisco: Council of State Governments, 1960.

Williams, Lee G. "Recent Legislation Affecting the Mexican Labor Program." *Employment Security Review* 29(February 1962):29–31.

Zeller, Belle. "Regulation of Pressure Groups and Lobbyists." *Annals of the American Academy of Political and Social Science* 319(September 1958):94–103.

Zuckerman, John. "The Migrant Worker in Relation to the Labor Problems of the Farmer." In *Proceedings: Western Interstate Conference on Migratory Labor*, pp. 35–40. San Francisco: Council of State Governments, 1960.

NEWSPAPERS AND PERIODICALS

El Universal [Mexico City], 1951–1954; 1962–1964.
Excelsior [Mexico City], 1950–1954.
Hispanic American Report, 1948–1964.
Hispano Americano [Mexico City], February, 1951; June, 1963.
New York Times, 1942–1965.

INDEX